Archaeological Survey of Western India

INSCRIPTIONS

FROM

THE CAVE-TEMPLES OF WESTERN INDIA,

WITH

DESCRIPTIVE NOTES, &c.

BY

JAS BURGESS, LL.D., M.R.A.S., F.R.G.S.,
MEM, DE LA Soc. Asiat.,

ARCHAEOLOGICAL SURVEYOR AND REPORTER TO GOVERNMENT,

AND

BHAGWANLAL INDRAJI PANDIT

GYAN

Published by

GYAN

Gyan Publishing House
5, Ansari Road
Daryaganj, New Delhi-110002
Phone: 011-47034999, 9811692060
E-mail: books@gyanbooks.com

Distribution Network
gyanbooks.com
India, USA, Canada, UK, Australia, France

ISBN : 978-81-212-2528-1 (HB)
First Published, 1881

2nd Impression 2021

Printed at: Gyan Press, Delhi.

Inscriptions from the Cave-Temples of Western India
Author: Jas Burgess

Archæological Survey of Western India.

INSCRIPTIONS

FROM

THE CAVE-TEMPLES OF WESTERN INDIA,

WITH

DESCRIPTIVE NOTES, &c.

BY

JAS. BURGESS, LL.D., M.R.A.S., F.R.G.S., MEM. DE LA SOC. ASIAT.,
ARCHÆOLOGICAL SURVEYOR AND REPORTER TO GOVERNMENT,

AND

BHAGWANLAL INDRAJI PANDIT.

Bombay:
PRINTED BY ORDER OF GOVERNMENT
AT THE GOVERNMENT CENTRAL PRESS.

1881.

PREFATORY NOTE.

The descriptive notes in this memorandum were prepared in February 1880, and are necessarily fragmentary, as being supplementary to the information in *The Cave Temples of India*, and chiefly intended to preserve additional notes which have either come to hand since that work was sent to the press, or which could not conveniently be wrought into it. In several cases their object is chiefly to indicate distinctly the position of each inscription.

The inscriptions from the various caves have been prepared by Paṇḍit Bhagwânlâl Indraji and myself, as explained in the text. I am indebted, however, to Dr. G. Bühler, C.I.E., for notes and suggestions; to J. F. Fleet, Esq., C.S., for the preparation of the Mârasiṁha grant and the revisal of the proofs of the three inscriptions that follow it; and to Dr. E. W. West for the translations of the Pahlavi inscriptions at Kaṇheri which were supplied to the *Indian Antiquary*, while these notes were passing through the press, and incorporated at p. 63; and also for the use of numerous notes and drawings from which part of the materials used have been drawn. The impressions of the Kuḍâ inscriptions taken by the Archæological Survey in 1877-78, being in England, Dr. West's very excellent copies have been employed in their place.

It is the first time that any large collection of the cave-inscriptions has been made in one paper, and it is only to be regretted that want of time has prevented the completion of them here. The Nâsik, Kaṇheri, and Nânâghâṭ inscriptions yet remain to be translated; but fac-similes have been taken of all except of a portion of those at Kaṇheri, and these, I hope, will be made this season.

From the abraded and fragmentary character of many of these inscriptions, it will be understood that the translations are to a certain extent only tentative. They suggest many points of interest which must be discussed elsewhere: it has been my main object to supply the materials for such discussion. The fac-similes alone ought to be valuable as a contribution to Indian palæography, especially from the later Maurya period about B.C. 200 to the 7th century A.D.

The plates were printed off and a large portion of the following pages were in type before I left Bombay on 1st May last, but only about a third of the matter had been printed off. Since then, owing to my distance from the press and other causes, the printing has been carried to completion more slowly than I had expected.

J. BURGESS,

Archæological Surveyor.

Edinburgh, 20th April 1881.

CONTENTS.

B 761

PLATES.

* By an oversight, Inscription No. 20 on this Plate has been printed upside down.

CAVES AT MAHÂD

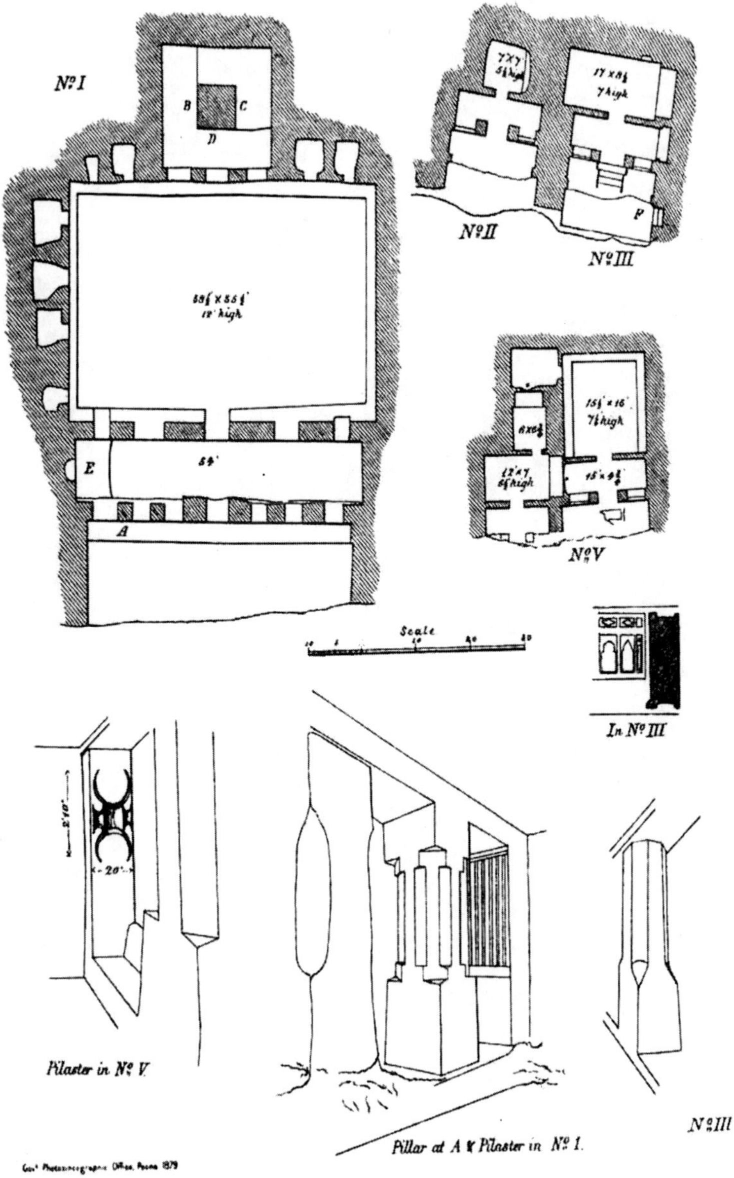

Govt Photozincographic Office, Poona 1879

1.—NOTES ON THE ROCK-TEMPLES AT MHÂR AND KUḌÂ AND THEIR INSCRIPTIONS.

THE small village of Pâl is about a mile north-west from Mhâṛ. Near it is a group of caves excavated in the almost perpendicular scarp of a hill, and numbering about twenty-eight in all. As they have never been described in any detail, the following rough notes may be of use. Beginning from the south end of the series :—

Excavation No. I is the largest in the group. It is unfinished and seems to have been suddenly stopped (see plan, Plate I). A seat 1½ feet high runs round three sides of the main chamber. Floor of cells 3 feet above the hall. Right side of the hall was being extended by cutting away a layer of 8 or 9 inches. E is a raised portion of the verandah floor ; it seems as if the floor was being lowered a foot, and a part at E left unfinished. The shrine contains a rough square mass, as if for a dâgoba. Upon the front of it at D is rudely sculptured a Buddha in bas-relief. On the sides at B and C are standing attendants. This is the only sculpture in any of the caves here. There are six rough columns in the verandah : the left one (A) is finished (see sketch). Most of the other five columns have a bracket left at the top.

In front of Cave I, at a lower level, are three tanks 14 or 15 feet square each. Two have small square entrances, the other is perhaps partly broken in.

Cave II. See plan : inner cell unfinished.

Cave III. The most perfect of the series. At F is the entrance to a well. A stair-case leads not only to No. IV, but still lower to the level of the tanks in front of No. I. Its exit has been ruined, but the steps there are now built up with loose stones. The inner verandah is now chunamed and panelled (see plate). The door into the hall has sockets for posts. An irregular recess at the right end of the verandah contains a seat, beaded, and has pilasters ; seats inside the parapet also beaded ; column of verandah as in the plate.

No. IV. Verandah has two columns—broken. Sockets for posts in the floor and ceiling, just inside the front door. The partition wall is broken through in two places.

No. V. Verandah has two octagonal columns with bases 20 inches square. Square pilasters both ornamented in the style so common at Kanheri and Junnar (see plate). Parapet with seat inside, between pillars and pilasters. Front of verandah is smoothly polished and still very perfect. The hall is rough and has been plastered with clay. A seat runs round three sides 18 inches high, with plain beading. Front door has sockets in the floor and in the top of door jamb for posts. The front of this cave has been almost exactly similar to No. III, and to one or two others in the series.

No. VI. A small unfinished cell, about the same level as the tanks in front of No. I.

No. VII. A larger unfinished cell, having a tank at the left side of the front, half filled with mud.

No. VIII. A larger irregular cave with verandah.

No. IX. Two carved pillars in front are broken away. Capitals are of the Nâsik and Junnar lotâ-shape type. Pilasters ornamented as those in No. V, which also occurs in another cave. The hall has a seat round back and two sides: three cells in the left and as many in the right side: large recess from the hall in the back wall for dâgoba, which has been removed, but the umbrella remains attached to the roof: on each side of this recess is a cell. There are small holes as if for a screen across the front of the recess. All the cell doors have sockets for frames as in No. III. The following inscription of four lines and two letters is on the back of the hall to the right:—

MHAR INSCRIPTION.[1]

Trnsliteration.

सिधं कुमारस काणभोअस व्हेणुपालितस
(ए)स लेण चेतिएघर ओवरका च अठ ८ वि[2] कंम नियु-
तं ले[3][ण]स च उभतो पसेसु पोढियो बे २ लेणस
अलिंगणके पयो च दतो एतस च कुमारस देय
धंम

Sanskrit.

सिद्धम् कुमारस्य काणभोजस्य विष्णुपालितस्यै-
तल्लयनं चैत्यगृहमपवरकाश्चाष्टौ ८ इति कर्म नियु-
क्तं लयनस्य चोभयतः पार्श्वयोः प्रही द्वौ २ लयनस्य
आलग्नकः(?) पन्याश्च दत्तः एतस्य च कुमारस्य देय-
धर्मः ॥

Translation.

"To the Perfect one! Prince Kâṇabhoa Vheṇupâlita's[5] Leṇa, chaityagriha, and eight (8)[6] cells; this much work is endowed, and two (2) cisterns on each side of the Leṇa, also a passage connected[7] with the Leṇa are presented. It is a charitable gift of that Kumâra (*or* Prince)."[8]

[1] Transliterated and translated by Bhagwânlâl Indraji Paṇḍit.

[2] Read ति.

[3] I believe that the writer has by mistake omitted the letter *ṇa* after *le* in this word.

[4] Or ०लु०.

[5] Sans. Kâṇabhoja Vishṇupâlita. The Sanskṛit Vishṇu is changed into Veṇhu in Prâkṛit, whereas we here find Vheṇu in the name Vheṇupâlita. This must either be a mistake or a local style of spelling. From the titles *Kumâra* and *Kâṇabhoa* it seems that Vishṇupâlita must have been of royal family, for it is not customary to affix *Kumâra* to any but princes. Kâṇabhoja must be the name of the family similar to *Mahâbhoja* found in the Kuḍâ inscriptions, and it is highly probable that this family was ruling in Mhâṛ (where the inscription is found) and the other surrounding minor districts.

[6] After the figure 8, a letter like *vi* is visible, but it seems to be a mistake for *ti*; *ti* in Prâkṛit is used for Sanskṛit *iti*, "this much," "so much."

[7] *Aligaṇaka* or *alugaṇaka* might be a corruption of the Sanskṛit *âlagnaka*, "attached," which seems to be a suitable word in the place.

[8] The characters of this record seem to be of about the time of Vâsishṭhîputra the Andhrabhṛitya.

There are ten more caves at this level,—one, a small open cell with a dâgoba 5 or 6 feet high.

In the next level, the seventh contains a short *inscription* at the right end of the verandah, and at the other end of the same verandah is a small dâgoba in relief. One of the preceding six is a cell with a dâgoba, as above.

The most northerly cave next to this last and containing the inscription, is at a much lower level—the lowest in the series.

There are 27 or 28 caves in all, exclusive of tanks. Nos. II and III are the highest. They are in a straight portion of the hill, with an easterly aspect, less than a mile from Mhâḍ. The parapets in front of two of the undescribed caves are carved in the "rail pattern" with thin uprights.[1]

At the foot of the hill, under some trees, are three fallen dâgobas, which must have stood close to where they now lie.

Kôl,—a small village across the Sâvitrî, south-east from Mhâḍ. In a hill behind it are two small groups of caves—the first to the north-east of the village consists of a few dilapidated cells; the other to the south-east contains one cell larger than any of the others, but all are apparently unfinished. In this second group are *three* short inscriptions. One of them reads thus:—

Transcript.[2]

Gahapatiputasa seṭhisa.

agharakhitasa deyadhamaṁ lena(ṁ).

Translation.

"A cave, the religious gift of Śeṭh Sagharakhita (*Saṁgharakshita*), son of Gahapati."

In a hill to the north-east of Mhâḍ are a few cells and cisterns, and there is a cell in a hill to the south, near the road leading to Nâgotanâ.

Kuḍâ is on the east side of the north-east arm of the Râjapur creek. A small branch creek runs up through mangrove bushes nearly to the village. The caves are about 150 to 200 feet above the sea level in a hill which is about 250 feet high at this point. They face to west-south-west, and the whole 26 caves are within about 200 yards in two lines of elevation,—Nos. I to XV below, and Nos. XVI to XXVI some forty feet higher up the hill. The view from the caves is splendid, the wide expanse of the Râjapur creek, like a mountain lake, some 5 miles wide, is right in front, entirely shut in by hills from 200 to 600 feet in height, which in most places run down nearly to the water, and a rocky islet occupies nearly the centre of the seeming lake. From the top of the hill, the hill fort of Ṭhala is plainly visible, and another to the north. The creek is called Kâlwa khâḍî, and the hill north-east of the caves Mohola.

---

[1] I have largely availed myself of Mr. A. A. West's very full notes in this account; the plate also is from his drawings. Conf. Dr. Wilson's account, *J. B. B. R. A. S.*, vol. III., pt. ii, p. 43.

[2] Translated by Dr. G. Bühler, C. I. E.

Cave No. I. Debris in front 2 feet higher than the floor of cave; little or no court. Front of the verandah, broken away; has had two plain octagonal columns and square pilasters with ornament—as in Mhâṛ caves—broken. At the left end is a plain cell with recessed bench or bed towards the back of the cave. Inscription (No. 1)[1] in two lines[2] is over the door of this, and extends along the back as far as the central door (2nd plate). It is deeply cut on a smooth surface and very distinct; the upper line seems complete, but some letters are wanting at the end of the second line, where the wall is broken away.

Inscription No. 1.

Transcript.

[१] महाभोजीय सडगेरिय विजयाय पुतस महाभोजस मंदवस खंदपालितस लेखकस[3]

[२] सुलसदतपुतस उतरदतापुतस च सिवभूतिस सह भयाय णंदाय देयधंमं [लेणं]

Sanskrit.[4]

महाभोज्या सडगेर्य्या विजयायाः पुत्रस्य महाभोजस्य माण्डपस्य स्कन्दपालितस्य लेखकस्य सुलसदत्तपुत्रस्य उत्तरदत्तापुत्रस्य च शिवभूतेः सह भार्य्यया नन्दया देयधर्मो [लयनम्] ॥

Translation.

"This cave is the meritorious gift of Sivabhûti, the son of Sulasadata and Utaradatâ, and writer to Mahâbhoja Mandava Khandapâlita,[5] son of Mahâbhoja Sadageri Vijayâ—together with his wife Namdâ."

Remarks.

Mahâbhoja is a title probably equivalent to *râja*.[6] It occurs also in No. 2 of the Bedsâ inscriptions, under the form *Mahâbhoya*.

Sadageri is apparently connected with the epithet *Sâdakara*, given to Mahâbhoja Sudaṁsana in inscription 19: it may be a family name or title.

Mandava may be either the Sanskrit *Mâṇḍavya* or *Mâṇḍapa*. In the first case the epithet would characterise Khandapâlita as a member of a Brahmanical *gotra* or race; in the second it might indicate that he was lord of a town called Maṇḍapa. This latter seems the preferable explanation as *Maṇḍapa* is a very common name for towns all over India, and three small villages called Mâdâḍ or Manḍâdh, *i.e.*, probably *Maṇḍapagaḍh*, lie close to Kuḍâ. Moreover, we have Bhag-Mândala and Kol-Mândala or Mândana near the mouth of the Sâvitrî or Bânkot River, which appear to correspond to the 'Mandabad' of Barbosa (1514); and a little to the south of the same river are Madangaḍh and Mândivali.[7]

---

1 The accompanying plates of inscriptions are from a series of very excellent copies, made many years ago by the Messrs. West and very kindly handed over to me with all their notes and drawings by Dr. E. West and A. A. West, Esq.

2 Prof. H. Jacobi of Munster has tranliterated and translated this inscription in *India Antiquary*, vol. VII., p. 253.

3 The *ka* wants the cross stroke in the copy, but the stone is injured here and there can be no doubt that the letter is *ka*.

4 The translations and remarks are the work of Paṇḍit Bhagwânlâl Indraji: I have rendered them into English.

5 Sans. Skandapâlita.

6 See Prof. Jacobi's remarks, *Ind. Ant.*, vol. VII., p. 254.

7 The Mandagara of Ptolemy is to be sought for in this neighbourhood.

Kudâ Inscriptions

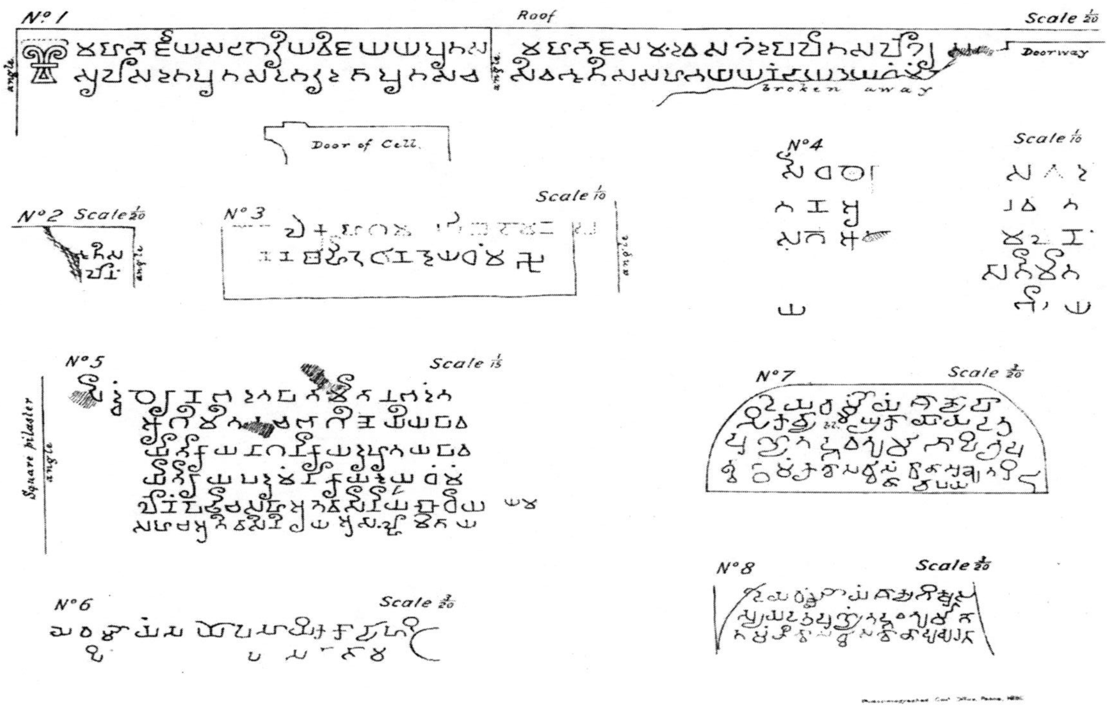

Leṇam at the end is broken away, but part of the letter *le* is still left.

The doorway in the centre is 7 feet wide, with sockets for door-posts. Plain square hall, leading at the back into an ante-chamber the full width of the hall, with two plain octagonal columns in front on a raised sill, and two square pilasters with the same ornament as the outer ones, but perfect: one of the columns fallen. The antechamber is plain, with remains of plaster on the walls. In the middle of the back is a 9½-feet doorway, without holes for wood-work: a bench runs round the ends and remainder of the back. The shrine is nearly square, with a middle-sized dâgoba in the centre.

No. II adjoins No. I and is on the same level; court very small. The front room or verandah has a door and a large open window; it has a recessed bench at the left end. Behind, towards the right side, is a cell with stone bed in the left side. Both doors have sockets for wooden frames, and there are traces of plaster on the walls of the outer room.

No. III, close adjoining, 1 foot lower level. Court small. On the left-hand side wall outside, is a fragment of an inscription (No. 2), being the ends of two lines deeply cut on a rough surface,—the rest is peeled off :—

INSCRIPTION No. 2.

Pâli.	*Sanskrit.*
......भूतिस	......भूतेः
......ळेनं	......लयनम्॥

The first line ending in *bhûtisa* suggests the name of Sivabhûti, as in the first inscription. In the second *lenaṁ* only is left. The cave was probably the gift of a member of the same family.

No. IV, about 12 feet to the right, and at 10 feet higher level; has a court with a bench on each side; steps up to the verandah, broken. The verandah has two octagonal pillars with square bases, and square pilasters with the same ornament as at Mhâṛ. A thin parapet joins each column with its corresponding pilaster, with rail pattern outside—the uprights carved with the ornament of the pilaster only doubled in the height. At the back of the verandah is a large central door, with a window on each side of it. Hall 1′ 6″ higher than the verandah—plain, square, with bench round back and two sides. Three recesses begun in the back wall with square pillars between them. No plaster in this cave, which was evidently never completed.

No. V close adjoining, and at 6 feet lower level; has a court with a tank of good water in a recess in the left. Inscription No. 3 is above the level of, and to the right hand of, this recess; it has been cut moderately deep on a rough surface, and is much weather-worn—many of the letters are very uncertain.

INSCRIPTION No. 3.

This is too much damaged to be decipherable. In the second line we might read :—

poḍhio be 2 deya dhamaṁ.

"The charitable gift of two (2) cisterns."

The 3rd letter resembles *ba*, the next is either *hi* or *dhi*, the lower stroke of the next letter is rather long for *a*, and the following two characters may be also misreadings in the copy.

Inscription No. 4 is on the opposite or right-hand wall: it has been deeply cut, but is so weather-worn that only a few letters at the ends of five lines can be made out.

INSCRIPTION No. 4.

सिधं थेरा[णं भदंत] सिवद-
तण अ[ते वासिनो] पव[इ]त-
स गोआ........[इ]म लेणं
...................सातिमित
य.......................यिय

Sanskrit.

सिद्धं स्थविरा[णां भदन्त] शिवद-
त्तानां अ[न्ति वासिनो] प्रव्रजित-
स्य गोआ........[इदं] लयनं
.......................स्वातिमित्रा
या.......................

This inscription is damaged: in the middle of the first line there is space for four letters, and this and the second are completed in the transcripts. The name of one of the donors in the 3rd line is lost. He was "an ascetic and disciple of the Thera (Bhadañta) Sivadata," and the other donor was "Sâtimitâ,[1] a female disciple."

Remark.

Thero, i.e. sthavira, is a term frequently applied to aged monks among the Buddhists and Jainas, and their names are always in the *plural majestatis. Bhadañta* is applied both to Bauddha and Jaina monks, and means "reverend," "worthy of worship." A vicarious form is *bhayañta,* (see below, inscription No. 25,) from which the Jaina Prâkṛit form *Bhañte* has been derived.

The verandah has one square pillar to the right of the centre, and a pilaster at the left side. In the left end of the verandah is inscription No. 5. It is in six lines on a decaying surface, but only three letters are much injured.

INSCRIPTION No. 5.[2]

सिद्धं थेराणं भदत[3] पातिमितन भदंत
आगिमित[न][4] च भागिणेयिय पाव
यितिकाय नागनिकाय दुहुतय[5] पाव
यितिकाय पदुमंनिकाय देय धंमं
लेणं पोढी च सहा अतेवासिनिय बोधिय[6]
सह च अतिवासिनिय असाल्हमिताय

---

[1] Sans. Svâtimitrâ.

[2] This is Prof. Jacobi's 2nd inscription (*Ind. Ant.,* vol. VII., p. 254).

[3] Read भदंत. [4] Read ०तान; the surface of the rock is injured here. [5] Read ०तुय.

[6] Two letters *ya-ma,* added beyond the end of this line, are only lightly cut and look recent; if inserted where the mark indicates they make Mayabodhi: if we read *Mâtuya bodhi-ya* it might be translated by "her female disciple's mother Bodhi and of her female disciple Asâlhamitâ."

KUDÂ

1. RAIL IN CAVE VI.

2. SCULPTURE IN CAVE VI

3. ON RIGHT WALL OF CAVE VI.

Photozincographed, Govt. Office, Poona, 1879.

Sanskrit.

सिद्धं स्थविराणां भदन्तप्रातिमित्राणां भदन्ता-
ग्निमित्राणां च भागिनेय्याः प्रव्र-
जितिकाया नागिनिकाया दुहितुः प्रव्र-
जितिकायाः पद्मिनिकाया देयधर्मो
लयनं प्रहिश्च सह अन्तेवासिन्या बोध्या
सह च अन्तेवासिन्या आषाढामित्रया ॥

Translation.

"To the Perfect! A Lena and cistern, the charitable gift of the female ascetic (*or* nun) Padumanikâ[1], daughter of Nâganikâ[2] the ascetic, the sister's daughter of the Thera Bhadanta Pâtimita[3] and Bhadanta Âgimita,[4] and, of her female disciples Bodhi and Asâḷhamitâ.[5]"

Remarks.

Siddhaṁ is here translated as an abridgment of *Siddhaṁ namaḥ.*[6] Buddhists and Jainas distinguish those persons who have arrived at the state of perfection by the name *Siddhas.* And it is a common practice among them to salute them at the commencement of any writing. This word is also found in the Brahmanical inscriptions of later date, and it is highly probable they derived it from the Buddhists. They apply the name, however, to their great Yogîs or sages. It is true that according to Pâṇini it is not grammatically correct to say *siddaṁ namaḥ*; still it is in common use. Both Buddhists and Brâhmaṇs teach their pupils to repeat the phrase before commencing their lessons in the alphabet.

At the right end of the verandah is a recessed bench. Behind the verandah at the left end is a small open room, with a bench on the right side; behind this is a cell with a bench or bed at the back; and to the left of this is another inner cell with a bench or bed on the right of it. In the right end of the verandah back wall a door leads into another cell, with a very small one beyond it having a recess in the back wall. There are traces of plaster on the walls and ceiling of this cave.

No. VI. Close adjoining the last and at 3 feet lower level, the next has a court in front with the head and forelegs of a standing elephant, 11 feet high, projecting from each side wall—that on the right nearly gone; trunk and tusks of the other broken. On the front of the cave, behind this left elephant, is a sculptured figure of Buddha, 18" high, seated on a throne with his feet on a lotos, over a wheel, with three deer on each side, and upheld by Nâga figures with others below (see 3rd plate,[7] *fig.* 2). At each side of Buddha a *chauri*-bearer stands on a lotos, the left one being Avalokitêśwara, holds a lotos stem with his left arm. Two *Vidyâdharas* hold a crown over Buddha's head; and above this is a segmental arc

[1] Padminikâ. [2] Nâginikâ.

[3] Prâtimitra—Pâtimita is probably a mistake for Sâtimita—G. B.

[4] Agnimitra. [5] Ashâḍhamitrâ.

[6] Some scholars will differ from this opinion of the Paṇḍit's, which was also held by Dr. Stevenson.—The proper translation of *siddham* is 'hail!' In the phrase *siddham namaḥ* or, as the Lekhâvalis have it, *namaḥ siddham*, the word *siddham* refers to the well-known Sûtra *siddhovarṇasamâmnâyaḥ*, 'established (and auspicious) is the record of the letters.'—G. B.

[7] The illustrations of this cave (3rd and 5th plates) are from drawings made by the Assistants in the Archæological Survey.

supported by *makaras* on each side, and two flying figures above it. Inscription (No. 6) is beneath to the left. It has been faintly cut and is much decayed.

INSCRIPTION NO. 6.

[दे] यधर्मोयं सघोपसायिककार्य हारि

......पि.....प.. ...स....ताम

This inscription is in a later alphabet than the preceding ones, and in Sanskrit. It is partly illegible. In the beginning we have [*de*]*ya dharmoyam*, 'this meritorious gift,' and then *sa*[*m*]*ghopaśâyikakârya*, 'the honourable tranquillizer of the Sangha.' The rest is illegible.

The steps up are broken. The verandah has two octagonal pillars with square bases, and square pilasters. Between the pillars and pilasters is a thin parapet, ornamented outside with rail pattern, and with a bench on the inside as in Cave III at Nâsik—which cave belongs to about the same age as this.

On the left pilaster is a Buddha, seated cross-legged on a cushion, 13 inches high, with a *chauri*-bearer on each side standing on a lotos—the left one, Avalokitêśwara, holding a lotos stem with his left arm. Above is a segmental arch with Gandharvas on each side. The cushion rests on a high four-footed stool or table, between the legs of which is a lotos with a deer on each side of its stem. The legs of the seat stand on the ornament or semi-circular moulding at the bottom of the pilaster, which contains inscription (No. 7), and outside the lower end of each leg is a small kneeling figure with joined hands. The inscription is in four lines and some odd letters, faintly cut and indistinct.

INSCRIPTION NO. 7.

देयधर्म्मोयं शाक्योपा-

सिक[1]व्याघ्रकाया[2] यदत्र

पुण्य[3] तद्भवतु मातापितृपू-

र्व्वङ्गमं कृत्वा सर्व्वसत्वानां अनुत्तरि[4] ज्ञा-

नावापय[5]

Translation.

"This is the meritorious gift of the female Sâkya worshipper[6] Vyâghrakâ[7]: may its benefit be for the attainment of supreme knowledge, first by her father and mother and then by the whole sentient world."

On the inner side of this pilaster, the upper group of sculpture consists of a Buddha seated cross-legged, 8 inches high, with a standing *chauriwâlâ* on either hand. The lower group has a similar Buddha, 11 inches high, on a lotos, with two standing *chauriwâlâs*—the left one being Padmapâni. Under each side lotos is a kneeling figure with joined hands.

On the face of the right pilaster near the top are two 8-inch Buddhas seated on cushions, separated by a pillar, and with a kneeling figure in the outer lower corner of each compartment. Below these is a 13-inch Buddha seated on a *sinhâsana* with feet on lotos, and two *chauriwâlâs*, one with lotos as before and

---

[1] Read °का. [2] Read व्याघ्रिकाया. [3] Read पुण्यं. [4] Read °र. [5] Read ज्ञानावाप्तये.

[6] *Sâkyopâsikâ* is properly a devout Buddhist laic. [7] Sans. Vyâghrika.

Kudâ Inscriptions

N°9 Roof Scale 1/20

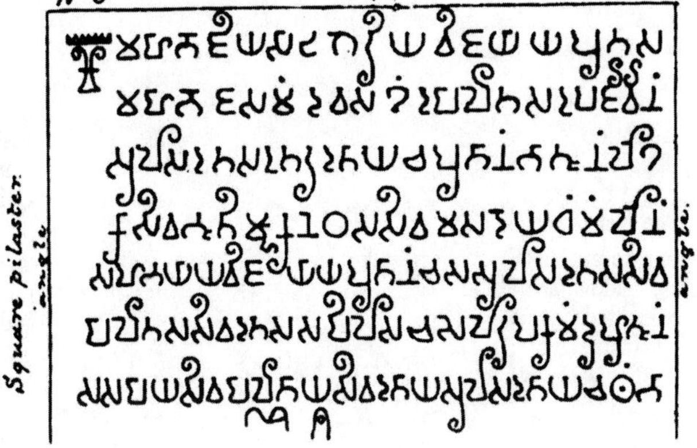

N°10 Scale 1/20

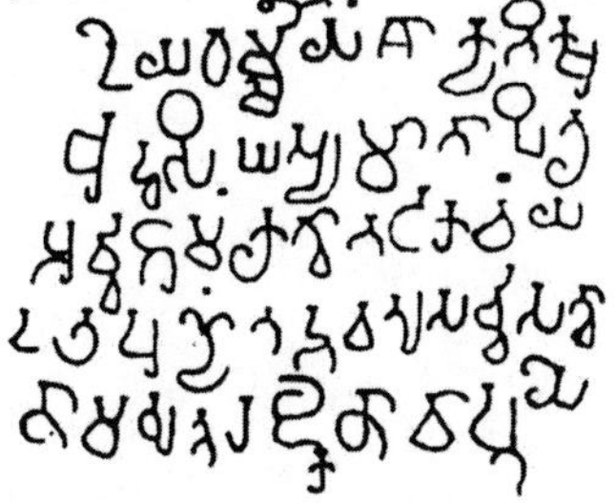

N°11 Scale 1/20

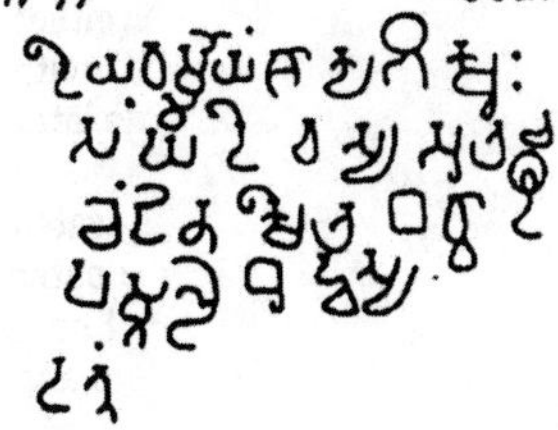

N°12 Scale 1/20

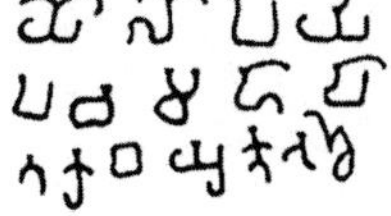

each standing on a lotos. Overhead is a triple tiara carried by two *Vidyâdharas*, with a *makara toraṇa* above, as before, and four *Vidyâdharas* carrying festoons above the arch. Below the lotoses, on the left side of the stem of the central one, is a deer couched, with a man kneeling behind it and presenting some offering. Behind him is a kneeling female with joined hands. On the right side are corresponding figures; animal defaced. Below these are mouldings and, in a panel, three deer, and on the bottom semi-circle is inscription No. 8 in three lines, faintly cut and imperfect at the ends.

Inscription No. 8.

देयधर्म्मोयं शाक्याभिक्षुस ......
स्य यदत्र पुण्यं तद्भवतु माता[पितृपूर्वं]
ङ्गमं क्रित्वा[1] सर्व्वसत्वाना[मनुत्तरज्ञानावाप्तये]

Translation.

"This meritorious gift of the Śâkya Bhikshu... : may its benefit be for the attainment of supreme knowledge, first by his father and mother and then by the whole sentient world."

In the left end of the verandah is inscription No. 9 in seven lines[2] (see 4th plate) beautifully cut on a smooth surface and perfect :—

Inscription No. 9.

महाभोजिय[3] साडगेरिय विजयाय पुतस
महाभोजस मंदवस खंदपालितस उपजीवीनं
सुलसदतस उतरदताय च पुतानं भातूनं लेख
का सिवभूतिम्हा कनेठस सिवमस देयधंमं लेनं
सह भयाय[4] विजयाय पुतानं च स सुलसदतस सिव
पालितस सिवदतस सपिलस च सेलरूपकमं दुहुतूनं
स सपाय सिवपालिताय सिवदताय सुलसदताय च थंभा.

Sanskrit.

महाभोज्याः साडगेर्या विजयायाः पुत्रस्य
महाभोजस्य मांडपस्य स्कन्दपालितस्य उपजीविनां
सुलसदत्तस्य उत्तरदत्तायाश्च पुत्राणां भ्रातृणां [मध्ये] लेख-
काच्छिवभूतेः कनिष्ठस्य शिवमस्य देयधर्मो लयनम्
सह भार्यया विजयया पुत्राणां च स सुलसदत्तस्य शिव-
पालितस्य शिवदत्तस्य सार्पिलस्य च शैलरूपकर्म दुहितॄणां
स सर्पायाः शिवपालितायाः शिवदत्तायाः सुलसदत्तायाश्च स्तंभाः ॥

---

[1] Read कृत्वा.

[2] This is the 3rd of the inscriptions translated by Prof. Jacobi (*Ind. Ant.*, vol. VII., pp. 254-5). For his remarks on Sulasâ, see *Ind. Ant.*, vol. IX., p. 28.

[3] Read ° भोजिय, see No. 1. [4] Read भायाय.

INSCRIPTION No. 10.

देयधर्म्मोयं शाक्यभिक्षु[1]
बुद्धसिघस्य[2] मातापितृ
पूर्व्वङ्गमं कृत्वा भटाकर्च[3] य
दत्र पुण्यं तद्भवतु सर्व्वसत्वा
नामनुत्तरज्ञानावाप्तये

Translation.

"This meritorious gift of the Śâkyabhikshu Budhasiṅgha; may the merit of it be for the attainment of supreme knowledge by father, mother, and Bhaṭârka, and then to the whole sentient world."

Remarks.

Bhaṭṭâraka is a title applied to a Banddha high priest: it was not so used in very early times, but by the later Digambara and Śvetâmbara Jainas and Buddhists it came to be so employed, as it had been previously to kings, and again in more recent times even to a proud consequential person. Bhaṭârka seems to be a provincial and corrupt spelling of this word.

After this comes another group of sculpture, the same as the last as far as the *Nâganîs*; between the left Nâganî and left *chauriwâlâ* is inscription No. 11, and between the right hand ones is No. 12. They are but faintly cut.

INSCRIPTIONS NOS. 11 AND 12.

देयधर्म्मोयं शाक्यभिक्षुः[4]
संघदेवस्य अत्र च
चैडिनक्षेत्रं[5] बध्वा दी
पमूल्य[6] बुद्धस्य[7]
दत्तं
यो लोपयें[त्]
पंचमहापा
तकयुक्तो[8] भवे[त्] ॥

Translation.

"This (*image*) is the meritorious gift of the Śâkyabhikshu Saṅghadêva, and the Chendina field is given for the expense of lights to Buddha. Who cuts off (*this grant*) is guilty of the five great sins."

Under the left Nâganî is a kneeling figure offering a lotos bud; behind the right one is another kneeling figure, and below it a female. Third: a Buddha, 19 inches high, same as the first down to the lotoses; below, the Nâgas appear to have torn up the lotos stem and are bearing it aloft; the Nâganîs kneeling behind as before (see 3rd plate, *fig.* 3). Below are two kneeling figures on each side looking upwards.

---

[1] Read भिक्षो.° [2] Read ° सिंहस्य. [3] Read भटार्कस्य च.
[4] Read ° क्षोः. [5] Read ° त्रं. [6] Read ल्यं. [7] We should have बुद्धाय here. [8] Read क्तो.

At the back of the hall is a low screen wall supporting two octagonal pillars and pilasters with the Mhâṛ pattern on them. An entrance between them leads to the antechamber of the shrine, and a low parapet or rail behind the bench is carved with animals. The left side is shewn in the third plate, *fig.* 1. The other side has 1st, (from left,) a *śârdûla* driven by a dwarf holding its tail; 2nd, a maned tiger with a dwarf holding its tail and brandishing a club; 3rd, a bull similarly driven; and 4th, a tiger.[1]

On the return of the back wall on each side, which meets this parapet, are two figures, male and female, similar to what we find on the front screens in the Chaitya Caves at Kaṇheri and Kârlê. In the left corner is a male 5′ 4″ high and female 5′ 2,″ allowing for head-dresses, with a child holding the woman's foot at the right lower corner. The attitudes and dress of these and the corresponding pair (male 5′ 4,″ female 5′ 0,″) in the right corner, are shewn in the fifth plate. Are they dancing? These seem older than any of the other wall sculptures.

The floor of the antechamber is level with the top of the bench in the hall, and had also benches on the inner sides of the thin parapets. At the left end is a cell benched on the right side; and just above this bench is an entrance, 18 inches square, into a smaller cell filled with stones and rubbish. A doorway, about 9 feet wide, leads into the shrine with a plain dâgoba in it, reaching to near the roof, and joined to it by the staff of the umbrella which is carved on the rock above. There are trees of plaster and painting on all the walls, roofs and columns of this cave.

No. VII. Close to the last and at 5 feet higher level is Cave VII, with a water tank to the right of the entrance. The court is plain, with steps up to the entrance at the left end of the verandah, which has two octagonal columns with square bases and square pilasters, with the ornament already shewn on a pilaster at Mhâṛ (1st plate). Between the pillars is a thin plain parapet with a seat inside. A door in the back of the verandah, to the right, leads into a cell with a stone bench on the left side. Traces of plaster are on the walls; and there are sockets for the door frame. In the right end of the verandah is a recessed bench. On the left end wall is inscription No. 13[2] (see 6th plate) in four lines, very deeply and clearly cut on a smooth surface, and entire:—

INSCRIPTION No. 13.

मामकवेजीयस वेजस इसिरखितुपासक
स पुतस वेजस सोमदेवस देयधंमं लेणं
पुतस च स नागस इसिरखितस सिवघोसस च
दुहुतुय च इसिपालिताय पुसाय धंमाय सपाय च

Sanskrit.

मामकवैद्यकस्य वैद्यस्य ऋषिरक्षितोपासक-
स्य पुत्रस्य वैद्यस्य सोमदेवस्य देयधर्मो लयनम्
पुत्रस्य च स नागस्य ऋषिरक्षितस्य शिवघोषस्य च
दुहितुश्च स ऋषिपालिताया पुष्याया धर्माया: सर्पायाश्च ॥

---

[1] Figured in *The Cave Temples*, Plate III., *fig.* 1.

[2] This is Prof. Jacobi's No. 4 (*Ind. Ant.*, vol. VII., p. 255).

Kudâ Inscriptions

No 13 Scale $\frac{1}{20}$

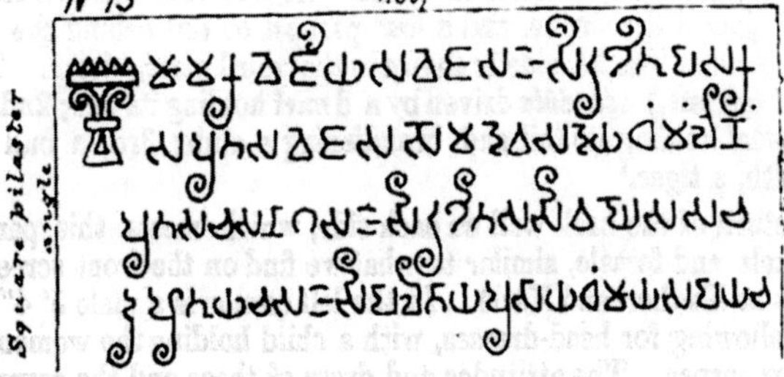

No 14 Scale $\frac{1}{20}$

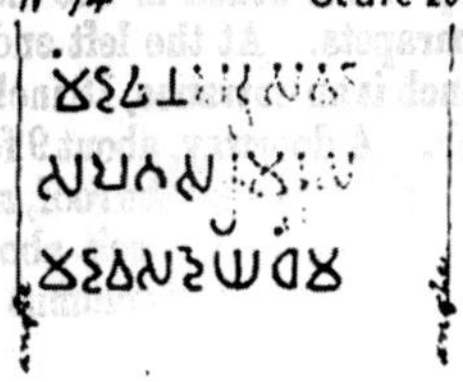

No 17 Scale $\frac{1}{15}$

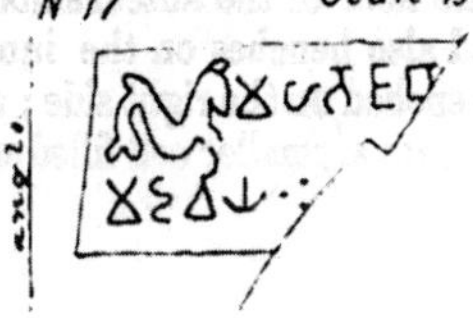

No 15 Scale $\frac{1}{10}$

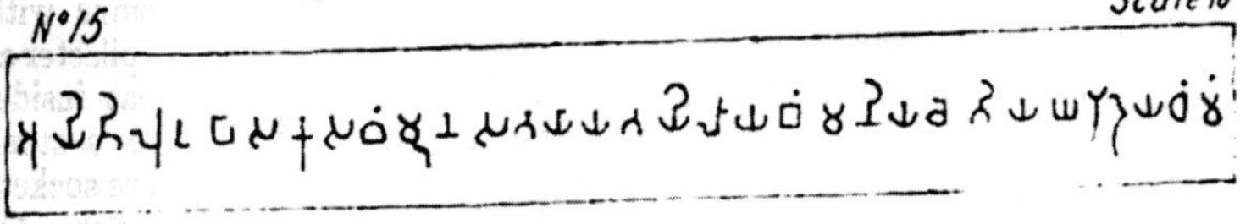

No 16 Scale $\frac{1}{15}$

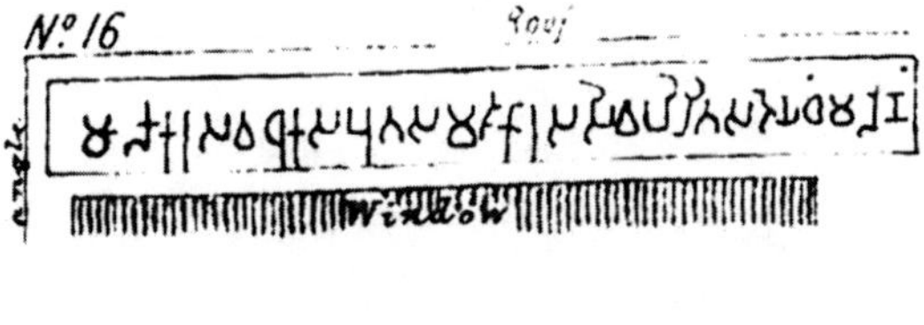

No 18 Scale $\frac{1}{10}$

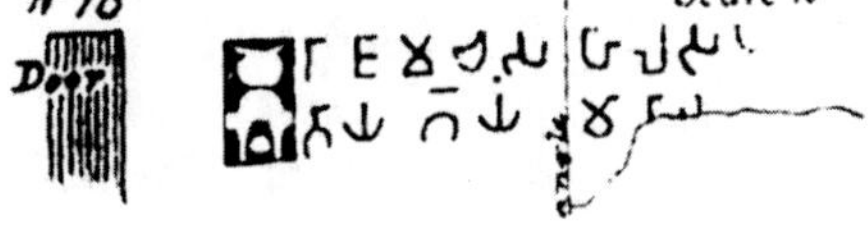

Translation.

"The meritorious gift of a cave by the physician Somadeva, the son of the Mâmakavejiya physician and worshipper Isirakhita,[1] and his (*Somadeva's*) sons Nâga, Isirakhita, and Sivaghosa, and daughters Isipâlitâ,[2] Pusâ,[3] Dhammâ,[4] and Sapâ.[5]"

Remarks.

Mâmakavejiya, an epithet of Isirakhita, is equivalent to the Sanskrit *mâmakavediya*. Mâmaka may be the name of some once famous *vaidya*, or physician, who gave the name to his family; or if *mâmaka* be some branch of medicine not now known, the term would mean one of a family skilled in that branch.

Upâsaka is a Bauddha and Jaina title for a householder or layman of the sect. In the *Chaturvidha Sangha* there are four classes of people—Bhikshus, Bihkshunîs, Upâsikas, and Upâsikâs.

Just beyond the tank outside this is another cistern, dry and broken in, with inscription No. 14 on the back of the recess over it. It is deeply cut but much weatherworn, so that the latter half of the first two lines is indistinct and the copy conjectural; the 3rd letter in the 2nd line was probably *pu*, and the 5th *ku*, as read; and in the next line the first syllable must have been *maṁ*.

INSCRIPTION No. 14.

मंदवानं परस[सि?]वम-
स प[पु]तस कुमारस
मदवस देयधम.

Sanskrit.

मांढपानां पराशिवम-
स्य पुत्रस्य कुमारस्य
मांढपस्य देयधर्मः

Translation.

"The meritorious gift of Maṅdava Kumâra, son of Sivama, the chief of the Mandavas (?)"

No. VIII is just beyond the last tank and 3 feet lower than No. VII. It consists of an oblong chamber, with a door near the right end and a window to the left, now broken into one; at the left end is a stone bench. A door in the back, towards the right, leads into a cell having a short recessed bench on the left. Half the length of this bench has been cut to a depth of 19 inches, leaving a 3 inch wall at the front of the bench, and fitted for receiving a trap lid 3" thick, which would complete the bench and form a box 21" square and 16" deep.

No. IX is close to the last and at 6 feet higher level. Entered from the left side of the court is a cell with a stone bench at the back; the front wall is nearly gone, but it had a window to the right of the door. In the right side is a window and a door leading into the verandah which has two octagon columns with cushion bases and capitals and plain octagon pilasters. A large door at the back,

---

[1] Sans. Ṛishirakshita. [2] Ṛishipâlitâ. [3] Pushyâ. [4] Dharmâ. [5] Sarpâ.

with sockets for a frame, leads into a chamber containing a plain dâgoba, the abacus of the capital reaching to the roof. The dâgoba is towards the back of the shrine, but about equidistant from the back and sides. There are traces of plaster on the walls. Inscription No. 15 is at the right end of the verandah of this cave, deeply cut on a smooth panel.

INSCRIPTION No. 15.

अयितिलु उपासकस बंम्हनस भयाय भयिलाय बंमनिय चेतियघरो देयधंमं

Sanskrit.

आर्यतिलूपासकस्य ब्राह्मणस्य भार्याया भ्राजिलाया ब्राह्मण्याश्चैत्यगृहं देयधर्मः

Translation.

"The meritorious gift of a Chetiyaghara[1] by Bhayilâ,[2] a Brâhmaṇî, wife of the Brâhmaṇa Upâsaka Ayitilu.[3]"

No. X is close to the last, but at 5 feet lower level. It has a small court in front, with a door towards the right, now broken into a large window to the left of it. Inside is an oblong chamber opening towards the right into a cell, with a stone bed at the back. Over the window is inscription No. 16, deeply cut on a rough surface. The 13th and 14th letters are probably *mâ-lâ*, as in the transcript, and the 20th may perhaps be *pâ*.

INSCRIPTION No. 16.

माळाकारस वधुकस पुतस म[मा]लाकारस सिवपिरितस देयधंम लेणं

Sanskrit.

मालाकारस्य वधुकस्य पुत्रस्य मालाकारस्य शिवपालितस्य देयधर्मो लयनम्

Translation.

"The meritorious gift of a Lêṇa by Sivapirita,[4] gardener, son of the gardener Vadhuka."

No. XI is close by, and at 2 feet lower level. It consists, first, of an open verandah with inscription No. 17 on the right end wall, which is mostly broken away, as is also the back wall of this verandah, which was pierced by a door and window into an oblong room with a bench along the back, now much destroyed; then, to the right of the verandah is another larger plain open chamber. This might properly be regarded as two caves.

INSCRIPTION No. 17.

This inscription is deeply cut on a smooth panel, but part of it is broken away: the donor was a daughter of a Mahâbhoja[5] of the family or town of Mandava:—

महाभोजवा [लिकाय]

मंदविय इ ....

No. XII, close adjoining and at the same level, is similar to the first part of No. XI, but the verandah is nearly gone except a stone bench at the right end, over the recess above which, and partly on the back wall is inscription No. 18, cut on a rough surface and distinct, but injured at the ends of the lines.

---

[1] San. Chaityagṛiha. [2] Sans. Bhrâjilâ. [3] Sans. Âryatila. [4] Sans. S'ivapâlita(?)

[5] Conf. Inscrip. No. 19.

The door into the room behind has sockets, and to the left of it is a large window, partly broken into one. The inner room has a bench at the back.

INSCRIPTION No. 18.

राजमचस हालस [दुहु]
ताय गोयंमाया [लिणं]

Sanskrit.

राजामात्यस्य हालस्य दुहि-
तुर्गौतमाया लयनम्

Translation.

"The Lêna of Goyammâ,[1] the daughter of Hâla, the royal minister."

Remarks.

This inscription has an odd representation of a lion at the commencement. The 'râja' was perhaps one of the Mahâbhojas. Of *dutaya* (daughter) the *du* is partially visible and *tâya* appears in the copy for *tuya*. After *Goyammâyâ*, *le* is also partially legible in the copy.

No. XIII, close to the last and at 2 feet higher level, has an open verandah with a short bench at the right end. Traces of plaster on the walls. Steps lead down in front from the right end of the verandah. Inscription No. 19 is on the back wall over the window, which is to the left of the door leading into a nearly square chamber with bench at the back (see 7th plate). It is rudely cut on a rough surface.

INSCRIPTION No. 19.

महाभोयस साडकरस[2] सुदंसणस दुहुतुय विजयानिकाय देयधंमं छेन

Sanskrit.

महाभोजस्य साडकरस्य सुदर्शनस्य दुहितुर्विजयिनिकाया देयधर्मो लयनम्.

Translation.

"The meritorious gift of a Leṇa by Vijayanikâ, daughter of Mahâbhoya[3] Sâḍakara Sudaṁsaṇa.[4]"

Remarks.

Vijayanikâ is apparently the same as the Vijayâ of Nos. 1 and 9: the epithets Mahâbhoya and Sâḍakara, applied to her father here, corresponding with the feminine forms Mahâbhojî and Sâḍagerî applied to Vijayâ.

No. XIV is close to and on the same level with Cave XIII, and is exactly similar in plan. Inscription No. 20 is on the left end wall and round the back over the window. It is but lightly cut on a smooth panel, but distinct.

---

[1] Sans. Gautamâ.

[2] There is a hole in the stone, as if for an *anusvâra*, over the *ra* in this word. The *u* of *hu* in the fourth word and the *tu* following, are broken; the mark over the *vi* in the last word is a hole in the surface.

[3] Sans. Mahâbhoja. [4] Sans. Sudarśana.

INSCRIPTION No. 20.[1]

करहाकडकस लोहवाणियियस माहिकस
देयधंमं लेणं

Sanskrit.

करहाकटकस्य लोहवणिजो महिकस्य
देयधर्मो लयनम्

Translation.

"The meritorious gift of a cave by Mahika of Karahâkaḍa, ironmonger."

Remarks.

Karahâkaḍa or Karahâkaṭa is Karâḍ in the Sâtârâ district, near which are many Bauddha caves.

About 5 feet further is a tank containing water, and with inscription No. 21 on the back of its recess, deeply cut on a rough surface, but weather-worn and indistinct.

INSCRIPTION No. 21.

ग[ह]पतिनो वसुलस
सेठिनो सना[नपोढी]

Sanskrit.

गृहपतेर्वसुलस्य
श्रेष्ठिनः स्नानप्रहिः

Translation.

"Of the merchant (*sêṭh*) Vasula,...a bathing tank."

Remarks.

The first legible letter is *ga*, the next *hapa* wants the first part of the *ha*; after *seṭhi* there is apparently a weather-worn *no*, followed by *sanâ*, and *na poḍhî deya dhammam* is peeled off. A *snânaprahi*, Pâli *nâna poḍhi*, is a tank where the bhikshus could bathe,—open above, with a large aperture and stair down into the water.

About 20 feet from No. XIV is a small recess (apparently a tank now buried) nearly filled with earth and roots, with inscription No. 22 on the back of it, cut on a very rough weather-worn surface.

This has not been read.

About 45 feet beyond No. XIV is a recess like a cell, nearly filled with earth and boulders.

No. XV. About 55 yards beyond No. XIV and at 20 feet higher level is another dâgoba cave. The verandah has had four plain octagonal pillars, of which one is gone; at the ends are square pilasters with the same ornament as before. At each end of the verandah is a cell with a stone bench at the back.

---

[1] Prof. Jacobi's No. 7 (*ut. sup.*, p. 256.) Prof. Jacobi has remarked that the first six and ninth letters in this inscription differ considerably from the rest, and resemble those used in Aśoka's edicts.—J. B.

Kudâ Inscriptions

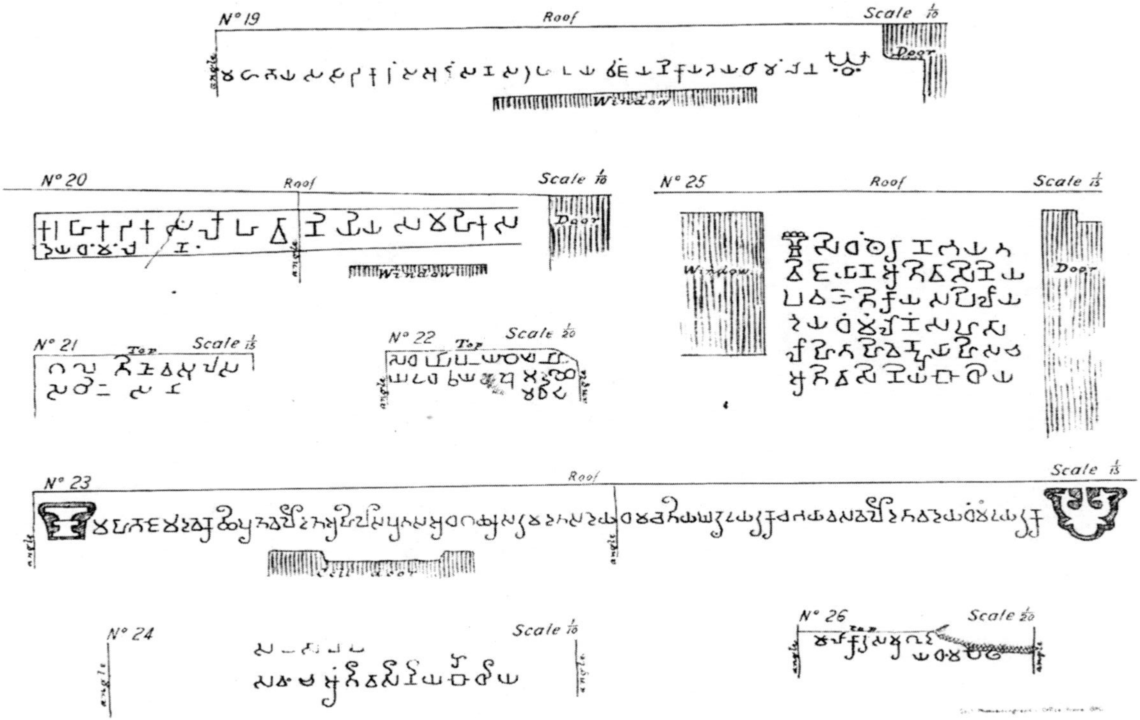

Inscription No. 23[1] in one long line on the left end and left of back walls near the roof. It is deeply cut on a smooth surface, and very distinct.

INSCRIPTION No. 23.

महाभोजे मंदवें[2] कोछिपुते वेलीदतेअहिलस पुतस अघगछकस रामदतस देय
धम चेतियघरो उयरको च भयाव स वेलीदताव[3] देयधंमं उयरको

Sanskrit.

माहाभोजे मांडपे कौत्सीपुत्रे वेल्दित्तेहिरलस्य पुत्रस्य अर्धगच्छकस्य रामदत्तस्य देय
धर्मश्चैत्यगृहमपवरकश्च भार्यायाश्च [स ?] वेलीदत्तायाश्च देयधर्मोपवरकः ॥

Translation.

"The meritorious gift of a Chêtiyaghara and cell[4] by Râmadata the Adhagachhaka,[5] the son of Ahila,[6] when Velîdata,[7] son of Kochî,[8] was Mahâbhoja Mandava; and by his wife Velîdatâ the meritorious gift of a cell."

Remarks.

Ahila may be Sanskrit *Âbhîra*, as in early times they were spread over this part of the country, and as testified by an inscription at Nâsik, they were even powerful. Their proper names, like the two mentioned here, often ended in *-data*. But it may, also, be a diminutive *ahi*, 'snake,' and an equivalent of Sapila (Sarpila) in No. 5.

Adhagachhaka is the name of a religious sect. The Jainas are divided into *gachhas*.

A wide doorway in the centre leads into the shrine containing a plain dâgoba of which the abacus is against the roof. There are traces of plaster on the walls and roof, and of painting on the columns.

The next four caves are about 30 feet above the level of No. XV, and in a position between XIV and XV but further back towards the summit of the hill, and are here numbered from left to right as an upper range. No. XVI has a tank with good water to the left of the entrance to the court; and another to the right. Both tanks have inscriptions Nos. 24 and 26 on the backs of their recesses. The court is plain, with a low bench across the front of the cave, which consists of an oblong chamber with door and window, and a bench or bed at the left end. Between the door and window is inscription No. 25, very deeply cut and distinct. A door near the left end of the chamber leads into a cell with a bench in its left side. There are traces of plaster on the walls of the chamber and cell.

---

[1] Jacobi's No. 8 (*u. s.*, p. 256).

[2] The connexion between the *anusvâra* and the *ma* is a flaw or break on the surface of the stone.

[3] Regarding *bhayâva* and *Velîdatâva* see Prof. Jacobi's remarks, *ut sup.*

[4] *Uyaraka*, Sans. *apavaraka*.

[5] Sans. Ardhagachhaka. [6] Sans. Âbhîra(?). [7] Sans. Vairidattâ(?). [8] Sans. Kautsi.

INSCRIPTION No. 24.

स...सा..............ण्हु......

सवं च आंतिवासिनीय बोधिय

Sanskrit.

....

सर्वं चान्तेवासिन्या बोध्या: ॥

The last line only is deeply cut, the others are peeled off and decayed: a *hu* below the last line but one suggests the name Veṇhu (Vishṇu). In the last we have "and all, of the female disciple Bodhî."

INSCRIPTION No. 25.[1]

सिधं थेराण भयत

विनयाण आतिवासिणिय

पवइतिकाय सपिलाय

देयधंमं लेणं सह सा

लोहिताहि वेण्हुयाहि स[ह]च

आतिवासिणिय बोधिय

Sanskrit.

सिद्धम् स्थविराणां भदन्त

विजयानामन्तेवासिन्या:

प्रव्रजितिकाया: सर्पिलाया

देयधर्मो लयनं सह सा

लोहिताभिर्विष्णुकाभि: सह च

अन्तेवासिन्या बोध्या ॥

Translation.

"To the Perfect! The meritorious gift of a Leṇa by the nun Sapilâ,[2] the female disciple of Thera Bhayanta Vijaya, with Lohitâ and Veṇhuyâ,[3] and her (*Sapila's*) female disciple Bodhî."

Remark.

As Lohitâ and Vehṇuyâ are in the plural majestatis, they may have been fellow-disciples with Sapilâ, or perhaps relations.[4]

INSCRIPTION No. 26.[5]

This has been deeply cut, but is weather-worn and broken, though fairly distinct.

मालाकारस मुगुदा......[दे]

यधंम पोढि

---

[1] Jacobi's No. 9 (*u. s.*, p. 256.) [2] Sans. Sarpilâ.

[3] Sans. Vishṇukâ. Dr. Bühler proposes, "with her venerable kinswoman Veṇhuyâ."

[4] Prof. Jacobi had already remarked this (*Ind. Ant.*, vol. VII., p. 256).

[5] This is Prof. Jacobi's No. 10 (*u. s.*, p. 256-7).

Kudâ Inscriptions

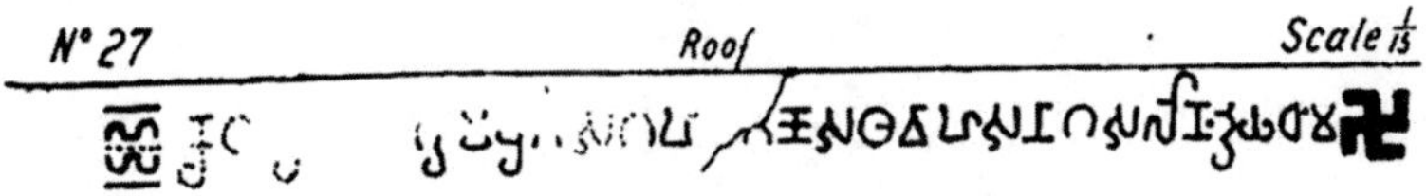

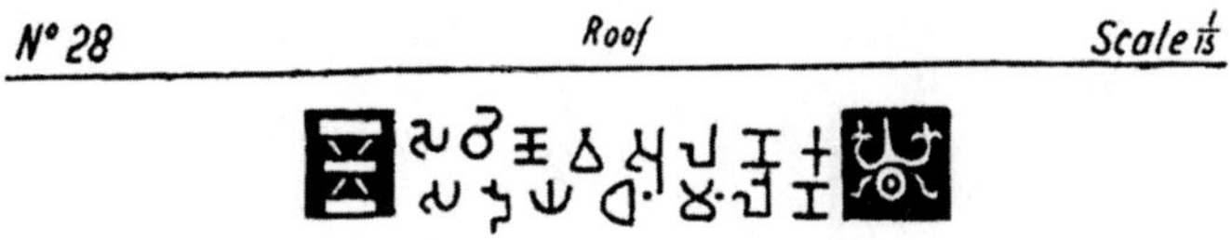

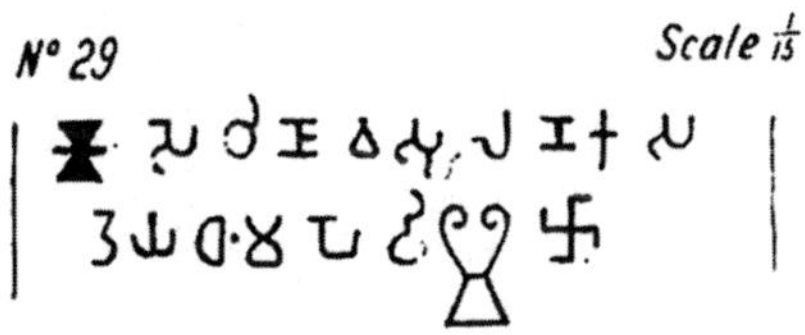

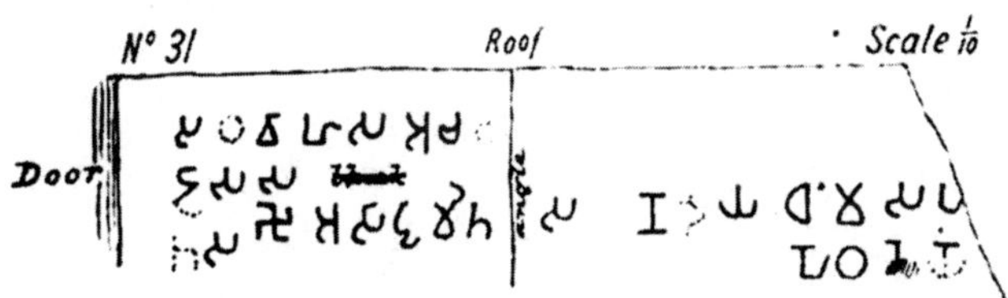

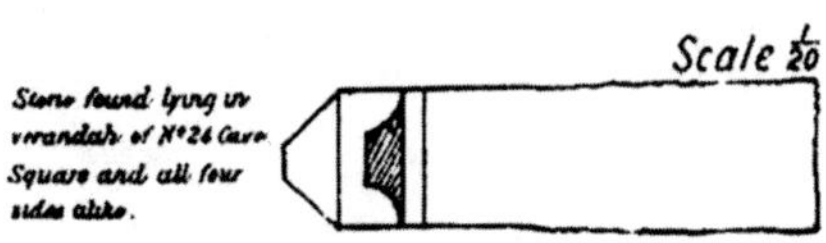

Sanskrit.

मालाकारस्य मृगदा [सस्य] दे

यधर्मः प्रहिः ॥

Translation.

"The meritorious gift of a cistern by the gardener Mugudâ(sa).[1]"

No. XVII. About 7 feet beyond the tank to the right of this last, and on the same level as that cave, is No. XVII, very like the last, only with a very large window to the left of the door. The doors have no sockets. Traces of plaster on the walls. The right end of the verandah is broken into that of the next cave. Inscription No. 27[2] is on the back wall of the front chamber close to the ceiling and to the left of the cell door (see 8th plate). It has been deeply cut on a smooth surface, but much of it is peeled off.

INSCRIPTION No. 27.

After the first letters we can read—

कोट .... स्वामिपुतस गहपतिणो सथवाहस नागस लेणं देयधंम

Sanskrit.

.... स्वामिपुत्रस्य गृहपतेः सार्थवाहस्य नागस्य लयनम् देयधर्मः ॥

Translation.

"The meritorious gift of a leṇa by Nâga, the trader and householder who ....son of Svâmi......."

Remark.

Sathavâha, Sans. *Sârtha-vâha*, is 'a great merchant,' 'leader of a caravan,' and is often applied to a ship-owner or trader.

No. XVIII is close to, and on the same level as, the last, but there is no bench or step up into the verandah, which is therefore 1 foot lower. The door is between two large open windows, and there is a bench at the left end. The cell at the back, towards the right end, has had a large window, now broken into the door, and a bench at the back. Both doors have sockets. There are traces of plaster on the walls. Inscription No. 28 is on the back wall of the verandah to the left, and close under the roof[3] it is deeply cut and distinct.

INSCRIPTION No. 28.

सेठिणो वसुलणक

स देयधंमं लेण

Sanskrit.

श्रेष्ठिनो वसुलणक-

स्य देयधर्मो लयनम् ॥

Translation.

"The meritorious gift of a cave (*leṇa*) by Vasulaṇaka, the merchant (*séṭhi*)."

---

[1] Sans. Mṛigadâsa.

[2] Jacobi's No. 11 (*ibid*, p. 257); his copy, however, was defective.

[3] Jacobi's No. 12 (*ibid*, p. 257); but his copy was imperfect.

No. XIX is close to XVIII; court 13 feet wide, plain, and at 1 foot 6 inches higher level than the last; verandah 14′ 9″ by 6′ 6″ like No. XVII; door to right and large window to left, with rough square pillar between them. At the left end a passage 3′ 9″ wide leads back with a recessed bed 6′ 2″ by 2′ 3″ on the right side. To the right a door in the back leads into a cell 6′ 9″ square, with a recessed bench at the back, 4′ 8″ long. Both doors have sockets: traces of plaster on the walls.

No. XX is about 57 yards further and at 10 feet higher level; difficult of access; front of verandah gone, and most of the back wall, which has had a door in the centre and a window to the left of it opening into a small square room.

No. XXI is about 27 yards further and 5 feet higher than No. XIX. The court is plain and the verandah has two roughly hewn square pillars. A doorway in the middle of the back wall leads into an unfinished chamber, with a square mass in the centre of the back wall and, being worked out on both sides, was probably intended for a dâgoba. To the left of the entrance is a tank choked up with inscription No. 29, on the back of the recess; it has been deeply cut, but is weather-worn.

INSCRIPTION No. 29.

सेठिणो वसुलणकस

देयधंम पोढि

Sanskrit.

श्रेष्ठिनो वसुलणकस्य

देयधर्मः प्रहिः ॥

Translation.

"The meritorious gift of a cistern by Vasulaṇaka, the merchant."

No. XXII close to the last and at 3 feet lower level; division of the courts broken; bench at left side of the court. A door to the right and window to the left are now broken into one. Inside is a chamber with a bench at the back. Between this and the next is a tank in a recess with good water.

No. XXIII. Just beyond the tank and at same level as the last is a cave with central door and two large windows. At the back of the outer oblong room is a nearly square one, with door and window and a recessed bench at the back. Over the left-hand window is inscription No. 30, cut on a rough surface.

INSCRIPTION No. 30.

सथवाहस वेहमितस[1] बितियिकय सिवदताय पु-

सणकमातुय देयधमं लेणं

Sanskrit.

सार्थवाहस्य वेशामित्रस्य द्वितीयकायाः शिवदत्तायाः पु-

ष्यणकमातुर्देयधर्मो लयनम् ॥

[1] The *mi* is badly formed and the *â* after *ta* is perhaps only a indentation on the rough surface of the rock; in *bitikuya* read °*kâya.*

Translation.

"The meritorious gift of a cave by Sivadatâ, the mother of Pûsaṇaka,[1] and second (daughter *or* wife) of Vehamita,[2] the trader."

Remark.

Bitiyika, Sans. *dvitîyakâ*, 'the second,' probably means the wife or second person in the household, or possibly daughter.

No. XXIV is 12 feet further on and at 4 feet higher level. It is similar to the last, only the front room or verandah is broken in, and the recessed bench is on the right of the inner cell. Inscription No. 31 is to the right of the door and partly on the right end: it is much weather-worn and indistinct.

INSCRIPTION No. 31.

सठवाहस अच[ल]

दासस

असाळमितस [ले]णं देयधंम सह

तस...पायो देय

Sanskrit.

सार्थवाहस्य अचल-

दासस्य

अषाढमित्रस्य लयनं देयधर्मः सह ....

तस...............पाठ देयो ॥

Translation.

"From the trader Achaladâsa's son Asâḷamita, the meritorious gift of a cave and a path (?)."

Remark.

After °*dâsasa* a *pu* seems to be omitted, and in the middle of the 3rd line a *le* after *sa*.

No. XXV is close adjoining and at the same level. The front of the verandah is gone; bench at left end; large open window and door in back wall leading into a chamber with recessed bench at the back.

No. XXVI adjoins; verandah broken into from the last; bench at right end of ruined verandah; window and door at the back enter a small plain chamber.

Lêṇa, Sans. *layanam*, 'an abode,' among Bauddha caves, a residence for Bhikshus. The other description of cave is the *chaityagṛiha*, which contained a dâgoba and was used for worship only. Later in the history of Buddhism when Lêṇas came to be made very large, a dâgoba, with the *dharmachakra* and *sinha* on either side of it (as in Caves III and VIII at Nâsik), were carved on the wall, or were set into a separate cell or shrine as at Bagh. From the fifth or sixth century, the Mahâyâna sect introduced colossal images of Buddha into the shrines of the *lêṇas*, or *vihâras*. The root *vihṛi* means to 'walk about,' 'go apart,' and the term *vihâra* was applied to large monastic halls, where the monks

[1] Sans. Pushyaṇaka. [2] Sans. Vêdamitra.

could walk about, to which they *betook* themselves for the rains, or, perhaps, the name arose from the legends invented respecting Buddha's having visited and *walked about* in the locality of each monastery. These vihâras served the double purpose of being temples for the images of Buddha and places of abode for the Bhikshus. On this plan the Nepâl monasteries are now formed: but the word *vihâra* does not seem to have been in general use before the sixth century A. D.

Gaṇḍakûṭi is a small apartment for an image of Buddha only, but with no accommodation for a monk.

Saṅghârâma is analogous to the Jaina *dharmaśâlâs* at their great *tirthas*, having a temple and residences for Bhikshus and Śrâvakas when the great *saṅghas* or pilgrimages visited them. Nothing of this sort, however, now remains in connection with any of the caves of Western India.

2.—BHAJA CAVES AND THEIR INSCRIPTIONS.

The small group of caves at Bhâjâ, about a mile south of the railway, or three miles south of the Kârlê caves, are cut in a low spur of the hill which is crowned by Îśapur fort.

The whole of the caves seem to have been the work of the Hînayâna sect, and do not appear to have been altered by the Mahâyânas of later times. The Chaitya-cave is of a very early type, and has had a wooden front. There are no inscriptions upon it. To the east of it are several ruined vihâras,—none of them large, nor with pillars in their halls,—and the only carving in them are 'Chaitya arches' over the cell doors and string courses of 'rail pattern' connecting them, after the style of Cave XII at Ajaṇṭâ. To the west is a group of fourteen dâgobas cut out of the solid rock; those in front are exposed, but the five behind are under the rock, and in some cases their capitals are joined to it. Several of these have inscriptions, much weather-worn and abraded, which the Paṇḍit has deciphered pretty completely.

Still further west, a small vihâra cave was discovered, and excavated in December 1879. The verandah had a half-arch roof, ribbed, and with dâgobas and Caryatides alternately, arranged along the upper part of the back wall, which is pierced below by two doors and a latticed window. There is also a cell at the right end of the verandah, on each side the door of which and extending along part of the front wall is a large scene carved in low relief, in which are numerous figures; to the right of the cell door elephants and wild beasts, sacred trees, human figures, both male and female, some with short broad swords, one female with a horse or ass's head, &c. On the left side, female demons of hideous proportions seem to be carrying off a chariot and its occupants.

To the left of the window a small square stone seat was carved, but is much broken. On each side the central door, and to the left of the side door is a dwârapâla, also in low relief, with very rich turban, necklaces, bracelets, &c. That on the right holds a bow; the one between the doors (much injured) held two spears; the figure was much damaged and the stone cracked before excavation, but shortly afterwards some mischievous person pushed or knocked it out and destroyed it. The third, to the left, holds two spears with barbed heads. In the left end of the verandah is a small recess, with a pillar and two pilasters in

Bhâjâ Inscriptions.

1

2

3

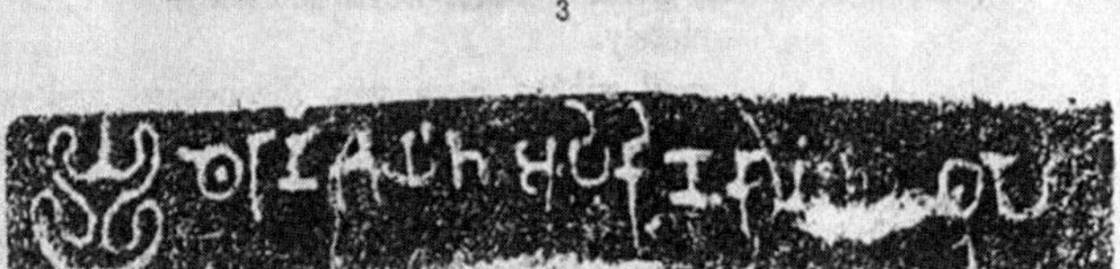

4

5

6

7

Photozincographed Survey Office Poona 1879

front. The capitals of the pillar and right side pilaster (the left one is broken) are carved with a sort of centaurs or sphinxes, having the bodies of cows or buffaloes, and human female busts. This recess is raised from the floor, and the plinth below is carved with numerous figures executed with much minuteness, and all in a very early style of sculpture.

Inside is a square room with a bench along the left side, over which are two low recesses, and two loftier panels carved each with an armed man. These recesses and panels are each surmounted by a Chaitya arch, projecting well forward. On the back and right side are two cells, and between their doors are recesses also, either for moveable images, or, possibly, for setting vessels and utensils in. All four walls are carved with 'Chaitya arches' connected by string courses of 'rail pattern.'

Altogether, this cave is one of the most curious, and apparently most ancient vihâra cave in Western India, and thus tends to support the theory I put forth some years ago, that the Bhâjâ caves were not, as had been previously suggested, an offshoot from those of Kârlê, but quite an earlier foundation.

The inscriptions are only eight in all, short, and of little immediate historical importance,[1] though they may yet turn out to have connections with others. The first is in the more ancient form of characters; the second is of a later date, the alphabet bearing a near resemblance to that used by the Ândhrabhṛityas.

Inscription No. 1.

Over a cell door in Cave XVII, west of the Chaitya-cave. It is a good deal mutilated, but pretty legible[2]:—

नडसवस नायस
भोगवतस गाभो दानं

Sanskrit.

नटशर्वस्य ज्ञातस्य
भोगवतस्य गर्भो दानम् ॥

Translation.

"The gift of a cell from Nádasava, a Nâya of Bhogavatî."

Remarks.

Nâya is the name of a caste, otherwise known as Jñâta. *Bhogavataasa*—'a native of Bhogavatî.'

---

[1] Two of the Bhâjâ inscriptions (our Nos. 2 and 8) were copied by the late Professor L. W. Westergaard, and Nos. 1 and 2 by M. D'Ochoa, in 1844, and given to Dr. J. Bird, who gave what he believed to be translations of them (*J. B. B. R. A. S.*, vol. I, pp. 439-443). No better specimens of the results of the ignorance and self-assurance of pedantry could well be produced. He seems to have allowed himself, like Dr. Inman, to be entangled by a theory as to what the inscriptions ought to say, and each word had to be taken up in a particular way and manipulated to suit his system. He claims to differ from Westergaard in his readings both of vowels and consonants, and then transliterates inscription No. 2 as—

Mahâratha sûkasâkâ pûtasâ
tânamdâtasa dayyâdamâpâda,

and translates it: "The righteous gift of a symbol and vehicle of the purified Sâka Sâka *Sakra or Indra*), the resting place of the giver."—J. B.

[2] The photozincograph of these inscriptions (9th plate) is not quite satisfactory. The first letter looks like ना and भोगवतस like भागततस. The actual readings have been ascertained by an inspection of the original.

Bhâjâ Inscriptions.

No. 8

Bedsâ Cave Inscriptions.

No. 1

2

3

Photozincographed, Govt. Office Poona, 1880.

Inscription No. 5.

On the base of the fourth dâgoba, very indistinct :—

थेरानं भयंत संघदिनानं

Sanskrit.

. स्थविराणां भदन्तसंघदत्तानां [स्तूपः] ॥

Translation.

"[*The Thupo*] of the venerable reverend Saṅghadina.[1]"

Inscription No. 6.

On the capital of one of the dâgobas in the second row, under the rock :—

No. 6.

थेरानं भयंत

Sanskrit.

स्थविराणां भदन्त ॥

Translation.

"The venerable reverend.[2]"

Inscription No. 7.

Over the right-hand cell door in the back of the vihâra Cave No. VI, to the east of the Chaitya :—

बाधया [बोधिया] हालिक जयाया दानं

Sanskrit.

बोध्या हालिक जायाया दानम् ॥

Translation.

"The gift of Bâdhâ (Bodhi), the ploughman's wife."

Inscription No. 8.

On the *garbha* or dome of the large dâgoba which stands first in the front row, much weather-worn and scarcely legible.

3.—THE INSCRIPTIONS AT BEDSA CAVES.

The Beḍsâ caves are on the south side of the range of hills in which those of Bhâjâ and Pâtan are, and a few miles south-west from the Khaḍkâlê railway station. Next to Bhâjâ and Koṇḍânê in age, the group is but a small one, and its special peculiarity is a vaulted vihâra. This vihâra is very much like a Chaitya cave, having an apsidal back; but it is low and has no pillars. The cells are arranged round the sides and back; have the chaitya-arch ornament over

---

[1] Saṅghadina is the Prâkṛit for Saṅghadatta.

[2] This fills the line; the name of the Bhadanta has never been added.

each; and pilasters of the antique pattern shewn in the accompanying plate, with a portion of the shaft cut away at the corners. Between these pilasters are grated windows of the pattern shewn in the drawing.[1]

There are only three inscriptions, of which two were copied by the late Professor Westergaard and interpreted by Dr. James Bird in his usual style; for he found no difficulty in getting Pâli inscriptions to support an esoteric meaning in accordance with his theory.

INSCRIPTION No. 1.

Consisting of two lines on the rock behind a dâgoba; weather-worn and the beginning of each line lost:—

.... य गोभूतिनं आरणकान पेण्डपातिकानं मारकुडवासीनं थुपो

.... वासिना भतासाळमितेन कारित

Sanskrit.

........गोभूतीनामारण्यकानां पैण्डपातिकानां मारकूटवासीनां स्तूपः

........वासिना भट्टाषाढमित्रेण कारितः ॥

Translation.

"The Thûpo of Gobhûti, native of Mârakuḍa, an Åraṇaka (*and*) Peḍapàtika. Caused to be made by Asâlamita Bhata,[2] inhabitant of......."

Remarks.

Peḍapâtikânaṁ, Sans. *piṇḍapâtikânâṁ*, is one who lives on alms, and is here used in the plural majestatis. *Áraṇaka*, Sans. *âraṇyaka*, a dweller in forests.[3] *Mârakuḍa*, Sans. *Mârakûṭa*, the hill of Mâra, is perhaps the old name of that in which the Beḍsâ caves are.

Bhata—must be *bhaṭṭa*—a warrior. The name of his birth-place is lost.

INSCRIPTION No. 2.

This consists of three lines, and is cut in the rock over a water cistern near the Chaitya, and tolerably distinct:—

महाभोयबालिकाय म[हा]देवि-

य महारठिनिय सामडिनिकाय

[दे]यधम आपदेवणकस बितियिकाय-

Sanskrit.

महाभोजबालिकाया महादेव्या

महारथिन्याः सामडिनिकाया

देयधर्म आपदेवणकस्य द्वितीयकायाः ॥

---

[1] This plate is from the notes of the Messrs. West.

[2] Sans. Ashâḍhamitra Bhaṭṭa;—*Bhata* is probably Sans. *bhakta*, 'devoted.'—G. B.

[3] Gobhûti must have been rather a notable ascetic in the eyes of his countrymen, having a double title to sanctity.

Window from Bedsâ Caves

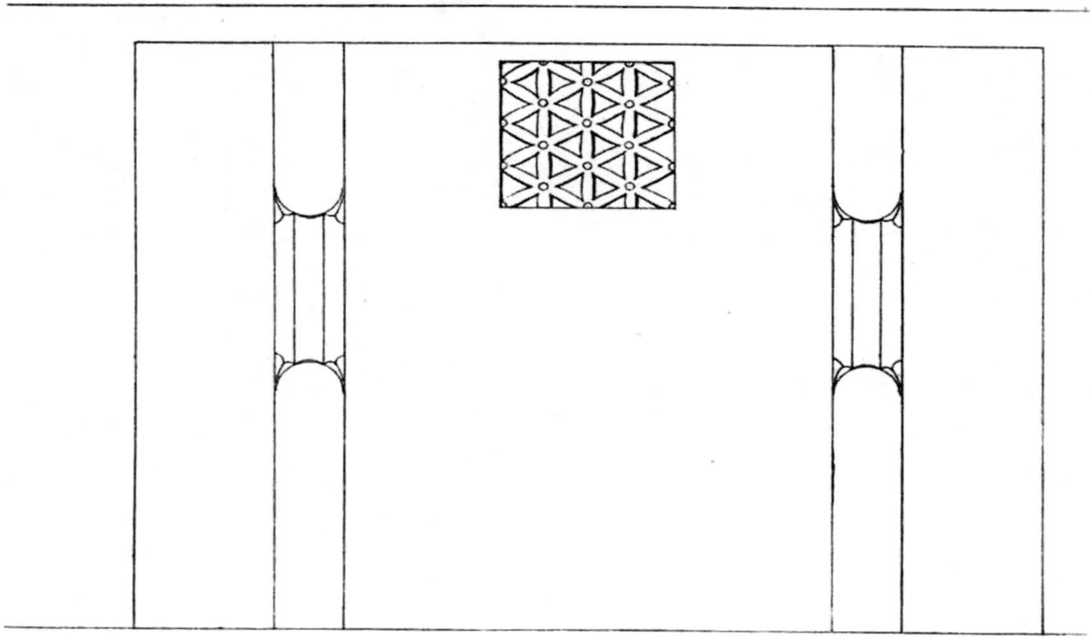

Photozincographed, Govt. Office, Poona, 1880

Scale 1 Inch to a foot

Translation.

"The religious gift of Mahâbhoya's daughter (*bâlikâ*) Sâmaḍinikâ, the Mahâdêvî (or princess) Mahârathini[1] and second wife of Âpadêvaṇaka.[2]"

Remarks.

Madêvi is a mistake of the engraver's for *Mahâdêvi*. *Mahâbhoya* must have been a râja in this part of the country, whose daughter's name Sâmaḍinikâ may also be read Sâmesinikâ, but the third letter is more like *di* than *si*, and the second, if intended for *me*, is not regularly formed.

INSCRIPTION No. 3.

Over the door of a cell in the right end of the verandah of the Chaitya:—

नासिकान अनदस सेठिस पुतस पुसणकस दान·

Sanskrit.

नासिकस्यानन्दस्य श्रेष्ठिनः पुत्रस्य पुष्यणकस्य दानम् ॥

Translation.

"A gift of Pusaṇaka,[3] son of Anada[4] Seṭhi, inhabitant of Nâsik."[5]

Remark.

The fourth letter looks like *ta*, but the sense requires us to read *na*, perhaps indicated by the last stroke being somewhat lengthened.

4.—THE INSCRIPTIONS IN THE BAUDDHA ROCK-TEMPLES AT KARLE.

The Rock-Temples of Kârlê are so well known and have been so often described that nothing need be added here respecting them. The carvings on the front wall of the great cave are manifestly of very various ages: those of Buddha and his attendants being evidently the latest. Whether the pairs of figures on each side the doors, and on the inside of the ends of the outer screen, are of the same age as the rest of the front is doubtful. Similar pairs are carved higher up on each end of the verandah, but they are carved in a much better style; and in the case of at least two of those below, we have

---

[1] This title may mean wife [or daughter] of a great warrior.

[2] Compare the above transcript and translation with those of Dr. J. Bird (*J. B. B. R. A. S.*, vol. I., p. 441):—

Mahâtya palakaiyya manuva
ya mahâratanayya sâmaddhinakaiyya
dayâdhama upada manâkâsa vâtya kaiyya

(though one hardly knows whether he meant the Devanâgarî spelling or the Roman to be followed, or why he makes them different). His translation is:—

"A righteous gift of a small offering to the moving power (body), the intellectual principal, the cherishing material body, the offspring of Manu, the precious jewel, the supreme heavenly one here."

By those who know as little of the language as Dr. Bird, any meaning apparently can be extracted from an inscription; and the publication of such stuff leads to sensible people entertaining doubts of all tanslations from languages like cuneiform but little known.—J. B.

[3] Sans. Pushyaṇaka.

[4] Sans. Ananda.

[5] Conf. Dr. Bird's reading, *J. B. B. R. A. S.*, vol. I., p. 440.

inscriptions stating that they were added by a Bhadanta or cleric,—whether whilst the excavation of the cave was going on or long after, we do not know.

The inscriptions, however, on the famous Chaitya-cave and its neighbouring monastic dwellings have never been translated. Dr. Stevenson and Dr. J. Wilson attempted one or two of the most prominent, but not with much success. Whilst camped in the neighbourhood in December 1879, Paṇḍit Bhagvânlâl Indrâjî took fresh facsimiles of the whole series of twenty-two inscriptions, and transliterated them into Devanâgarî, then turned them verbatim into Sanskrit, and with his assistance in rendering them literally I have made the following English versions from his vernacular :—

Inscription No. 1.

On the left end of the verandah of the great Chaitya-cave, on a deep flat moulding over the heads of three large elephants :—

बेजयंतिता सेठिणा भूनपालेना सेलघरं परिनिठापितं जबुदिपम्हि[1] उत्तम

Sanskrit.

वैजयन्तीतः श्रेष्ठिना भूतपालेन शैलगृहं परिनिष्ठापितं जम्बुद्वीप उत्तमम्॥

Translation.

"Sêṭh Bhûtapâla, from Vejayanti,[2] has established a rock-mansion, the most excellent in Jambudvîpa."[3]

Remarks.

Vejayantitâ—vaijayantitaḥ—' from Vaijayanti '; *seṭhi—śreshṭhin*—is now usually applied only to merchants. But the original meaning of *śreshṭhi* is 'great, excellent, chief, best,' and so might be applied to any man of high rank.

On the opposite end of the verandah, facing this is the word *sidhaṁ*, in large letters, as if an inscription had been just begun, but never carried further than the invocation.

Inscription No. 2.

On the lion-pillar, or *sinhastambha*, on the left of the entrance :—

महारठिस गोतिपुत्रस अगिमित्रणकस सिहथभो दानं

Sanskrit.

महारथिनो गोतिपुत्रस्याग्निमित्रणकस्य सिंहस्तंभो दानम्॥

---

[1] Read जंबु०.

[2] Dr. Bühler has suggested this rendering, and that the correct reading is doubtless *vejayantito* 'from Vejayanti,' as the fac-simile shows: *Vaijayantî* occurs both in Brahmanical and Jaina books as the name of a town on the coast of the Koṅkaṇ (see *Petersb. Dict.* sub voce; and Mr. K. T. Telang's 'Kadamba Inscriptions,' *J. B. B. R. A. S.* vol. XII., p. 321). It is probably the Greek Byzantion.—G. Bühler.

[3] This dedication is strikingly brief: this 'rock-mansion' is undoubtedly (*Jambudîpamhi uttama*) 'the most excellent in Jambudvîpa'; but we wish the princely merchant had told us a little more of himself,—in whose reign he lived, or when.—J. B.

Kārlé Cave Inscriptions.

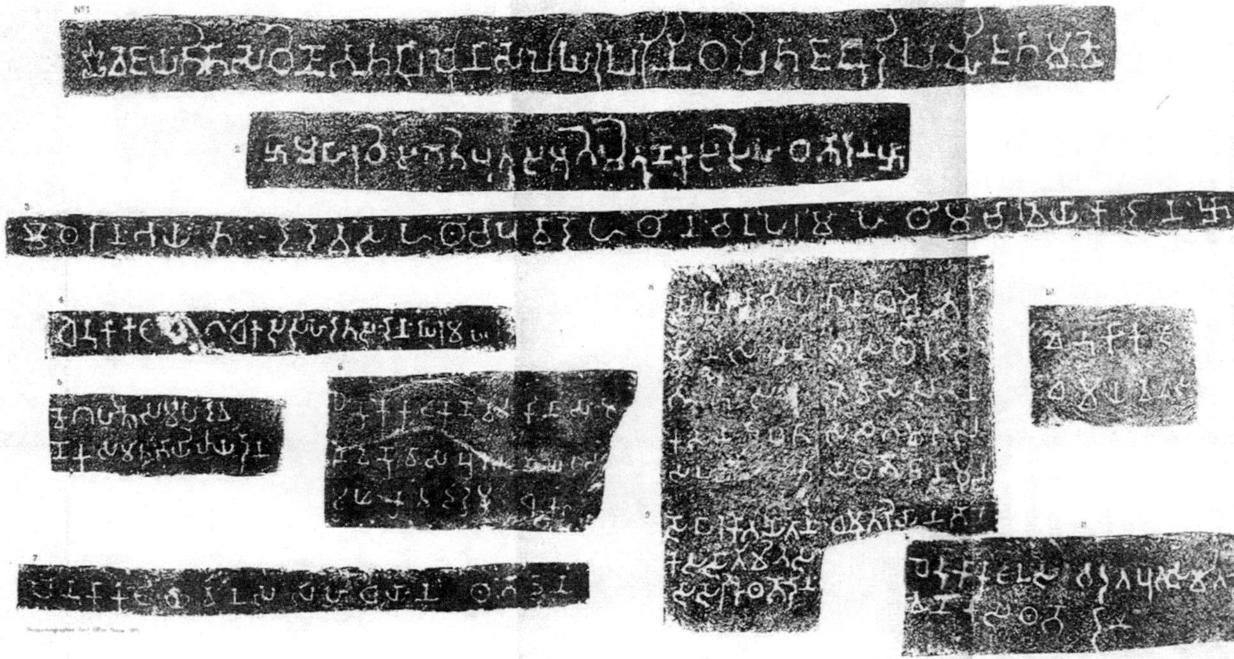

Translation.[1]

"From Agimitraṇaka, son of Goti, a great warrior, the gift of a lion-pillar."

Remarks.

Agimitraṇaka, Sans. *Agnimitraṇaka* : the syllable *-naka*, added to the name seems to have been a usual practice in those early times. In No. 5 we have *Mahâdêvanaka* for *Mahâdêva*, and in No. 8, *Mitadêvanaka*.

Inscription No. 3.

On the right end of the verandah below the feet of the elephants :—

थेरानं भयंतइंददेवस हथि च पुवा दो हथिंन च
उपारिमा हेथिमा च वेयिकादाने

Sanskrit.

स्थविराणां भदन्तेन्द्रदेवस्य[देवानां] हस्तिनौ च पूर्वौ द्वौ हस्तिनां च
उपरितना अधस्तना च वेदिकादानम् ॥

Translation.

"The gift of, first, two elephants,[2] and above and below the elephants, a (*rail-pattern*) moulding, by the venerable reverend (*bhadanta*) Indadêva.[3]"

Remarks.

Over the plinth on which this inscription is, are *three* elephants, of which the first two, with the rail-pattern belt above and below, were the gift of this *Bhadanta*. The word *vedi* here used is applied in Sanskṛit to an altar, seat, dais, &c., but in this place and elsewhere it evidently applies to bands or string-courses carved with the rail-pattern.[4]

Inscription No. 4.

Over the right-hand side door into the Chaitya :—

धेनुकाकटा गंधिकस सिहदतस दानं घरमुघ

Sanskrit.

धेनुकाकटात् गान्धिकस्य सिंहदत्तस्य दानं गृहमुखम् ॥

Translation.

"The gift of a door by Sihadata,[5] a perfumer, from Dhenukâkaṭa."

---

[1] This inscription was translated by Dr. Stevenson : "The Chief Agimitra, son of the great king Bhoti, erected this lion-crowned pillar." *J. B. B. R. A. S.*, vol. V., pp. 3, and 426, 427.

[2] *Hathi* seems to stand for *hathî* and to be nominative plural. As the plural might be used to denote the number *three*, the translation might thus be : '*Three* elephants, and below and above the first two elephants, a moulding the gift of, &c'.—G. Bühler.

[3] Sans. Indradêva.

[4] It is perhaps from the root *ve* 'to weave, bind together' as a railing.

[5] Sans. Siṅhadatta.

Remarks.

Gandhika is literally a dealer in perfumes, but in early times it was nearly equivalent to our modern druggist, for the perfumer, along with the perfumes he obtained from distant countries, had facilities for obtaining medicinal drugs also, and naturally added them to his stock in trade until he engrossed this part of the business of the *vaidya*, or physician, who would at first sell also the drugs he prescribed. *Gharamugha*, Sans. *grihamukha*, 'a façade,' implies also the architrave and sculpture round the door, with the arch above and its enclosed lattice work.

Inscription No. 5.

The upper inscription on a pillar of the open screen in front of the verandah:—

गहतस महादेव-
णकस मातु भायिलाया दानं

Sanskrit.

गृहस्यस्य महादेव-
णकस्य मातुर्भ्राजिकाया दानम् ॥

Translation.

"The gift of Bhâyilâ[1], the mother of Mahâdêvaṇaka, a householder."

Remark.

Gahata may be a corruption of *grihastha*. The gift must be the pillar bearing this inscription.

Inscription No. 6.

On the same pillar, but lower down:—

धेणुकाकटकेण वढकिना सामि[के]
ण वेणुवासपुतेण घरस
मुघं कतं दारमुधुकस...

Sanskrit.

धेनुकाकटकेण वर्द्धकिना स्वामिके-
न विष्णुवासपुत्रेण गृहस्य
मुखं कृतं द्वारमूर्द्धक...

Translation.

"Sâmika[2], son of Veṇuvâsa,[3] a carpenter, a native of Dheṇukâkaṭa, made the doorway and.........above the door."

The end of this inscription after the word *dâramudhukasa* is destroyed. The door referred to is perhaps that entering the Chaitya on the left, on which there is no inscription.

---

[1] Sans. Bhrâjilâ. [2] Sans. Svâmika. [3] Sans. Vishṇuvâsa (or Veṇuvâsa).—G.B.

INSCRIPTION No. 7.

On the fourth pillar inside the Chaitya on the left hand :—

धेनुकाकटा यवनस सिहधयान थंभो दान

Sanskrit.

धेनुकाकटाद्यवनस्य सिंहध्वजानां[यस्य] स्तंभो दानम् ॥

Translation.

"The gift of a pillar by Sihadhaya,[1] a Yavana, from Dhenukâkaṭa."

Remarks.

Sihadhaya's name is in the plural, while *Yavana* is singular, perhaps by a mistake of the engraver. *Yona* or *Yavana*, 'a Greek,'—probably an Indo-Baktrian, many of whom were converts to Buddhism.

INSCRIPTION No. 8.

On the shaft of the fifth pillar on the left or north side of the nave :—

सोपारका भयतान धमुतर-
यान संमानयस थेरस [मा]-
तुलस अंतेवासिस भान-
कस नदापुतिस सातिमितस
सह [मातापि]तुय थभो दानमुलं

Sanskrit.

शोर्पारकाद्भदन्तानां धर्म्मोत्तरी-
यानां सन्मानार्थाय स्थविरस्य मा-
तुलस्यान्तेवासिनो भागिनेय-
कस्य नन्दापुत्रस्य स्वातिमित्रस्य
सह [मातापि]तृभ्यां स्तम्भदानमूल्यम् ॥

Translation.

"The gift of the cost of a pillar by Sâtimita,[2] from Sopâraka, out of respect for his maternal uncle the Bhadanta Dhamutaraya, by his (*i.e.*, the Bhadanta's) disciple and sister's son Sâtimita, the son of Nandâ, with his mother and father."

Remarks.

Sopâraka, or Sorpâraka, is Supâra rear Bassein, of which the Bhadanta was an inhabitant.

Samânathasa is in the genitive case, which is used in Prâkṛit for the Sanskrit dative *sammânârthâya* 'for respect to.' In Sanskṛit *sammânârtham* or *sammânâya* is used; but in Aśoka's inscriptions, *sûpâthâya* (Sans. *sûpârthâya*) 'for soup,' 'for the purpose of soup,' is found; so here, the pillar is *for* the purpose of respect.

Bhânaka in Prâkṛit, *bhâgineyaka* in Sanskṛit, of which *bhânaka* is a corruption; in modern Gujarâti, *bhâṇo* is used.

This inscription is much obliterated, probably intentionally, and beneath it, in clear cut letters, is the following, of the same Sâtimita :—

---

[1] Sans. Sinhadhvaja.

[2] Sans. Svâtimitra.

Inscription No. 9.

सोपारका भयंतान धमुतरियान भाण-

कस सातिमितस

ससरीरो थभो दानं

Sanskrit.

शोर्पारकाद्भदन्तानां धर्म्मोत्तरीयानां भागिने-

यस्य स्वातिमित्रस्य

सशरीरः स्तम्भो दानम् ॥

Translation.

"The gift of a pillar containing relics, by Sâtimita from Sopâraka sister's son of Bhadanta Dhamutaraya."

Remarks.

There is a hole or receptacle cut for the purpose of holding a relic in the centre of a lotos carved on the front of the pillar just where the inscription ends. No other example like this has been noticed elsewhere.

Inscription No. 10.

On the shaft of the third pillar on the same side :—

धेनुकाकटा

धंमयवनस

Sanskrit.

धेनुकाकटात्

धर्मयवनस्य ॥

Translation.

"(*The gift*) of Dhama, a Yavana from Dhenukâkaṭa."

Remark.

Here we have a Yavana with the Indian name of Dhama or Dharma.

Dhenukâkaṭa—now Dharanikoṭa near Amarâvati on the Kṛishṇâ, the old capital of the Ândhras. It is frequently mentioned in the cave inscriptions.

Inscription No. 11.

On the shaft of the seventh pillar on the left side :—

धेनुकाकटा उसभदतपुतस मितदे-

वणकस थभो दानं

Sanskrit.

धेनुकाकठादृषभदत्तपुत्रस्य मित्रदे-

वणकस्य स्तम्भो दानम् ॥

Kārlé Cave Inscriptions

Nº 12

13

14

15

16

Translation.

"The gift of a pillar by Mitadêvaṇaka[1], son of Usabhadata[2] from Dhenukâkaṭa."

INSCRIPTION No. 12.

On the inner face of the gallery :—

असाढमिताये भिखुणि[ये]....

Sanskrit.

अषाढामित्राया भिक्षुण्याः...

Translation.

"(*Gift*) of Asâḍhâmitâ[3], a nun......"

Remark.

This must refer to the belt of rail pattern just under the inscription. Some letters at the end of the line are destroyed—probably *veyi* (or *vedikâ*) *dânam*, 'gift of the rail.'

INSCRIPTION No. 13.

On the upper frieze to the right of the central door of the Chaitya and outside :—

[1] सिधं रञो खहरातस खतपस नहपानस जा[मा]तरा दिनिकपुतेन उसभदातेनात्रि-

[2] गोसतसहसदेण नदिया बणासयं सुवण[ति]रथकरेण [देवा]ण ब्रह्मणानं च सोळस गा-

[3] मदे[न] पभासे पूततिथे ब्रह्मणाणं अठभायाप[देण]गावसापि त्रिसतसहसं

[4] दापयिता वलूरकेसु लेणवासान पवजितान चातुदिससघस

[5] यापणय गामो करजिको दतो सवानं[व]सावासितानं.

Sanskrit.

[1] सिद्धम्। राज्ञः क्षहरातस्य क्षत्रपस्य नहपानस्य जामात्रा दिनीकपुत्रेण ऋषभदत्तेन त्रि-

[2] गोशतसहस्रदेन नद्यां वार्णशायां सुवर्णतीर्थकरेण देवेभ्यो ब्राह्मणेभ्यश्च षोडशग्रा-

[3] मदेन प्रभासे पूततीर्थे ब्राह्मणेभ्यो ऽष्टौ भार्याप्रदेन गवां चापि त्रिशतसहस्रं

[4] दापयित्रा वलूरकेषु लयनवासीनां प्रवृजितानां चातुर्दिशसंघाय

[5] यापनार्थं ग्रामः करजिको दत्तः सर्वेषां [व]र्षावासिनाम् ॥

Translation.

"To the Perfect. Usabhadata,[4] son of Dinika and son-in-law of the King Khaharâta Khatapa Nahapâna, the giver of 300,000 cows,—having given gold, and being a visitor to the *tirtha* at the Baṇâsâ river[5]; the giver of sixteen villages to gods and Brâhmaṇs; at the holy place Pabhâsa the giver of eight wives to Brâhmaṇs; and who caused 300,000 cows to be given;[6] and who at Valuraka

---

1 Sans. Mitradêvanaka.

2 Sans. Ṛishabhadatta.

3 Sans. Ashâḍhamitrâ.

4 Sans. Ṛishabhadattâ.

5 This conjecture *tirathakareṇa* is not a very probable one, as *tiratha* is a modern form and not used in the old Prâkrits. Probably the *ra* of *ratha* is a mistake for *ti*. The explanation of the word *suvaṇatitthakareṇa* is furnished by Nâsik inscription No. 17, where Usavadâta calls himself *nadyâṁ barnâśyâṁ suvarṇadânatîrthakara*, which in my opinion means 'the founder of a Tîrtha and giver of a gift of gold on the river Baṇâs'; or 'the founder of a *Tîrtha* by means of a gift of gold.'—G. Bühler.

6 Instead of *gâvasâpi* I read (*a*)*ṇuvasam pi* and translate, "who caused annually three hundred thousand (pieces of money) to be distributed." Nâsik inscription No. 17 reads *anuvarsham brakmaṇaśatasahasrîbhajâpayitrâ*.—G. Bühler.

gave the village of Karajaka to the *sangha* of ascetics from the four quarters residing in the *leṇa*, all dwelling there for the support during the rainy season."

Remarks.

Khaharâta Khatapa Nahapâna, Sans. *Kshaharâta Kshatrapa Nahapâna*—Khaharâta must have been Nahapâna's family name.

A *Baṇâsâ* river is in northern Gujarât, flowing from the base of Abu into the Raṇ of Kachh, and another in eastern Râjputânâ, flowing in the Chambal.

Prabhâsa-tîrtha is Somanâtha Paṭṭana, still known as Prabhâsa Pâṭaṇa. The 'giving of wives to eight Brâhmaṇs' means that he gave a money donation sufficient to defray the marriage expenses of so many. It is still a custom for wealthy persons to pay the *kanyâdâna* of poor Brâhmaṇs, giving a sum of money sufficient to defray the marriage expenses of a daughter, and on the marriage day the donor 'gives away' the girl to her husband.

Whom Usabhadata "caused to give" (*dâpayitâ*) 300,000 cows is not said: apparently, he did not give them himself.

Valûraka appears to be the ancient name of the monastic establishment at Kârlê. It occurs in the next two inscriptions also, and is in the plural majestatis; so also at Nâsik we have *Triraśmishu* (No. 17, l. 3, in *Tr. Int. Cong. Orien.*, p. 327).

Karajika, the village given to the monastery has not been indentified: It may be Karanj close to Beḍsâ.

INSCRIPTION No. 14.

To the left of the central door and over the sculptures:—

[1] रञो वासिठिपुतस सामिसिरि [पुळुमायिस] सवछरे सतमे ७. गिम्हपखे पचमे ५

[2] दिवसे पयमे १ एताय पुवाय ओखळकियान महारठिस कोसिकिपुतस मितदेवस पुतेन

[3] [म]हारथिना वासिठिपुतेन सोमदेवेन गामो दतो वलुरकासघस वलुरकलेनान सकरा[र]करो[र]सदेय मयो

Sanskrit.

[1] राज्ञो वासिष्ठीपुत्रस्य स्वामिश्रीपुळुमाविनः संवत्सरे सप्तमे ७ ग्रीष्मपक्षे पञ्चमे ५

[2] दिवसे प्रथमे १ एतस्यां पूर्वस्यां[तिथौ]औत्खलकीयानां महारथिनः कौशिकीपुत्रस्य मित्रदेवस्य पुत्रेण

[3] महारथिना वासिष्ठीपुत्रेण सोमदेवेन ग्रामो दत्तः वलूरकसङ्घाय वलूरकलयनानां संस्कारकारणाय देय एषः ॥

Translation.

"King (*râño*) Vâsiṭhîputa, the illustrious lord (*sâmisiri*) [Puḷumâyi] in the year seventh (7), of summer the fifth (5) fortnight, and first (1) day. On that day Somadêva, a great warrior, the son of Vasiṭhî and of Mitadêva the son of Kosikî, a great warrior of the Okhaḷakiyas,[1] gave a village to the *sangha* of Valuraka. This gift is for the repairs of the Valuraka Leṇas."

---

[1] The construction of this sentence will be clearer if we put the mothers' names as epithets of their sons, thus: "On that day, the great warrior, Vasiṭhîputa Somadêva, son of the great warrior of the Okhaḷakiyas, Kosikîputa Mitadêva, gave a village to the *sangha* at Valuraka."

Remarks.

This inscription is somewhat broken : the name of Puḷumâyi is gone, but the space left and the name of Vâsiṭhîputa before it, renders it almost certain that this is the name wanting.

The mention of the *5th* fortnight of Grîshma shows that the year was not divided into six seasons (*ritu*) but into three—Grîshma, Varshâ, and Hemanta.

Autkhaḷakiya or *Okhaḷakiya* must be a clan or sept name.

INSCRIPTION No. 15.

Over the male and female figures to the right of the right-hand side door. The characters used seem rather later, if anything, than those in the preceding inscription :—

भदसमस भिखुस देयधम ।मियून

Sanskrit.

भद्रसमस्य भिक्षोर्देयधर्मो मिथुनम् ॥

Translation.

" Gift of a pair by the Bhikshu Bhadasama.[1]"

INSCRIPTION No. 16.

This faces the last, being over another pair of figures on the inner side of the right end of the outer screen or front of the verandah :—

भदसमस भिखुस देयधम मियून

Sanskrit.

भद्रसमस्य भिक्षोर्देयधर्मो मिथुनम् ॥

Translation.

" Gift of a pair by the Bhikshu Bhadasama.[1]"

INSCRIPTION No. 17.

On a piece of rail-pattern carving below the sculptures to the left of the central door :—

...[स]मणाय मातुय दानं वेयिका

Sanskrit.

...श्रमणाया मातुर्दानं वेदिका.॥

The beginning of this inscription is destroyed ; what is left reads,—" ...... the gift of a *vêdikâ* by the mother of ...... Samaṇâ.[2]"

INSCRIPTION No. 18.

Low down and to the right of the central door of the Chaitya :—

कोडिय भिखुणिय घुणिकमातु वेयिका दाण नादिकेन क[त]

---

[1] Sans. Bhadraśra.

[2] Sans. Śramaṇâ.

Sanskrit.

कोड्या भिक्षुण्या घूणिकमातुर्वेदिका दानम् । नन्दिकेन कृता ॥

Translation.

"The gift of a *vêdikâ* (rail ornament) by the nun Koḍî, mother of Ghuṇika. Made by Nadika.[1]"

INSCRIPTION No. 20.[2]

In the most northerly upper Cave, No. XII:—

[1] सिधं रञो वासिठिपुतस सिरिपुळिमाविस सवछरे चतुविसे २४ हेमतान पंखे ततिये ३ दिवसे बि-
[2] तिये २ उपासकस हरफरणस सेतफरण पुत्तस्य सोवसकस्य अबुळामाय वयबस्य इम देयधम मटपो-
[3] नवगभ महासाधियान परिगहे सघे चतुादिसे दिनं मातापितुन पुजासवसवान हितसुघस्ठतय एकविसस
[4] वछरे निठितो सहत च मे पुन बुधरखितेन मातर चस्य उपासकय बुधरखितस मातु देयधम पाथो अनो

Sanskrit.

[1] सिद्धम् । राज्ञो वासिष्ठीपुत्रस्य श्रीपुळिमावेः संवत्सरे चतुर्विंशे २४ हैमन्तानां पक्षे तृतीये ३ दिवसे द्वि-
[2] तीये २ उपासकस्य हरफरणस्य सेतफरणपुत्रस्य सोवसकस्य अबुलामायां वास्तव्यस्यायं देयधर्ममण्डपो
[3] नवगर्भः महासंघिकानां परिग्रहे संघे चातुर्दिशे दत्तः मातापित्रोः प्रजासर्वसत्वानां हितसुखस्थितये एकविंशे सं-
[4] वत्सरे निष्ठितः सहितं च मे पुनर्बुद्धरक्षितेन मात्रा चास्य उपासिकया । बुद्धरक्षितस्य मातुर्देयधर्मः पाथोऽन्यः ॥

Translation.

"To the Perfect! The king Vâsiṭhiputa, the illustrious (*siri*) Puḷimâvi, in the year (*of his reign*) twenty-four (24), in the third (3) fortnight of the winter (*hemanta*) months, the second (2) day. This meritorious gift of a nine-celled maṇḍapa by the (*Upâsaka*) layman Harapharaṇa, son of Setapharaṇa,[3] a Sovasaka, native of Abulâmâ, for the possession of the *saṅgha* of the Mahâsaṅghas from the four quarters. For the continuance in welfare and happiness of father and mother and all people and living things. Established in the twenty-first year, and with me Budharakhita and his mother an Upâsikâ. And in addition the meritorious gift of another passage by the mother of Budharakhita."

Remarks.

The language of this important inscription differs from that usually employed and the varieties of spelling remind us of what occurs on the Kshatrapa coins;

---

[1] Sans. Naṅdika.

[2] Inscription No. 19—just over an image of Buddha which has been inserted at a later date between the central and right-hand door of the Chaitya-cave—is not yet ready. It is of the 19th year of Vâsishṭhîputra's time, and records a benefaction to the Bhikshus by the tâlukdâr of Mâmala—the modern Mâwal.

[3] Harapharaṇa and Setapharaṇa are clearly two Persian names. The former corresponds with the Greek Horophernes or Holophernes. The latter part of both *-pharaṇa* is the Persian *frana*, 'lord.' *Seta* is perhaps the ancient *khshaeta* and the modern *shîd*.—G. Bühler.

Kârlê Cave Inscriptions.

No. 17

18

19

20

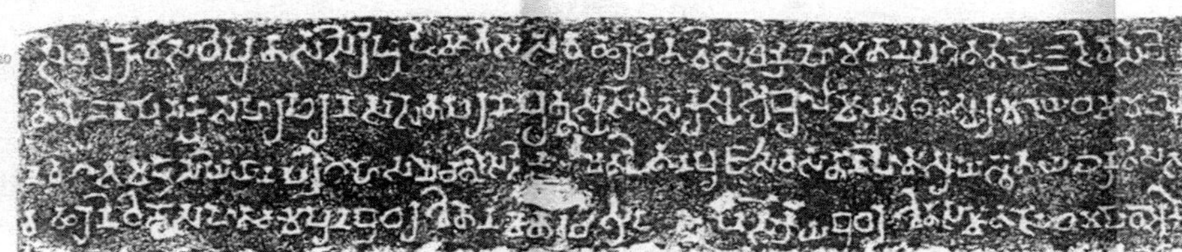

21

for in one place the genitive ends in *-sa* and in another in *-sya*, and we have *puta* in *Vâsiṭhîputasa* and *putta* in *Pharaṇaputtasya*.

The names of the Upâsaka Harapharaṇa and his father Setapharaṇa are unlike any in use in India, and may possibly be of Parthians. The name of their family *sovasaka* has a resemblance to *Śvâvaka*, but their native place Abulâmâ has not an Indian name. For *hitasughasṭhataya* we must read *hitasughasthataye* (in Sans. *hitasukhasthitaye*) *ekavisasavachare niṭhio*—established in the 1st year. The *vi* in *ekavisa°* is doubtful and might be read *ti*, making 31st year; but it is uncertain whether he reigned so long as 31 years.

Budharakhita and his mother seem to have been relations who aided Harapharaṇa in the work.

Inscription No. 21.

In a recess over a water cistern at the end of Cave XIII:—

....[सवछरे ?] ५ हेमाताण पखे......[एता]य पुवाय घ[भ]पत

.....हिणां अंतेवासिनिण लेण भगिने......साविकाण सदिगा

......घसु काले पवइताण संघाय ढु.........च देयधम पोढि

............परिवारेण उपय..................

...........अंतेवासिनिहि उसभाए.

Sanskrit.

......[संवत्सरे] ५ हैमन्तानां पक्षे .... एतस्यां पूर्वस्यां

......नां अन्तेवासिनीनां लयनं भागिने[या]: ......श्राविकायाः सादि...

......[निदा]घ[स्य] काले प्रव्रजितानां संघाय ढु...... च देयधर्मः प्राहैः

...................परिवारेण उपय...............................

.......................अन्तेवासिनीभिः ऋषभया ....

This inscription is so defaced that a consecutive translation is impossible. The sense runs thus:—

In the fifth year and of the Hemanta-paksha (of some râja—possibly Puḷumâyi), the female disciple of (*some*) Bhadanta, gave a leṇa; and a sister's daughter a Śrâvikâ (*or laic*) gave a cistern for the *saṅgha* of ascetics. With the donor several other names of relations are associated, (*but obliterated,*) with Usabhâ,[1] a female disciple.

Hematâṇaṁ—Sans. *haimantânâṁ*—is in the plural, 'of the months of winter.'

Inscription No. 22.

This is in Excavation No. III. to the south of the Chaitya:—

सिध पवइतस बुधरखितस देयधम

---

[1] Sans. Ṛishabhâ. The frequent occurrence of such names would seem to indicate some connection with Jainism;—the first Jaina being Ṛishabha.

Remarks.

Kuṇbi: this word is derived from the Sanskṛit *kuṭumbika*, meaning a person supporting a family; it is now generally used to indicate a particular caste. From the style of alphabet used in this inscription it appears to belong to somewhere between the times of Vâsishṭhîputra and Gautamîputra II. of the Andhra dynasty.

6.—INSCRIPTION FROM KOLHÂPUR.

In making some excavations about two years ago at Kolhâpur the foundations of a large Stûpa were turned up, and in the centre of it was found a square stone box containing a rock-crystal box, or relic-casket. On the square lid of the stone box was cut in pure Maurya or Aśôka characters an inscription (No. 1 on the plate), while on the side of the box was the letter *A*.

Bamhasa danaṁ.
Dhamagutena kâritaṁ.[1]

Translation.

"The gift of Bamha,[2] made by Dhamaguta.[3]"

7.—PITALKHORA CAVE INSCRIPTIONS.

The Pitalkhora Bauddha Caves are near the deserted village of Pâtna, 12 miles south of Châlisgâṅw in Khândesh. They are of a very early date, ranking with Bhâjâ and Khondâṇê.

On two pillars of the Chaitya-cave are short inscriptions[4] :—

INSCRIPTION No. 1 (No. 3 on the plate).

Transcript.

Patiṭhâṇâ Mitadêvasa
Gâdhikasa kulasa
[*ṭhab*]o dâna[*ṁ*].

Sanskrit.

प्रतिष्ठानात् मित्रदेवस्य
गाधिकस्य कुलस्य
स्तम्भो दानम् ॥

Translation.

"A pillar, the gift of Mitadêva of the Gâdhi family, from Patiṭhâṇa.[5]"

Remark.

This inscription shows pure Aśôka or Maurya characters.

---

[1] There not being room for *-ritam* in the second line, it has been inserted *between* the lines.

[2] Sans. Bramha.

[3] Sans. Dharmagupta.

[4] Translated by Dr. G. Bühler, C.I.E.

[5] Pratishṭhâṇa—Paiṭhâṇa.

Junnar

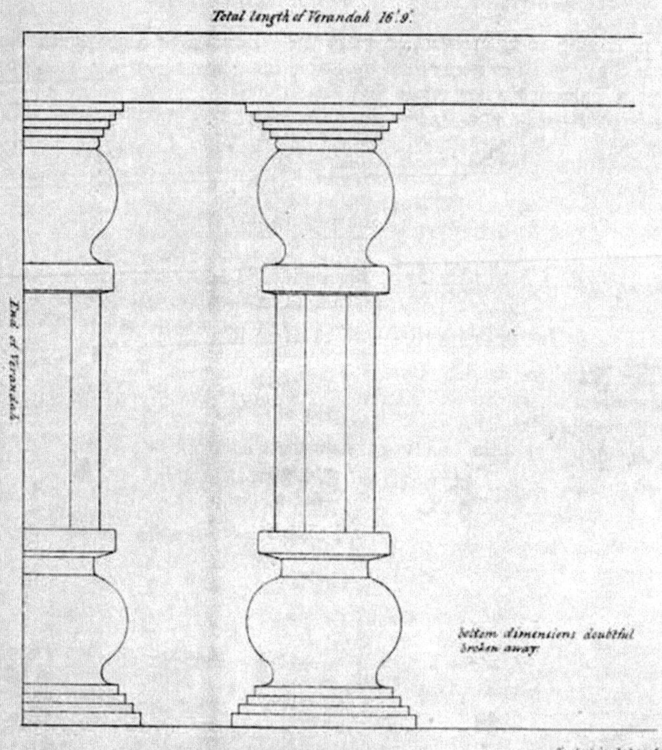

Scale ½ inch to a foot.

Chaitya cave G. No 3. 2 columns and pilasters of Verandah.

Photozincographed, Govt. Office, Poona, 1880.

INSCRIPTION No. 7.

रामवेजस वछी[पुतस म]गिलस पुतस दतकस दान

Sanskrit.

रामवैद्यस्य वात्सीपुत्रस्य मगिलस्य पुत्रस्य दत्तकस्य दानम् ॥

"Gift of Dataka[1], son of the royal physician Magila, the son of Vachhî."

Remark.

The alphabet of these inscriptions in the Vihâra differs very little from those in the Chaitya, and may belong to about 100 B. C., or earlier a little. At this time Paiṭhana was evidently the capital of the district.

8.—JUNNAR CAVES AND INSCRIPTIONS.

A number of inscriptions from the Junnar Caves were given in No. 1 of these *Memoranda*, and some of them were afterwards translated by Dr. Kern of Leiden.[2] The Paṇḍit having gone to Junnar with a memorandum of all those known to exist, he took fac-simile impressions of all the accessible ones and copies of the others.

INSCRIPTION No. 1.

This is in one of a group of caves near the base of the east scarp of Śivaneri hill towards the southern end, on the back of a recessed bench on the left side of a small cave consisting of three cells each about 7 feet square broken into one. The letters left are all clear and distinct, but the first portion of it is broken away.

......य भूतेनकस

......पोढि चा देयधम.

Sanskrit.

......ष भूतेनकस्य

......प्रहिष देयधर्मः ॥

It records the gift of a *poḍhi* or cistern and probably the *leṇa* by some person, perhaps named Bhutenaka.

The above inscription is in the fifth excavation of this group. The third is a chamber 20½ feet by 19½ and 11 feet high with the cylindrical base or drum of a dâgoba 5' in diameter near the back. It is 3½ feet high, with a small sunken recess in the flat top, which suggests the idea that the upper portion of it must have been structural. The entrance is 6 feet wide, and the verandah is 16½ feet by 4½ inside the pilasters, and with two columns in front (one destroyed) of the pattern so common here and at Nâsik. A drawing of one of these and the adjoining pilaster is given in the accompanying Plate.[3]

---

[1] Sans. Dattaka.   [2] *Ind. Ant.*, vol. VI., p. 39.

[3] This plate is a photolithograph from a drawing among the MS. notes of the Messrs. West.

Inscription No. 2.[1]

This is in one of the group in the upper scarp on the east side of the fort. It is in a chamber 21′ by 11′, exactly over a vihâra below, measuring 24′ by 22′, with seven cells, with which it communicates by a stair outside at the right end. The inscription is deeply cut along the upper part of the left wall.

[१] मुधकियस मलस गोलिकियस आनदस बेण नणान देयधम उपठाण.

Sanskrit.

मूर्द्धकीयस्य मल्लस्य गौल्लिकीयस्यानन्दस्य द्वयोर्जनयोर्देयधर्म उपस्थानम्.॥

"Gift of a reception-hall by Mudhakiya Mala and Golikiya Ânada, two men."

Remarks.

Mudhakiya, probably the Sanskrit *Mûrdhakîya*, and *Golikiya*, Sanskrit *Gollakiya* (the *li* is injured and might be *li* or *la*) are the names of the families to which Mala (Sans. Malla) and Ânada (Sans. Ananda) respectively belonged.

Upaṭhâṇa, Sans. *upasthâna*, 'sitting near,'—a place for receiving visits, a drawing-room—referring to the room in which the inscription is.

Higher up than the group in which Inscription No. 1 is found are a number of cisterns, recesses and caves, on one of which there is a small fragment of an inscription.[2] In the group known as the Bârâ-koṭri, on the same side of the hill is Inscription No. 3, of which Dr. Stevenson gives the first three lines as his No. 8, and the two last as No. 9.[3]

Inscription No. 4.

This inscription is in a Chaitya Cave 31′ by 20½′ with a flat roof described in my *Memorandum*. The accompanying drawing of one of the pillars in the front part of the cave will illustrate their style.[4] The roof is painted in square panels with a circular ornament in each panel, and the same with the roof of the outer verandah.[5] The inscription is on the back wall of the verandah near the right end.

वीरसेणकस गहपतिपमुघस
धंमनिगमस देयधंम चेतियघरो
नियुतो सवलोकहितसुखाय

Sanskrit.

वीरसेनकस्य गृहपतिप्रमुखस्य
धर्मनैगमस्य देयधर्मश्चैत्यगृहं
नियुक्तं सर्वलोकहितसुखाय ॥

"Of Vîrasenaka, a chief householder and upright merchant, the meritorious gift of a *chetiyaghara*, presented for the welfare and happiness of all."

---

[1] No. 11 in No. I., and *Ind. Ant.*, vol. VI, p. 38.

[2] *Ind. Ant.*, vol. VI., p. 38*b*.

[3] *Ind. Ant.*, vol. VI., p. 38*b*; *Jour. B. B. R. A. Soc.*, vol. V., pp. 160-ff. It is No. 6 among those given by Col. Sykes, *Jour. R. A. Soc.*, vol. IV., pp. 287-ff.

[4] From the MS. notes and drawings of the Messrs. West.

[5] No. 12 *ut. sup.* This is No. 7 of Dr. Stevenson's copies, and No. 7 of Col. Sykes's.

Junnar Cave Inscriptions.

1 Scale $\frac{1}{11}$

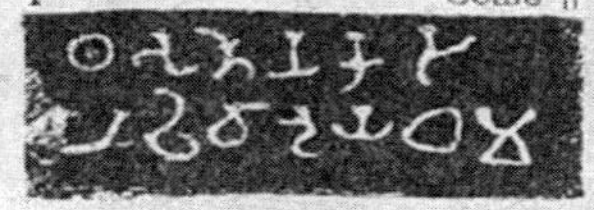

2 Scale $\frac{1}{12}$

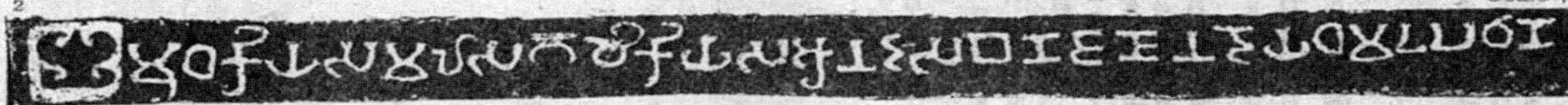

3 Scale $\frac{1}{8}$

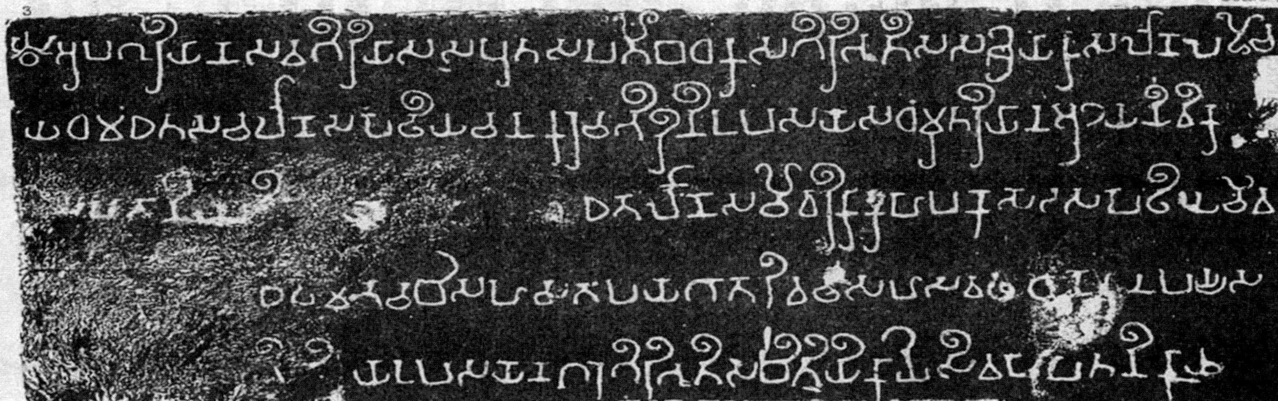

Photozincographed, Govt. Office, Poona, 1881

Junnar *Chaitya cave — B. No. 14 — Columns between inner Verandah and cave.*
2 columns and 2 halves forming pilasters. — Scale ½ inch to a foot.

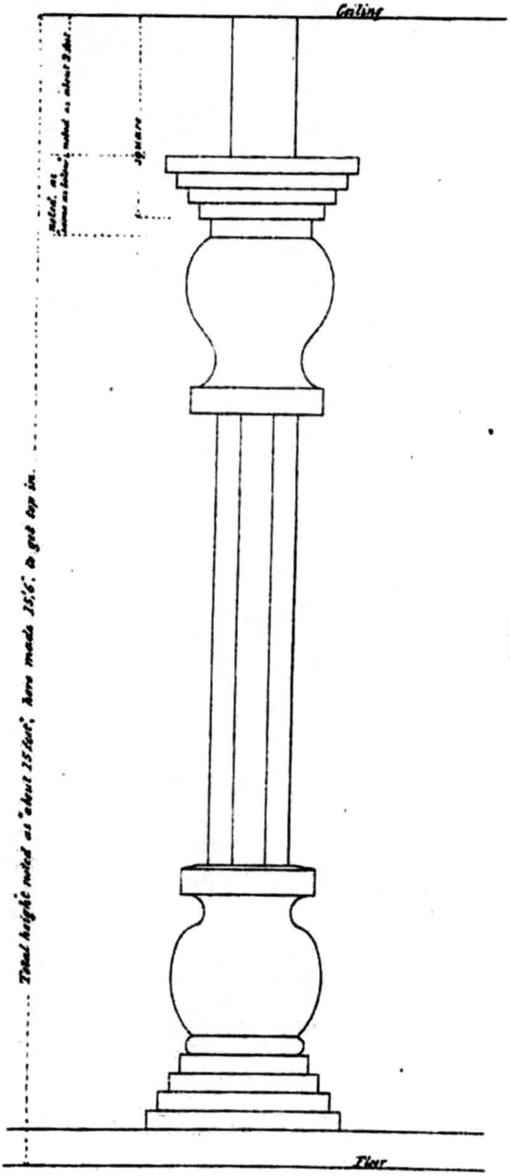

Photozincographed, Govt Office, Poona, 1890

Junnar Cave Inscriptions.

4 — Scale 1/11

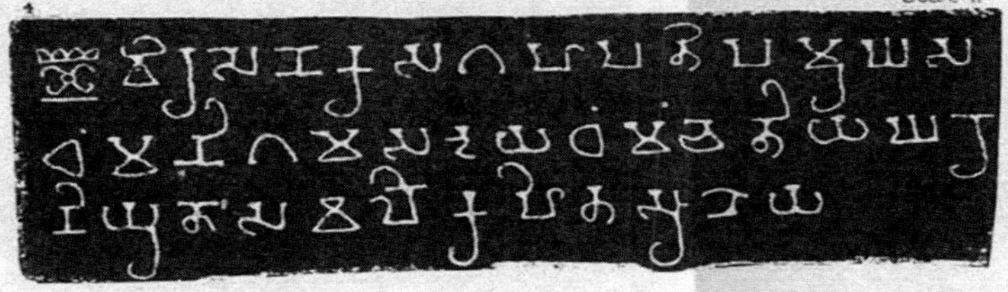

5 — Scale 1/8

6 — Scale 1/8

7 — Scale 1/6

8 — Scale 1/3

Photozincographed, Govt. Office, Poona, 1881.

Remark.

Dhamanigama, Sans. *dharmanaigama*, 'who trades uprightly'; *kûṭavâṇijya* and *dharmavâṇijya* are 'unjust' and 'just trading.'

INSCRIPTION No. 5.

This is near the extreme end of this row of caves, high up above a cistern. It is inaccessible and an eye copy could only be made. It is, however, clearly cut.

यवनस इरिलस गतान देयधम बे पोढियो

Sanskrit.

यवनस्येरिलस्य गतान (?) देयधर्मौ द्वी प्रही ॥

"The meritorious gift of two cisterns by the Yavana Irila Gatâna (?)."

Remarks.

Yavana is generally applied to foreigners, but it is impossible to say to what country this man belonged; he may have been a Parthian or Baktrian Greek.

Gatâna after the name Irila might be read *gabhânaṁ* (Sans. *garbhebhyaḥ*—the 6th case in Prâkṛit being used for the 4th in Sanskrit[1])—and we should then translate 'for the cells'; but this is doubtful, and in No. 33 the word is again used where such a meaning would not apply.

INSCRIPTION No. 6.

This is in the last excavation of the group, on the back of a recess above an open cistern. It is difficult to get at and much effaced. At the end of the second line are some letters like *kaṇḍavaví*.[2]

[१] अपगुरियान सवागिरियस पुतस पतिबधकस [गि]रिभूतिस [सह] भयाय सिवपालनिकाय

[२] देयधम पोढि लेन च एतस अखयनिवि............

Sanskrit.

अपगुरियाणां शर्वगिरियस्य पुत्रस्य प्रतिबंधकस्य गिरिभूतेः सह भार्यया शिवपालनिकया

देयधर्मः प्रहिल्यनं चैतस्याक्षयनीवि............

"The meritorious gift of a Leṇa and cistern by Patibadhaka Giribhûti son of Savagiriya of the Apaguriyas, with his wife Sivapâlanikâ; for this, a permanent capital................."

Remark.

Apaguriya may be the name of a clan.

INSCRIPTION No. 7.

On the façade of the Chaitya[3] at Mânmoḍi hill, on the central flat surface of a half lotus over the entrance—

यवनस चंदानं देयधम गभदा[र]

Sanskrit.

यवनस चन्द्राणां [न्द्रस्य] देयधर्मो गर्भद्वारः ॥

---

[1] See *Prâkrit Prakâśa* 64, VI.

[2] This is No. 8 of Col. Sykes's copies.

[3] See frontispiece to the *Cave Temples.*

"The meritorious gift of the façade of a (*garbha*) hall by the Yavana Chaṅda.[1]"

Remark.

The name Chanda is in the plural (conf. Kârlê Inscription No. 7). The *ra* at the end is broken away.

INSCRIPTION No. 8.

This is found in the series at caves in the southern spur of the Mânmoḍi hill about a mile east from the Chaitya in which is Inscription No. 7. It is on the back wall of an open verandah in a group of chambers now all broken into one. It is much defaced,[2] what is legible reads—

......[ग]हपतिपु[तानं] भातूणं दाण क

......सच प[च]गभं देयधंमं

Sanskrit.

......गृहपतिपुत्राणां भ्रातृणां दानं क

......स्य च पञ्चगर्भं देयधर्मः ॥

"...A five-celled (*house*)......the meritorious gift of the brothers, sons of Gahapati........."

On a large unfinished Chaitya in this group there are a number of inscriptions, many of them but indistinctly cut on a rough surface.

INSCRIPTION No. 9.

This is on the left end of the back wall of the verandah, just above the level of the door, faintly cut on a rough surface.[3]

गामे पुवानदेषु निवतनानि

पनरस १५ पलपस

देयधंमं अप[रा]जितेसु ग

ने पयोगोकहथे [दान ?]

Sanskrit.

ग्रामे पुवानदे निवर्त्तनानि

पञ्चदश १५ पल्लवस्य

देयधर्मः अपराजिते गणे

पयोगोक [पयोघोष ?] हस्ते दानम् ॥

"A meritorious gift of 15 *nivatanas* by Palapa in Puvânada village : the gift in the hand of Payogoka of the Aparâjita[4] sect."

Remarks.

The name of Puvânada, like that of all villages, is in the plural.

---

[1] Sans. Chandra.

[2] It is given as No. 2 of the Junnar inscriptions in Bird's *Caves of Western India.*

[3] This is No. 22 of Dr. Stevenson's, and No. 6 of Dr. Bird's copies.

[4] In the plural.

Junnar Cave Inscriptions.

9 Scale 1/11

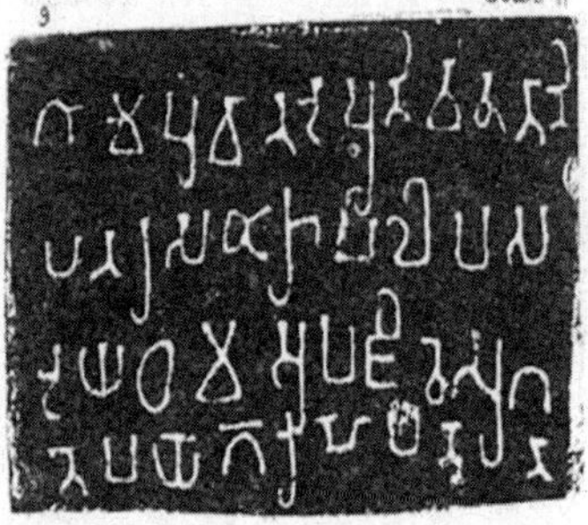

10 Scale 1/9

11

12 Scale 1/9

14 Scale 1/9

13 Scale 1/11

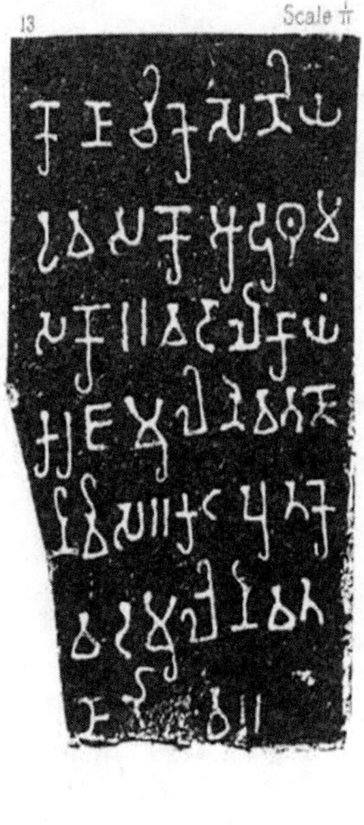

Photozincographed, Govt. Office, Poona, 1881.

4 *hâths* make 1 *daṇḍa*, and 30 *daṇḍa* make one *nivartana*; but sometimes 7 *hâths* are allowed to the *daṇḍa*.

Inscriptions Nos. 10, 11, 12.

These three inscriptions are on two octagonal pillars in front of the same large unfinished Chaitya Cave at the foot of the hill. They are in well cut letters, but the language is neither Pâli nor Sanskrit. No. 10 is on the left pillar, on the right side of it; No. 11 is on the right pillar corresponding side facing No. 10; and No. 12 is on the adjacent face towards the inner sides, but the lines do not align with those of No. 11.[1]

No. 10.	No. 11.	No. 12.
तावके	अपुराण	आस
केसुस	देसुका	ठाड
ततोभो	ह्रामणा	खुनेस
गादि	रोअठि	ण
	वादिमा	
	निकच	
	वीच	

Inscription No. 13.

On the left wall of the large recess over the door, and on the same level as the window; the letters are indistinct.[2]

कोणाचिकसेणिय
उवसको आडुयूप
सको ॥ वडालिकायं
करजमुलनिवतणा
नि विस ॥ कटपुतके
वडमुले निवत
णानि [न]व

Sanskrit.

कोणाचिकश्रेण्या
उपासक आडुयूप-
शकः ॥ वटालिकायां
करंजमूले निवर्त्तना-
नि विंशतिः ॥ कटपुत्रके
वटमूले निवर्त-
नानि नव ॥

[1] These are respectively Dr. Stevenson's Nos. 15, 14, and 13; Dr. Bird's No. 5; and Colonel Sykes's Nos. 3, 2, and 1.

[2] Dr. Stevenson's No. 21.

"By Aḍuṭhûma the Saka, an upâsaka of the guild of the Koṇâchikas (*a gift of*) 20 *nivotanas* in Vaḍâlikâ[1] near the Karanja tree, and in Kaṭaputaka, 9 *nivatanas* near the banyan tree."

Remarks.

What trade the *Koṇâchikas* were of, does not appear. The *Sakas* were perhaps foreigners but converts (*upâsakas*) to Buddhism : *Aḍuthûma* is a foreign name.

There is a Varâḍa 6 miles N. from Junnar, and a Katur, 5 miles S.S.W., which may be the Vaḍâli and Kaṭaputa (Sans. Kaṭaputra) of this inscription.

Inscription No. 14.

On the back of the recess over the door and alongside the window on its left. It is contiguous to No. 13. Many of the letters, especially in the lower lines, are very uncertain, as the rock is rough.[2]

महावेजे गामे जाबभति
उदेसेण निवतणानि षणुविस
सिधगणे अपराजिते
[नि]असतानि सेलस
मानमुकडस पुरतो
तलकवाडके निवत
णानि तिनि ॥ नगरस
......क...सेलउदे
सेण निवतणानि बे

Sanskrit.

महावेदग्रामे जाबभा·
त्युद्देशेण निवर्तनानि षड्विंशतिः
सिद्धगणे अपराजिते
न्यस्तानि शैलस्य
मानमुकुटस्य पुरत-
स्तलकवाटके निवर्त-
नानि त्रीणि ॥ नगरस्य
......क...शैलोद्दे·
शेन निवर्तने द्वे ॥

"In the village of Mahâveja, twenty-six *nivatanas* for Jâbabhati. To the Sidhagaṇa of the Aparâjitas, three *nivatanas* given at the hill-foot near Mânamukaḍa hill ; of the town......for...hill, two *nivatanas*..."

---

[1] Sans. Vaṭâlik.

[2] This is Dr. Stevenson's Nos. 19 and 20.

Junnar Cave Inscriptions.

15 Scale $\frac{1}{9}$

16 Scale $\frac{1}{9}$

17 Scale $\frac{1}{11}$

18 Scale $\frac{1}{11}$

Govt. Photozincographic Office, Poona, 188[illegible]

Remark.

The Sidhagaṇas evidently belonged to or were a division of the Aparâjita sect of Buddhists; *Aparâjita* (unconquered) is used as an adjective qualifying *sidhagaṇa*. *Mânamukaḍa* (Sans. *Mânamukuṭa*, 'crown of pride') appears to be the old name of the Mânmoḍa hill, where the inscription is. The donor's name is wanting,—possibly it was the same as in the previous inscription.

INSCRIPTION No. 15.

This is on the left side of the front of the arch round the window.[1]

Pâli.	*Sanskrit.*
आवि	आम्रि
काताति	काताति
निवत	निवर्त
णानि द्वे	ने द्वे
वाहत	वाहत
वचेडु	वचेडु-
कस	कस्यै-
एस	तत्

"Two *nivatanas* of mango trees (?)......this of Vâhata Vacheḍuka."

Remark.

Ambikatati, probably Sans. *âmrikatati*, but the *ta* may be *bha* and *âmbikabhati*—a mango field.

INSCRIPTION No. 16.

This is on the right side of the arch, opposite No. 15, but instead of being carved across the front, it is cut in three lines parallel to the arc of the arch.[2]

सेनिये वसकरस
मासे पाउनदुके
कासकारेसु सेनिय पादए[क]स

Sanskrit.

श्रेण्या वंशकारस्य
मासे पादोनद्विकम्
कांस्यकारेषु [काराणां] श्रेण्याः पादैक......

"The guild of bambu-workers, monthly, one and three quarters, and the guild of braziers a quarter......"

---

[1] This is Dr. Stevenson's No. 18, and Dr. Bird's No. 1.

[2] This is Dr. Stevenson's No. 17.

Remarks.

In *vasakarasa*, the anusvâra appears to be lost: Sans. *vaṁśakâra*, a bambu-worker; *kâsakâra*, Sans. *kâṁsyakâra*, braziers, hodie—*kâsâra*.

INSCRIPTION No. 17.

On the back of the recess to the right of the great arch.[1]

गामे वलाहकेसु कर
जभाति उदेसेण निवत
णानि बारस॥गामसे
उरकेसु निवतणानि
....

Sanskrit.

ग्रामे वलाहके करज
भृत्युद्देशेन निवर्त-
नानि द्वादश॥ ग्रामसे-
उरके निवर्तनानि
....

"In Valâhaka village, for *karajabhati*, twelve *nivatanas*. In Seuraka village ...*nivatanas*......"

INSCRIPTION No. 18.

On the right wall of the recess, to the right of No. 17. Many of the letters are doubtful.

अवारिलिव सरिख
डके निवतलानि च
तारि॥
अवरिल............
....
अवारिले ।िपुत्र-
क उदेसेण निवत
नानि अठ॥ गामक
डकेसु निवतणानि
बार देय............

[1] Dr. Stevenson's No. 16.

Junnar Cave Inscriptions.

19

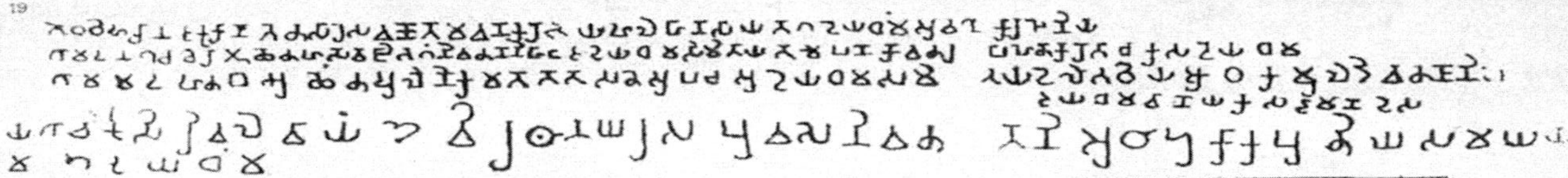

(eye copy)

under angle of moulding.

Doorway.

20 Scale 1/6

21 Scale 1/6

22 Scale 1/10

Sanskrit.

अपरास्य श्रिखे-
टके निवर्तनानि च-
त्वारि ॥
अपरास्य............
....
अपरास्ये जितपुत्र-
कोद्देशेन निवर्त-
नान्यष्टौ ॥ ग्राम-
कटके निवर्तनानि
द्वादश देय.............

"And on the west in Sirikaḍaka four *nivatanas*; west......for Jiputraka eight *nivatanas*; in Kaḍaka village, twelve *nivartanas*—a meritorious gift."

INSCRIPTION No. 19.

On a quadrantal moulding over the door-way, on a rough surface. The lower line and half are in larger letters than the lines above.[1]

(*Not Translated.*)

INSCRIPTION No 20.

To the right of the large unfinished Chaitya in which are the preceding inscriptions, is a verandah 15½' by 5' with two cells at the back. It is half filled with earth, and the front broken away. The inscription is on the back wall between the doors of the two cells.[2]

भारुकछकानं लंकुडियानं भातूणं
असासमस पुताण[3]
बुधमितस बुधरखितस च बिगभं देयधंमं

Sanskrit.

भारुकच्छकयोर्लंकुटिकयोर्भ्रात्रोर-
श्रश्रमस्य पुत्रयो-
र्बुद्धमित्रस्य बुद्धरक्षितस्य च द्विगर्भं देयधर्मः ॥

"A house of two cells, a meritorious gift by the brothers Budhamita and Budharakhita, Lankuḍiyas,[4] sons of Asasama, inhabitants of Bharukachha."

---

[1] This is Nos. 23 and 24 of Dr. Stevenson's, and Dr. Bird gives the 5th line of it as his No. 7.

[2] This is No. 9 of those in *Ind. Ant.*, vol. VI., p. 36, Dr. Stevenson's No. 12, and Dr. Bird's No. 3.

[3] This is inserted in much smaller letters between the lines.

[4] Probably Sans. *Laṅkuṭikas*—a sect.

Inscription No. 21.

This is another verandah alongside the last, 15½' by 8' with two cells at the back. It is on the back-wall between the doors of the cells, but has not been finished.[1]

सयितिगहपतिपुतस गहपतिस सिवदासस
वितियिकाय च सहा परिवा

Sanskrit.

सायितिगृहपतिपुत्रस्य गृहपतेः शिवदासस्य
द्वितीयिकायाश्च सह परिवारेण ॥

"(*Gift*) of the householder Sivadâsa, son of the householder Sayiti, and his wife with all his relatives..."

Inscription No. 22.

Next to the last verandah, is another 18' by 6½' with two columns and pilasters, without cells, and nearly full of earth. The inscription is outside close to the pilaster. The lower part of it is peeled off and so injured that a translation can hardly be attempted. It seems to have recorded the construction of a cave for Chetiyasa by a householder.[2]

गणाचरियानं थेरानं भ-
यंतसुलसानं तेविजा
नं अंतेवासिनं थेरान
भयंत चेतियसानं तेवि
जानं नंदनकानवक
......अ कोथल्की[3]
......च गहपति
......नतुनो नदणक
....
देयधम

Sanskrit.

गणाचार्याणां स्थविराणां भ-
दन्तसुल्सानां त्रैविद्या-
नामन्तेवासिनां स्थविराणां
भदन्तचैत्यसानां त्रैवि-
द्यानां नंदनकाणवक
......अ कौस्थलकी
......च गृहपति
......नप्तुर्नन्दनक
....
देयधर्मः ॥

---

[1] Stevenson's No. 11, Bird's No. 2, and No. 10, *Ind. Ant.*, vol. VI., p. 36.

[2] This is Stevenson's No. 10, and Bird's No. 8.

[3] This letter थ had been at first omitted and then cut above the line.

Junnar Cave Inscriptions.

23 Scale $\frac{1}{8}$

24 Scale $\frac{1}{8}$

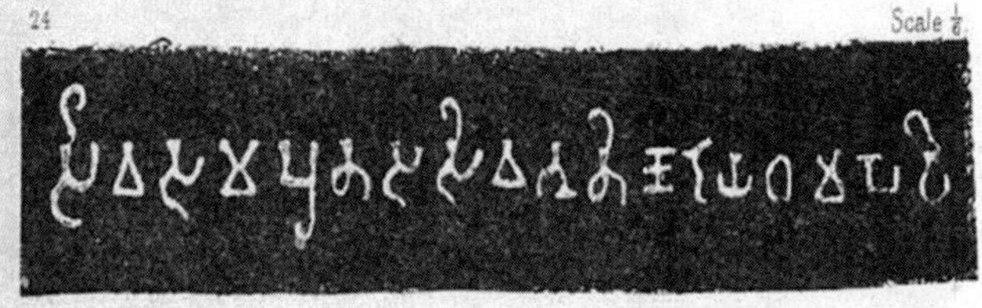

25 Scale $\frac{1}{9}$

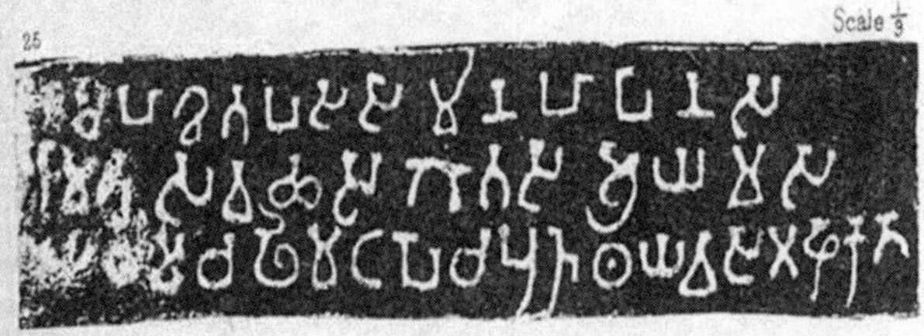

26 Scale $\frac{1}{6}$

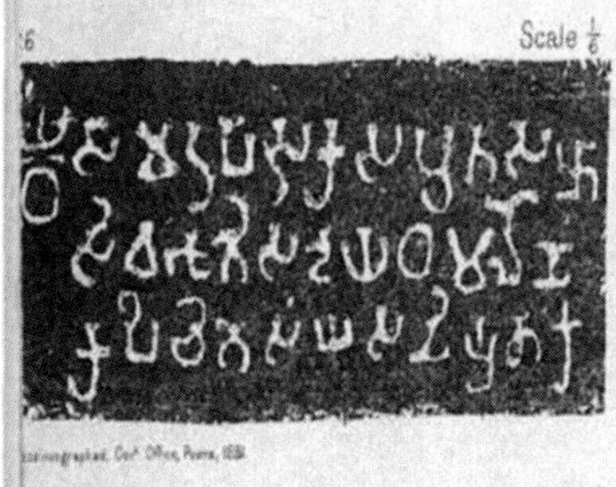

27 Scale $\frac{1}{9}$

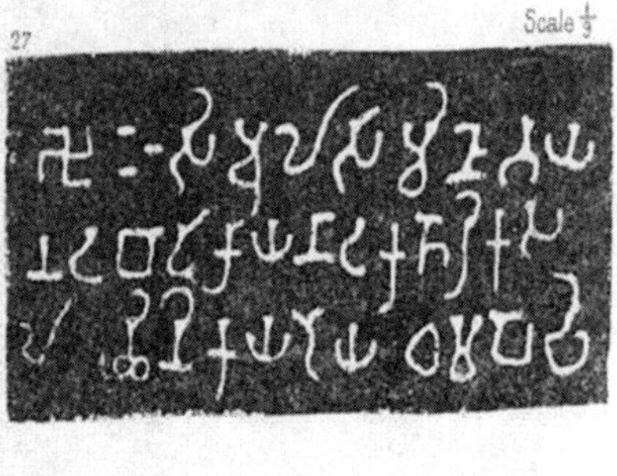

...ographed, Govt. Office, Poona, [illegible]

"The Âchârya of the Gaṇa, the venerable (*Thêra*) and reverend (*Bhayanta*) Tevidya[1] Sulasa: his disciple Thêra Bhayanta Chetiyasa, a Tevidya......*nadanakâṇavaka* ...*kothalaki*... and householder...... his grandson Nandanaka ...... the meritorious gift."

Inscription No. 23.

In the eastern slope of the southern spur of the Mânmoḍi hill is another series of caves. The first excavation is a verandah with two cells, and with two octagonal pillars and pilasters in front. The second is an unfinished Chaitya 33½' by 11½' with flat roof and a large square rough block of stone near the back. On the right hand wall outside the verandah, between the octagonal pilaster and the doorway into the next verandah and rather above the level of the door is an inscription in three long lines but nearly all obliterated. In the second line "son of Satamala" and in the third "son of Virabhuti" can just be made out.

सिधं उपासकस नेगम......
सतमल्पुतस ....
...पुत विरभुति......

Sanskrit.

सिद्धम् । उपासकस्य नैग[मस्य]......
शतमल्लपुत्रस्य (?)
...पुत्रवीरभूति...

Inscription No. 24.

Passing two chambers we reach a large recess, with a smaller one over it, on the back-wall of which, but inaccessible, is Inscription No. 24.[2]

सिवसमपुतस सिवभुतिणो देयधम पोढि

Sanskrit.

शिवसमपुत्रस्य शिवभूतेर्देयधर्मः प्रहिः॥

"The meritorious gift of a cistern by Sivabhuti, son of Sivasama."

Inscription No. 25.

Passing a cistern and two small recesses, we reach another recess with a bench round three sides, on the left side wall of which is the next inscription.[3] It is one of the most important of the series as the only one containing a royal name—that of Nahapâṇa, which we find also at Nâsik and at Kârlê.

[रञो] महाखतपस सामिनहपानस
[आ]मात्यस वछसगोतस अयमस
[दे]यधम च [पो ?]ढि मटपो च पुञयय वसे ४६ कतो

---

[1] 'Knowing the Tripiṭaka'— Sans. Traividya.

[2] No. 7 in *Ind. Ant.*, vol. VI., p. 35, Stevenson's No. 25, and Bird's No. 4.

[3] Stevenson's No. 26, and No. 8, *Ind. Ant.*, vol. VI, p. 35.

Sanskrit.

राज्ञो महाक्षत्रपस्य स्वामिनहपाणस्या-
मात्यस्य वत्ससगोत्रस्यायमस्य
देयधर्मः प्रहिर्मण्डपश्च पुण्यार्थाय वर्षे ४६ कृत : ॥

"The meritorious gift of a maṇḍapa and cistern by Ayama of the Vachhasagotra, prime minister of the king Mahâkhatapa (*great Satrap*), the lord Nahapâṇa; made for merit, in the year 46."

The next series of caves are those in the Leṇâdri hill about three miles north of the town. Taking the caves from west to east the following inscriptions occur :—

Inscription No. 26.

In the seventh excavation from the extreme end of the series, which is an open verandah 33½′ by about 4′, is Inscription No. 26 over a recessed bench in the back-wall. It is clearly cut.[1]

सामरूपासकस पुतस
सिवभूतिस देयधम लेणं
कपिचिते संघस निपुतं क [?]

Sanskrit.

श्यामोपासकस्य पुत्रस्य
शिवभूतेर्देयधर्मो लयनं
कपिचिते संघाय नियुक्तम् ॥

"The meritorious gift of a Leṇa by Sivabhûti, son of Sâmara[2] the Upâsaka, to the Saṅgha of Kapichita."

Remark.

Kapichita is probably the old name of the Leṇâdri hill, or of the monastic establishment there.

Inscription No. 27.

Passing a number of excavations we reach a recess over a dry tank which has been broken open. On the back wall of the recess the next inscription is clearly cut.[3]

इसिमुल्सामिनो भय-
नदत्राळिकाय नाडकतोरिकस
लछिनिक[4]य देयधम पोढि

[1] This is Dr. Stevenson's No. 6, and Col. Sykes's No. 13; also No. 6, *Ind. Ant.*, vol. VI., p. 35.

[2] Sans. Syâmala.

[3] Stevenson's No. 5, Sykes's No. 11, and No. 5, *Ind. Ant.*, vol. VI., p. 35.

[4] Read °काय.

Junnar Cave Inscriptions.

28 Scale $\frac{1}{6}$

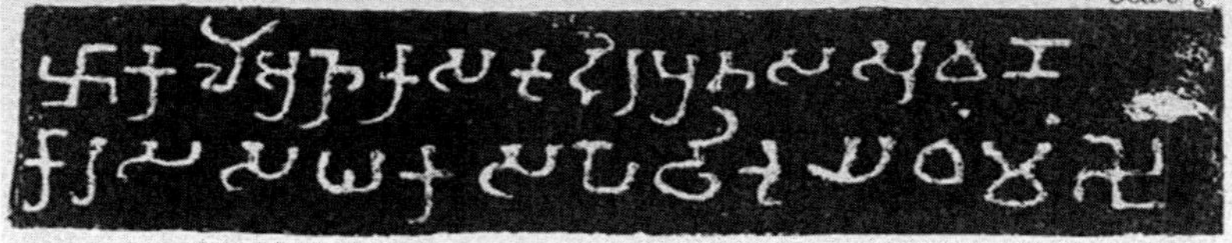

32 Scale $\frac{1}{8}$

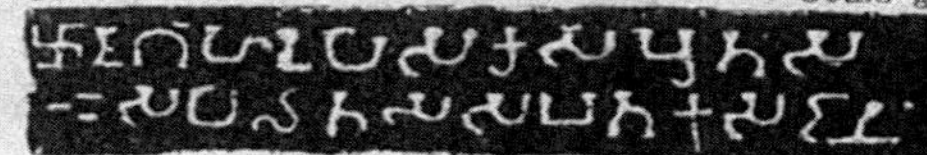

29 Scale $\frac{1}{8}$

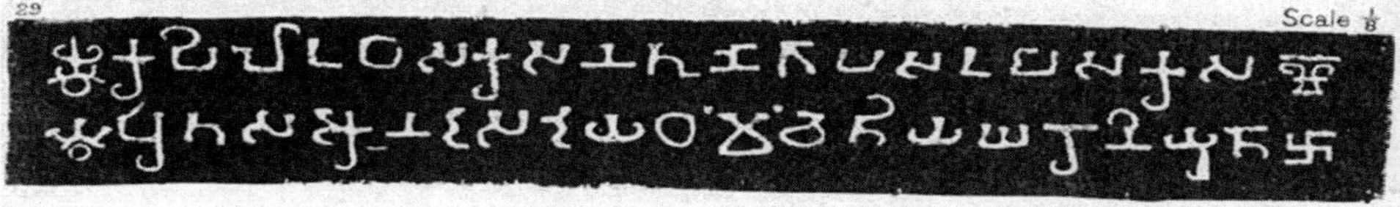

33 Scale $\frac{1}{11}$

30 Scale $\frac{1}{17}$

31 Scale $\frac{1}{11}$

34 Scale $\frac{1}{8}$

Photozincographed, Govt. Office, Poona, 1881.

Sanskrit.

ऋषिमूलस्वामिनो भार्या-
नन्दबालिकाया नाडक·तोरिकस्य
लक्ष्मिनिकाया देयधर्मः प्रहिः ॥

"The meritorious gift of a cistern by Lachhinikâ,[1] wife of Torika the Nâḍaka,[2] [*and*] Naḍabâḷikâ, wife of Mulasâmi Isi.[3]"

INSCRIPTION No. 28.

In the next recess also over a cistern, is an inscription, distinctly cut on the back wall and beginning and ending with a *svastika.*[4]

कलिअनकस कुडिरपुतस
सुवणकारस सघकस पोढि देयधंमं

Sanskrit.

कल्याणकस्य कुटीरपुत्रस्य सुवर्ण-
कारस्य सङ्घकस्य प्रहिर्देयधर्मः ॥

"The meritorious gift of a cistern by Saghaka,[5] a goldsmith, son of Kuḍira[6] of Kalyâṇa."

INSCRIPTION No. 29.

After the last are three chambers opening into one verandah; then a cell with an open verandah, and at a lower level is another cell with a verandah. The next is a flat roofed Chaitya, 22′ by 12′ with a dâgoba. The verandah measures 20′ by 3′ with two columns and pilasters in front, broken away. The inscription is on the back wall of the verandah, high up, and to the left of the door.[7]

कपिलउपासकस नतुनो तापसउपासकस
पुतस आनदस देयधंमं चेतियघरो नियुतो

Sanskrit.

कपिलोपासकस्य नप्तुस्तापसोपासकस्य
पुत्रस्यानन्दस्य देयधर्मश्चैत्यगृहं नियुक्तम् ॥

"The meritorious gift of a Chetiyaghara given by Ânad, son of Tâpasa the Upâsaka, and grandson of Kapila the Upâsaka."

After passing the large vihâra now appropriated as a temple of Gaṇapati a vaulted Chaitya is reached, near the top of the ascent. It measures 41′ by 22′

---

1 Sans. Lakshmiṇika. 2 Nâḍaka must be a caste name. 3 Sans. Ṛishi.

4 Stevenson's No. 4, Bird's No. 12, Sykes's No. 12, and No. 4 in *Ind. Ant.*, vol. VI., p. 35.

5 Sans. Sanghaka. 6 Sans. Kuṭira.

7 No. 3 in *Ind. Ant.*, vol. VI., p. 35, Stevenson's No. 3, and Bird's No. 11.

6" with stone ribs both over the nave and aisles. It has five octagonal free-standing and one attached columns on each side, with bases and capitals (see Plate), and six plain octagonal ones round the dâgoba. Above the capitals of the columns are pairs of animals, alternately elephants and tigers to each capital.

Inscription No. 30.

This is on the back wall of the verandah, over the door, deeply cut, and with a *svastika* at the beginning and end of the line.[1]

[१] कलीअनस हेरणिकपुतस सुलसदतस एकपुरिसस चेतियघरो नियुतो देयधम

Sanskrit.

कल्याणस्य हैरण्यकपुत्रस्य सुलसदत्तस्यैकपुरुषस्य चैत्यगृहं नियुक्तं देयधर्मः ॥

" The meritorious gift of a constructed Chetiyaghara by the distinguished Sulasadata, son of Heraṇika[2] of Kalyâṇa."

Inscription No. 31.

Passing a recess to the right of the Chaitya, the next excavation is a chamber 26' by 29' and 8' high, with a bench along both sides and back. It has two cells on each side and three in the back. There are two open windows in the verandah, over the left of which the inscription is distinctly cut.[3] There is a cistern with water outside the verandah to the right.

धंञिकसेणिय सतगभं पोदि च देयधमं

Sanskrit.

धान्यकश्रेण्याः सप्तगर्भं प्रहिश्च देयधर्मः ॥

"A meritorious gift of a seven-celled cave and cistern by the guild of corn-dealers."

Remarks.

Dhañika, Sans. *dhânyaka*,—a corn-dealer. *Satagabha*, Sans. *saptagarbha*,—of seven cells.

In the south scarp of Sivaneri hill there is another series of about sixteen excavations commencing from the tiled Hindu temple in the second line of fortification, the shrine of which temple is an excavation in the rock. Among these caves are three inscriptions, the first being on the back wall of a verandah 23½' by 3', with a cell behind. The inscription is to the left of the cell door, on a slightly sunk panel. The fourth letter of the second line only is broken.

---

[1] *Ind. Ant.*, vol. VI., p. 35, No. 3, Stevenson's No. 2, Bird's No. 9, and Sykes's No. 10.

[2] Sans. Hairaṇyaka.

[3] *Ind. Ant.*, vol. VI., p. 34, No. 2, Stevenson's No. 1, Bird's No. 10, and Sykes's No. 9.

Junnar

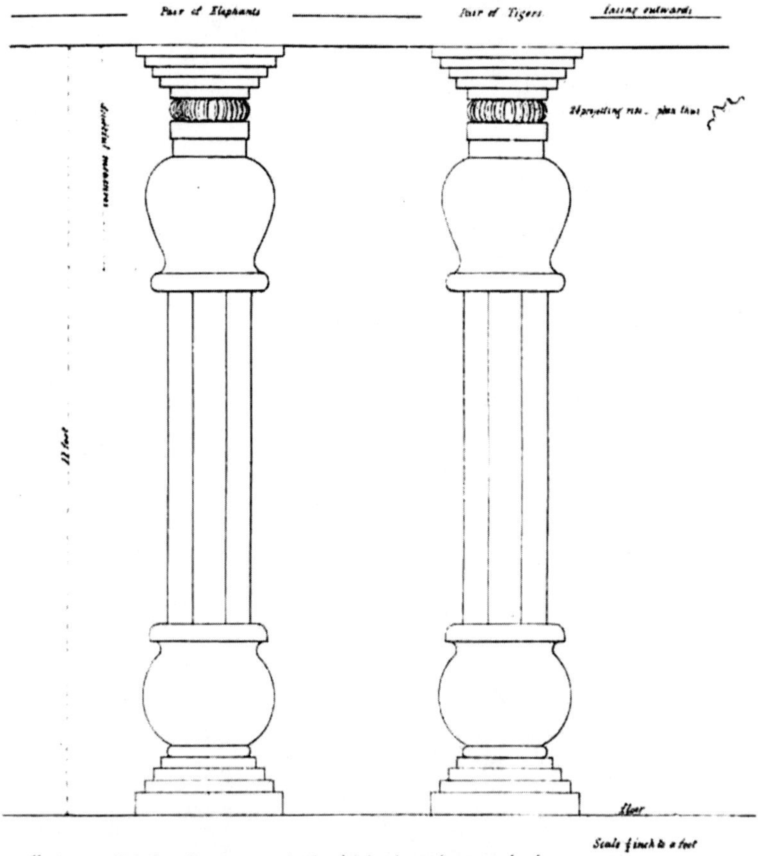

Chaitya cave No. A.31. 5½ columns on each side, 6 plain octagon columns round end alternately a pair of elephants or pair of tigers over each 2 columns and pilasters of Verandah, similar, with animals

Photozincographed Govt. Office Poona,

INSCRIPTION No. 32.

उगाहउपासकस पुतस

इसिपालितस सपुतकस दानं

Sanskrit.

उद्ग्राहोपासकस्य पुत्रस्य

ऋषिपालितस्य सपुत्रकस्य दानम् ॥

"The gift of Isipâlita[1] son of Ugâha[2] an Upâsaka with (*his*) sons."

INSCRIPTION No. 33.

The next is in an open chamber, 19′ by 14½′ and 8′ high, with a seat round the three inner sides. The front has been walled up in recent times, leaving a small doorway. On the left side wall is the inscription very clearly cut. No. 2, given above, is in a similar room but larger.

यवणस

चिटस गतानं

भोजणमटपो

देयधम सघे

Sanskrit.

यवनस्य

चिटस्य गतान [?]

भोजनमण्डपो

देयधर्मः संघे ॥

"The meritorious gift of a refectory by the Yavana Chiṭa Gatânam for the Sangha."

INSCRIPTION No. 34.

A little to the right of the cave in which is No. 32 is a Chaitya cave the front of which is built up. Over the door is this inscription[3]:—

उगाहपुतस इसिपालितस सपरिवारस चेतियघरो दानं

Sanskrit.

उद्ग्राहपुत्रस्य ऋषिपालितस्य सपरिवारस्य चैत्यगृहं दानम् ॥

"The gift of a Chetiyaghara by Isipâlita, son of Ugâha, with his family."

Remark.

The donor here is evidently the same as in No. 32.

---

[1] Sans. Ṛishipâlita. [2] Sans. Udgrâha.

[3] No. 1, in *Ind. Ant.*, vol. VI., p. 33.

9.—KANHERI CAVES.

The Kaṇheri Caves are too numerous to describe here in detail. Most of them are of a very simple type and were probably nearly all excavated by the early Hînayâna sect, but in after times as the Mahâyâna schools gained in popularity and influence, sculptures were introduced by them on the walls of many of the caves and especially in the verandah of the great Chaitya Cave and in the caves numbered 29, 35, 64, 66, 67, &c., and some of these and of the larger vihâras may have been entirely excavated by them. We do not, however, find here elaborately carved pillars and pilasters, such as are the rule in the later caves at Ajaṇṭâ, Aurangâbâd, Elurâ, Ghaṭotkacha, nor are pillars introduced into the halls except in the Mahârâja's or Darbâr Cave: stone benches too are common in the cells and occur even in No. 35, the walls of which are covered with sculptures of Buddha and attendants. And stone benches in the cells are found elsewhere only in Hînayâna excavations. Such ornament, however, as we do find here is not without interest, and should be compared with what we find at Nâsik, Junnar, and the Konkaṇ groups of caves.

The accompanying plates[1] will afford illustrations of these. On the first plate the first figure shows one of the most common of the pilaster ornaments and which is often found in very old caves both at Kaṇheri and elsewere. The next figure shows the same ornament in its most developed form from Cave 35.

The third is a sketch of a pillar in the verandah of No. 45, showing one of the most common forms of pillars in the early caves. The next is a slight modification of the same ornament as in the first figure. The fifth sketch is from a fragment of a pilaster in the verandah of Cave 42 and is an exception to the general rule of exceedingly plain shafts in these caves. The pilaster has been carved with much minuteness and care, though all its details show that it is of an earlier type than those of Ajaṇṭâ, &c. The last figure on this plate is a perspective sketch of the end portion of a stone bench in Cave No. 45.

The second plate gives further illustrations of the pilaster ornaments.[2] *Fig.* 1 gives the ornament in its simplest form and is from Cave No. 32. *Fig.* 2 is very similar and is from Cave No. 56.

No. 3 is from the Mhâṛ Caves and differs only in the wings being more widened: it is inserted here for comparison.

No. 4 is from Cave 59 at Kaṇheri, and instead of having a short flute in the centre it is hollowed out into a shallow flat-bottomed depression.

No. 5 is very similar and is from Cave 37.

No. 6 is also like the preceding two but has the wings more widened out: it is from Cave 50.

No. 7, from Cave 64, has two flutes in the centre.

No. 8, from Cave 29, has the bottoms of the flutes more squared out.

No. 9, from Cave 35, introduces additional curves above and below the neck, being a duplication of the original pattern.

---

[1] From the notes, &c., of the Messrs. West.

[2] The second half of this plate has been marked by mistake "Junnar." Though some of the patterns are also found at Junnar all the examples, except No. 3, here given are from the Kaṇheri caves.

PILASTER ORNAMENTS

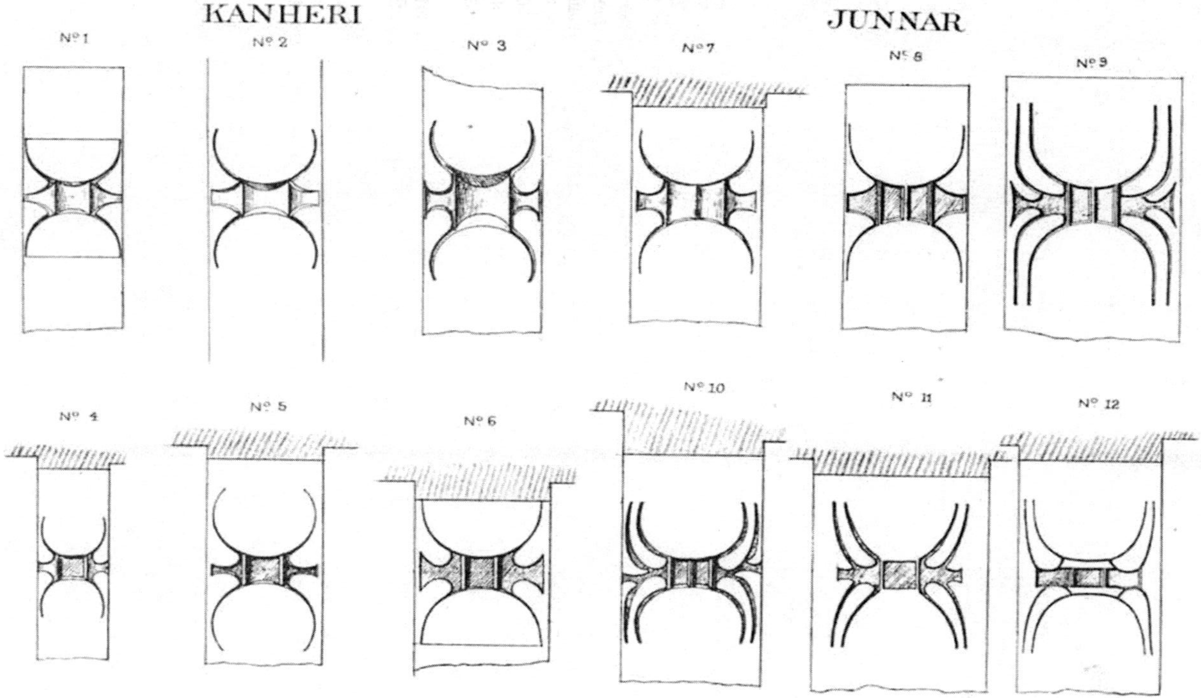

KANHERI

ORNAMENTS ON PILASTERS &c.

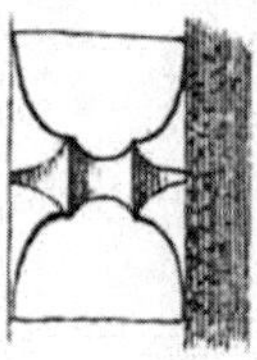

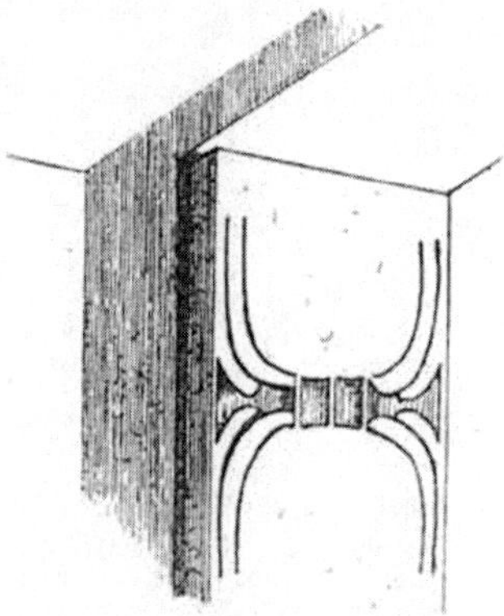

IN CAVE XXXV.

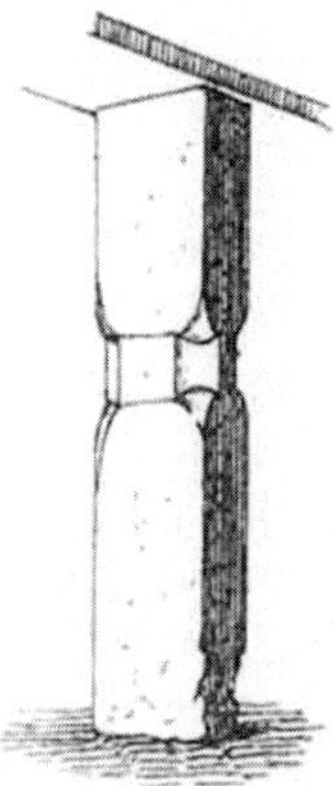

IN CAVE XLV.

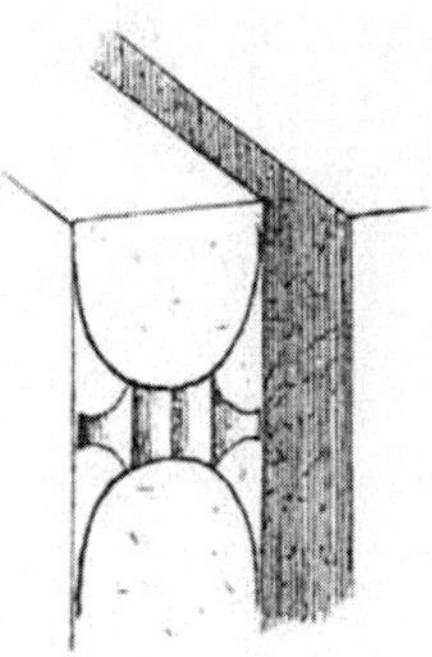

IN CAVE XLII.

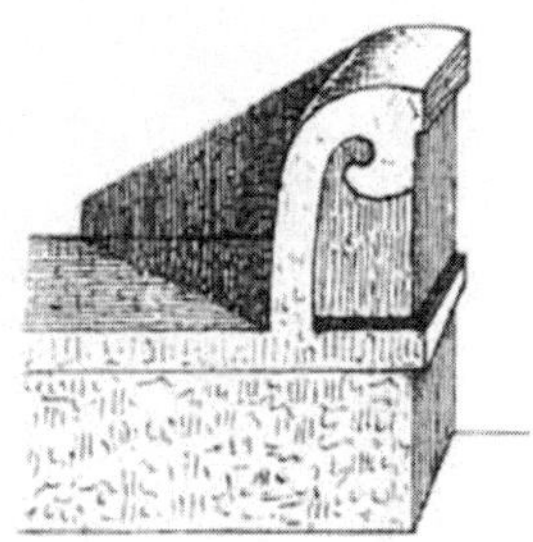

BENCH IN CAVE XLV.

Photozincographed, Govt. Office, Poona, 1879

Kanheri *(unfinished Column)* *Cave N° 1*

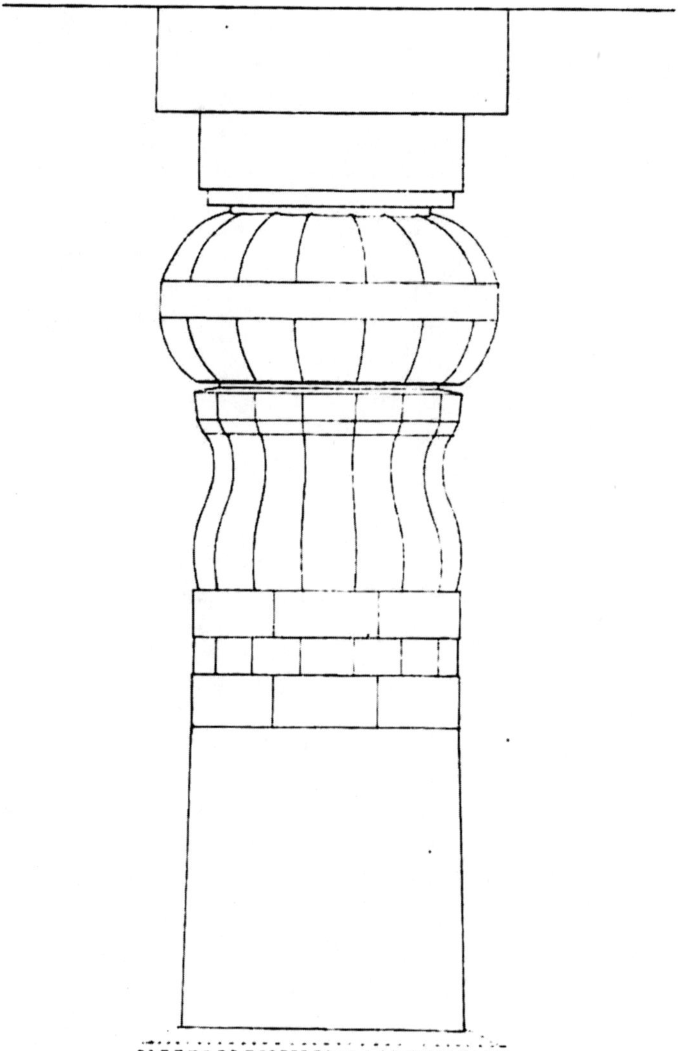

(Scale ½ Inch to a foot)

Nos. 10, 11, and 12, from Caves 76, 51, and 69 respectively, are stiffer and ruder forms of the same pattern.

The third of these plates is a careful drawing to a scale of half an inch to the foot of one of the unfinished columns in front of the verandah in Cave No. 1,—the unfinished Chaitya. It is evidently of a much later date than any of the preceding examples.[1]

1.—Copper-plate Inscription.

A copper-plate was found at Kaṇheri by Dr. James Bird in 1839. The following is his own account of the discovery[2]:—

"Immediately in front of the large arched cave, and on a ledge of the mountain, some thirty or forty feet below, there are several small *Thopas*, or monumental receptacles for the bones of a Buddha, or Rahat, built of cut stone at the base. These were once of a pyramidal shape, but are now much dilapidated, and appear like a heap of stones. Several years ago I thought of opening some of them, in expectation of obtaining coins or other relics; but found no favourable opportunity until lately, when several lengthened visits in company with Dr. Heddle gave me the desired means of doing so.

"The largest of the topes selected for examination appeared to have been one time between twelve or sixteen feet in height. It was much dilapidated, and was penetrated from above to the base, which was built of cut stone. After digging to the level of the ground and clearing away the materials, the workmen came to a circular stone, hollow in the centre, and covered at the top by a piece of gypsum. This contained two small copper urns, in one of which were some ashes mixed with a ruby, a pearl, small pieces of gold, and a small gold box containing a piece of cloth; in the other, a silver box and some ashes were found. Two copper-plates containing legible inscriptions in the *Lath*, or cave-character, accompanied the urns, and these, as far as I have yet been able to decipher them, inform us that the persons buried here were of the Buddhist faith. The smaller of the copper-plates bears an inscription in two lines, the last part of which contains the Buddhist creed."

What the first part of this inscription was we shall probably never learn: for Dr. Bird, like too many virtuosi, carefully retained the plates. He died in London about a dozen years ago, and they have not been heard of since.

Of the larger plate, he published a small lithograph in his *Historical Researches*, a copy of which lithograph he seems to have sent to the Asiatic Society of Bengal, where it was reproduced with a number of additional mistakes, and an interlinear transcription in Dêvanâgarî, and accompanied with what was called a "literal translation" by a Calcutta Bâbu: this was so nonsensical, however, that no one could accept it as a translation.

Failing to get a loan of the plate itself, Dr. Stevenson of Bombay[3] attempted to revise Dr. Bird's copy, and to a certain extent succeeded; but he made serious

[1] For further details respecting these caves, see *The Cave Temples of India*, pp. 348-360.

[2] *Jour. As. Soc. Beng.*, vol. X., pt. i., p. 94.

[3] *Jour. Bom. B. R. A. Soc.*, vol. V., pt. 16, p. 56.

errors in the transcription and translation. Using his copy[1] as a basis, Paṇḍit Bhagwânlâl Indraji ingeniously suggests the following amendments in the copy, making scarcely any marked changes in the shapes of the letters, and then transliterates it into intelligible Sanskṛit.

Line 1. In *Trikûṭa°*, the *tri* in Bird's copy looks like *stra*, but the upper part must be for the circle denoting *i*, badly formed. The whole character is depressed below its proper place in the line, but so also are the *ri* in *chatvâri*, and *gi*, *ri* in *Kṛishṇagiri*, in the same line. The *anusvâra* in *Trikûṭakânâṁ* is omitted either from the negligence of the copyist or in the original. In the copy we have *savvatsare*, where evidently has been misread as . In *dvaye*, the *e* is thrown back upon the *dva*.

Line 2. *Sindhuvishayântargatagramikaṇakavâstavya*, we should perhaps read *°gramika Naka*, *Bhoka* (or *Toka*), or *grame kaṇaka°*—'an inhabitant of the village of Bhoka or Toka in Sindh,' or of Kâṇaka.

The *bhâ* in *suprabhâyâḥ* is written as *bha*, the vowel mark being omitted in the *J. B. B. R. A. S.* copy; it appears in the *J. A. S. B.* one.

Line 3. For *Śrâvakâryagaṇyo*, the copy has *vrâvakâryyagaṅko*, having taken the place of and $=$*ṅko* that of $=$*ṇyo*. In *charaṇa*, *ra* is written ; and in *kuśalo* the *lo* is written as .

Line 4. *Śâradvatîputra* looks like *śaraṅśati*, being written for $=$*dva*.

Line 5. The *anusvâra* in *°kalinaṁ* is omitted; and in *yaksha*, for *ksha*, we have only *sha*.

Line 6. In *vaṅkaṇakâ* the last *ka* is written as *no*; the *śa* in *diśantva* is written ; and in *prachalita*, the *i* is attached to the letters *ṇa-ma* of the line above.

Line 7. In *ghûrṇṇitâ* the *i* circle is omitted over *°rṇṇa*. In *yâvadvâ*, the last syllable is wrongly written *dva*; and at the end of line 8 the *visarga* is omitted after the word *nâmnaḥ*.[2]

Transcript.

[१] नमस्सर्व्वज्ञाय ॥ त्रिकूटकानां प्रवर्द्धमानराज्यसम्वत्सरशतद्वये पञ्चचत्वारिंशदुत्तरे कृष्णगिरिमहाविहारे

[२] सिन्धुविषयान्तर्गतग्रामे काणकवास्तव्य[:] सुप्रभायाः बुद्धश्रिया ✕ पुष्यवर्मणश्च पुत्रोदशबलबालि-

[३] नो भगवतश्शाक्यमुनेस्सम्यक्सम्बुद्धस्य तद्धर्म्मश्रावकार्य्यगण्यो चरणपरिचरणकुशलो बुद्धरुचिरि-

[४] दं तस्यैव परममुनेरग्र्यश्रावकस्यार्य्यशारद्वतीपुत्रस्य चैत्यं घटितपाषाणेष्टकाभिराच-

[५] न्द्रार्क्कार्ण्णव क्षितिस्थितिसमकालीनं प्रतिष्ठापितवांस्तदस्य देवयक्षसिद्धविद्याधरगणमाणिभद्रपू-

[६] र्णभद्रपञ्चिकार्य्यवज्रपाणिवङ्कणकादयः स्वस्ति दिशन्त्वपि च यावद्वीचीसहस्रप्रचलितमकरा-

[७] घुर्ण्णितावर्त्ततोय[:] क्षीरोदः क्षीरतोयो बृहदुपलचित ✕ कर्क्कशो वापि मेरुः यावद्वा यान्ति नद्य-

[८] स्सुविमलसलिलास्सागरं तोयवत्यः तावत्कीर्त्तिः स्थिरेयं भजतु शुभकरी सत्सुतं पुष्यनाम्न[:]

दादा (?)

---

[1] The accompanying plate is an enlarged fac-simile of the one in Bird's book.

[2] It is inserted but in parentheses in the *J. A. S. B.* copy.

Copper Plate Inscription from Kanheri.

(Copied from Dr. J. Bird's "Historical Researches")

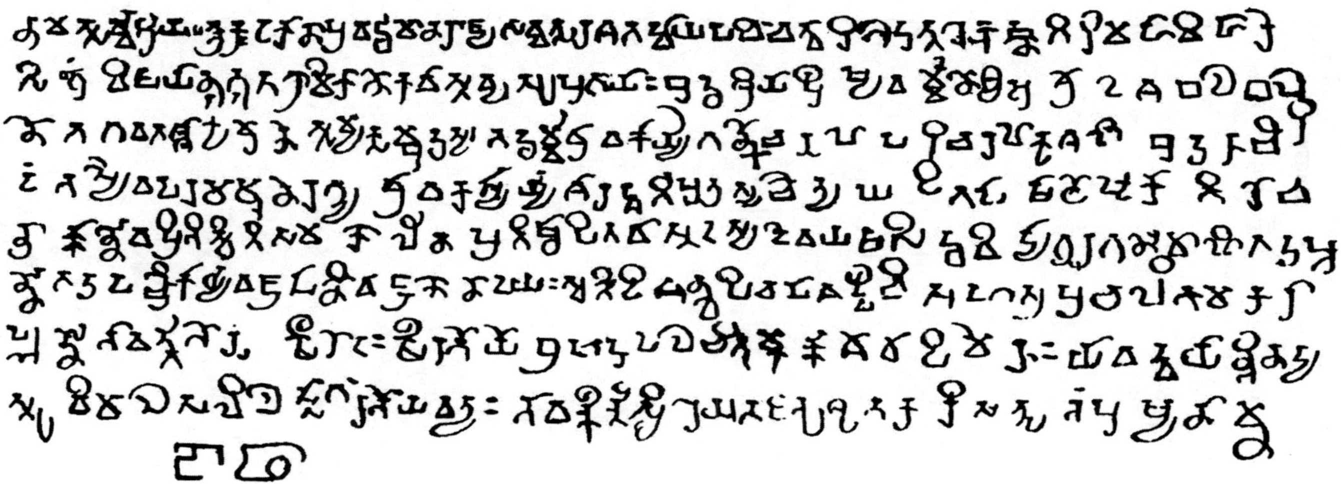

Translation.

"Salutation to the omniscient (Buddha)! In the year two hundred and forty-five of the increasing rule of the Trikûṭakas, in the great vihâra of Kṛishṇagiri, Buddharuchi—an inhabitant of Kanaka (? Kabhoka or Katoka) a village in the Sindhu country, the son of the glorious Buddhaśri and Pushyavarman, intent on religious duties, of the religion of Śâkya Muni (*who was*) strong in the possession of the ten powers, revered, possessed of perfect knowledge—an Ârya-gaṇa of his (*i.e.*, Ś. M.'s) Śrâvaks,—erected this Chaitya of dressed stone and brick, to last while moon, sun and ocean endure, to the great Śrâvaka of the Paramamuni (Buddha)—the noble Śâradvatîputra. Therefore let the Devas, Yakshas, Siddhas, Vidyâdharas, Gaṇas, and Mâṇibhadra, Pûrṇabhadra, Pañchika, Ârya-Vajrapâṇi, Vaṅkaṇaka,(?) &c., be propitious. Moreover, as long as the milky ocean, the waters of the whirlpools of which are whirled round by the sea monsters which are driven about by its thousand waves, is an ocean of milk; and as long as the rugged Meru is piled with great rocks; and as long as the rivers of clear water flow with water into the ocean;—so long may this enduring and auspicious fame attach itself to the excellent son of him named Pushya(varman)."

Remarks.

Almost the only word of importance in this inscription is the name of the *Trikûṭakas*, of which the dominion is said to have lasted 245 years. Hitherto no other reference has been made to any such dynasty. Among the great dynasties of which we have inscriptions, the Ândhras employ no date from a fixed epoch, nor do they mention such a title as Trikûṭaka. The Kshatrapas employ a fixed epoch, but the characters on their coins bearing dates about 250 of their era are of a much earlier type than those of this plate, which apparently belong to about the sixth century A. D. The Guptas style their era 'Guptakâla,' 'Guptasya-kâla,' 'Guptanṛiparâjyabhukti,' or 'Saṁ.,' but such a name as Trikûṭa does no occur in their inscriptions; nor among the numerous copper-plates of the Valabhi dynasty, whose power, moreover, is not known to have ever extended to the Koṅkaṇ. The Gurjara and Râshṭrakûṭa kings all dated in the Śakakâla, and the earliest known Râshṭrakûṭa king was Dantivarma early in the 7th century A. D.[1] The Śilahâras were only petty kings in the Koṅkaṇ, and Kapardi I., their earliest king, belongs to the ninth century (cir. 820 A. D.).[2]

Trikûṭaka—native of a town or country (Trikûṭa) 'on three hills'—must refer to some place in Aparânta, or the Northern Koṅkaṇ, not far from Kaṇheri where the plate was deposited.

Now, the *Raghuvaṁśa* (IV. śl. 52, 53, 58) says that Raghu, when he conquered the Koṅkaṇ, built a city called Trikûṭa[3] on a lofty site, as a tower of victory. The inference from this is that in Kâlidâsa's time, such a place as Trikûṭa really existed not far from the western coast. Aparânta was this western

[1] Govinda I. of the Râshṭrakûṭas (*Ind. Ant.*, vol. V., p. 144; vol. VI., p. 72) most probably flourished cir. 660 to 680 A. D., though it is not impossible that he may have been the Âppâyika-Gôvinda mentioned in the Aihole inscription (*Ind. Ant.*, vol. VIII., pp. 238, 244), who must have lived about A. D. 625. The Elurâ inscription gives us the name of his father Indrarâja, and of his grandfather Dantivarma.—J. B.

[2] From the form of the characters, I incline to think that this inscription may be dated in the Gupta era; the Trikûṭakas, like the Valabhi Senâpatis, may have continued to use the Gupta era on assuming independence; or it may have been adopted from Gujarât.—J. B.

[3] See also *Ind. Ant.*, vol. III., pp. 6, 7.

coast, which the Greeks called Ariake or Abarike, and the commentary on the *Raghuvaṁśa* mentions on the authority of the *Viśvakôsha* that the district in which was Sorpâraka (the modern Supârâ), was called Aparânta :—

Aparântâstu pâśchâtyâs te cha Śurpârakâdayaḥ.

Ptolemy and the *Periplus* both mention Tagara as a noted city in the west of India. Now, Tagara is a corruption of the Sanskṛit *Trigiri*—a synonym of Trikûṭa ; and Tagara may be identified with Junnar, which answers to the statement in the *Raghuvaṁśa*, in being built fully 2,000 feet above the sea, and surrounded by steep hills such as Śivanêri,[1] Mânmoḍi, &c., and is readily reached from the Konkaṇ by the Nânâghâṭ and Mâlsej Ghâṭ. The kings of this place, then, would be the Trikûṭakas, and their rule may have extended to Salsette; but of their history we know nothing.[2]

The Junnar cave inscriptions, however, belong to a much earlier date, and afford us no information about these Trikûṭakas.

2.—Inscriptions.

The following inscription was translated by Paṇḍit Bhagwânlâl Indraji and published in the *J. Bom. B. R. A. S.* in 1877 (vol. XII., p. 407). It is numbered 19 in Mr. West's collection and is found in cave No. 36, on the right hand side wall, outside the verandah, where it occupies a space about 3 feet 8 inches wide by 2 feet 6 inches high, but the surface is rough and in some cases, especially in the fourth, sixth and last lines, portions of it are much abraded. The letters are similar to those used in other Ândhrabhṛitya inscriptions.

Transcript.

सिधं रञो मादरिपुतस स्वामि (सिरि)सेनस
सवछरे ८ गिप ५ दिव १० एतायं पुवायं क-
लिपाणकस नकेमस वेण्हुनांदिस पुतस नेग-
मस गहपातिस (सात्त?)स लेणं पातेठापि-
तं सहा आप्यकेन (जसे)न सहा पितुना वेण्हुनं-
दिना सहामातुये बोधिसमाये सहा भा-
[तुना····] हथिना सहा सवेन (निकायेनेति)

Sanskrit.

सिद्धम् । राज्ञो मादरिपुत्रस्य स्वामिश्रीसेनस्य
संवत्सरे ८ ग्री. प. ५ । दिव. १० एतस्यां पूर्वस्यां क-
ल्याणकस्य नैगमस्य विष्णुनन्दिनः पुत्रस्य नैग-
मस्य गृहपतेः (सात्त?)स्य लयनं प्रतिष्ठापि-

---

[1] Possibly the first town was on one of these hills; if not actually so, Śivanêri must have been the citadel.—J. B.

[2] The Silâra or Śilahâra kings speak of themselves as "born in the family of Jîmûtavâhana, the Silahâra prince, (*Tagarapuravarâdhîśvara*) lord of the excellent city of Tagara" (conf. *Ind. Ant.*, vol. IX., p. 37). So the Kadambas in Canara took the epithet of *Banavâsipurâdhîśvara* (*J. B. B. R. A. S.*, vol. X., p. 54, and vol. XII., p. 57 and p. 305 ; *Ind. Ant.*, vol. IX., p. 43 ; and conf. vol. VI., p. 102 ; *J. R. A. S.*, vol. IV., p. 35). May they not have been descended at least from a dynasty ruling there? On Tagara see also *Arch. Surv. W. India*, vol. III., pp. 54, 55 ; *Ind. Ant.*, vol. VI., p. 75 ; vol. VII., p. 103 ; and vol. VIII., p. 144.—J. B.

तं सह आर्य्यकेण(यशसा) सह पित्रा विष्णुन-
न्दिना सह मात्रा बोधिसमया सह भ्रा-
[त्रा....] हास्तिना सह सर्व्वेण (निकायेनेति) ॥

Translation.

"Siddham! In the 8th year of king Mâḍhariputta, the lord Sirisena, in the 6th fortnight of Grishma, the 10th day. On the above (*day*) a merchant householder the son of Veṇhunandi,[1] merchant, a resident of Kalyâṇa, constructed a cave of Satta (?) with the respectable.....[2] with his father Veṇhunandi, with his mother Bodhisamâ, with his brother ....-hathi, with an assembly of all (*nikâya*) co-religionists."

Portions of other two inscriptions have also been translated by the Paṇḍit (*J. B. B. R. A. S.*, vol. XIII., p. 11). They are among the latest at Kaṇheri, both belonging to the 9th century, and to the Śilâhâra kings of the Koṅkaṇ, who were tributaries to the Râshṭrakûṭas of the Dekhan. They are interesting as giving us the names of two kings in each of these dynasties as well as two dates, twenty-four years apart, in the contemporary rule of one sovereign in each family. Kapardî II., the Śilâhâra king, whose capital was probably Chemula or perhaps "Puri," the son of Pulaśakti, was evidently reigning during the whole interval A. D. 853-878; and apparently Amoghavarsha ruled during the same period. He is distinctly the son or successor of Jagattunga: Amoghavarsha I. was son of Govinda III., one of whose *birudas* was Jagattunga, but he must have ruled cir. 810-830; and Amoghavarsha II. was the son of Indra II. Indra either bore the *birudas* of Jagadrudra and Jagattunga, or was succeeded by a son of that name; but the dates seem to point to Indra II. himself who may have borne the *biruda* of Amoghavarsha, and he succeeded Jagattunga about 850 A. D.[3]

The first is No. 15 of West's collection, and is from the architrave over the verandah of Cave No. X.—the Darbâr or Mahârâja's cave. It consists of eight lines: three upper ones 11 feet long, then three others 11 feet 7 inches long, and two additional lines 5 feet 6 inches long, to the left of the second three, and on the same level.[4]

Translation.

"May it be propitious (*svasti*)! On the 2nd day of the dark half of Mârgaśîrsha in the Prajâpati year, after seven hundred and seventy-five years, in figures—Saṁvat 775[5] of the Śaka king had passed: during the victorious and happy reign of Amoghavarshadêva, the great sovereign, the great king of kings, the noble lord, meditating on the feet of the great sovereign, the chief of kings, the majestic lord, the illustrious Jagattunga, he presented the whole of the Koṅkaṇ, during the flourishing and victorious reign in it of Kapardî, who has gained the five great titles, a jewel among the great chiefs of districts, meditating on the feet of Pulaśakti, the gem of the great chiefs of districts............"

---

[1] Sans. *Vishṇunandi*. [2] The name here is obliterated.

[3] See *Arch. Reports*, vol. III, p. 32. [4] *J. B. B. R. A. S.*, vol. VI., p. 6.

[5] Prajâpati, according to Telinga rule, agrees with 773, and Śrimukha with 775 Śaka; Angira, by the Jyotishṭava rule, agrees with 775, and Prajâpati with Śaka 774.—J. B.

The next is No. 43 in West's enumeration, and is on the architrave over the verandah in Cave 78, just opposite to the last. It is in an inscription of two 7 feet lengths, of five lines each, each length being over an intercolumination, and the short line below being on the capital of a column. It is faint and indistinct in places, and is in the same late alphabet as No. 15. Only the first portion is here translated.

Translation.

"May it be propitious! After seven hundred and ninety-nine, in figures 799 years of the Śaka king had elapsed, during the prosperous and victorious reign of the illustrious Amoghavarshadeva, the great lord, the chief of great kings, (*by whom*) was presented the whole of the Koṅkaṇ, in the circle of which Kapardî a jewel among the chiefs of districts, during his victorious and prosperous reign................."

The whole of the inscriptions have not all been taken in fac-simile yet, and therefore are not translated here.

The other inscriptions are in preparation and will be published when ready.

3.—Pahlavi Inscriptions in the Kanheri Caves.

In Cave 66 there are three Pahlavi inscriptions of which Dr. E. W. West of Munich has supplied the following account with translations.[1]

These three Pahlavi inscriptions are all dated, and consist chiefly of the names of certain Pârsis who visited the Kaṇheri Caves early in the eleventh century. They are all three inscribed in vertical lines, to be read from the top downwards; Pahlavi writing being read from right to left. As they would be more conveniently read if the lines were horizontal, the reason for inscribing them in vertical lines is not obvious; but it may be noted that a few short Pahlavi inscriptions, in the same comparatively modern character,[2] are found in Persia, which are also inscribed in vertical lines.

The earliest date is that in the inscription on the verandah pilaster to the right of a person entering the cave. This inscription is so faintly cut that the greater part of it would be illegible if it were not for the fact that the names it contains are the same as those in the second inscription.

With the assistance of that inscription it may be read, line for line, as follows[3]:—

Transliteration.

Pavan shem-î yazatô.
Pavan tag mûrvâk va nadûkô da*d*ak denman shnat 300
70 8-î Yazdaka*rdô* bidanâ Mit*r*ô yôm
Aûha*r*mazd ham-dînîkân va*l* denman *j*inâk yâtûn*d*

---

[1] These inscription have been translated by Dr. E. W. West, for the *Indian Antiquary*, where they will also appear with his remarks in full. Mr. K. M. Kama also kindly supplied me with versions of the three longer inscriptions prepared by Pârsi scholars.

[2] Not the Sasanian inscriptions, which are always in horizontal lines.

[3] As some sounds are written more ways than one in Pahlavi, italics are used to express such variants; thus, *d* is used for d written like t, *j* for j written like y, *l* and *r* for l and r written either like n or like an Avesta o, *v* and *z* for v and z written like ch.

No. 1

Kanheri. Pehlavi Inscription

Govt. Photozinco Office, Poona, 1880.

hômand Yazdân-pânak. va Mâh-aîyyâr-î
Mitra-aîyyâr,[1] Panj-bûkhtŏ va Padar-bûkhtŏ-î
Mâh-aîyyâr, Mardân-shâd-î Hîrâd[2]-Bâhrâm
va Hîrâd-Bâhrâm-î Mardân-shâd Mitra-aiyyâr-î
Bâhrâm-panâh va Bâhrâm-panâh-i Mitra-aîyyâr,
Falân-zâd[3] va Zâd-sparham-î Âtûr[4]-mahân,
Nûk-mâhân va Dîn-Bâhrâm va Bajûrg-âtûr va Hîrâd-mard
va Bêh-zâdŏ-î Mâh. . . . .

This inscription is evidently incomplete, as it stops in the middle of a name and also omits the names contained in the last two lines of the next inscription. Nearly the whole of the first two lines have been broken away and removed since 1870, and the copy of them could not, therefore, be corrected in 1875; so that the reading of so much of the second line as does not occur in the next inscription, is doubtful.

In the following translations of these three inscriptions, as transcribed, the words in italics are understood, but not expressed, in the original Pahlavi :—

Translation.

"In the name of God.[5]

"Through strong omens and the good Judge this[6] year 378 of Yazdakard, *on* the day Aûharmazd of the month Mitrô (10th October 1009), *there* have come to this place the co-religionists[7] Yazdân-pânak and Mâh-aîyyâr *sons* of Mitra-aîyyar, &c. (as in No. 2, as far as) Bêh-zâd *son* of Mâh[8]. . . . . "

The next date, which is only forty-five days later, occurs in the inscription in the recess over the water-tank alongside the cave (No. 1 on the plate). This inscription, though likewise cut faintly, is much more distinct than the last, and is numbered with the Pahlavi cipher for "two" preceding the invocation in its first line. It contains the same names as the last inscription, with a few others added at the end to complete the list, and may be read as follows:—

---

[1] *Aîyyâr* is merely a provisional reading for the Pahlavi equivalent of Pers. *yâr*, until its true sound is ascertained. In the second inscription it is always circumflexed, as if to be read *aîdbâr*.

[2] Or, perhaps, *Khîrâd* or *Aîr-aê*, as the final d (not being *d*) is doubtful after a vowel.

[3] In the second inscription the l is distinctly noted by a diacritical mark, otherwise it would be better to read *Farukhŏ-zâd*, a common Pahlavi name.

[4] Hitherto I have generally read this word *âtarô* direct from the Avesta, but it occurs in Sasanian inscriptions, not only in a form which can be read either *âtarô* or *âtûr*, but also in another form which *must* be read *âtûr*; it is also transcribed by Syriac writers as *âdûr* or *âdur*. The second part of the name is here written *mahân*, but is *mâhân* in the next inscription and in the next name here.

[5] The Pahlavi word is here in the singular number.

[6] As already stated, the reading of this first phrase is doubtful. Another guess would make it mean "in a good omened and happy state I write."

[7] This word is doubtful, but *hamdînîkân* seems to be the only intelligible reading for it as it stands in No. 2.

[8] Breaking off in the middle of a name.

Transliteration.

2. Pavan shem-î yazatô.[1]
Shnat 300 va 70 8-î Yazdaka*rdô* bidanâ Âvânô
va yôm Mit*r*ô hamdînîkân va*l* denman *j*înâk yâtûn*d*
hômand Yazdân-pânak va Mâh-aîyyâr-î
Mit*ra*-aîyyâr, Panj-bûkhtô va Pa*d*ar-bûkhtô-î
Mâh-aîyyâr, Mar*d*ân-shâ*d*-î Hîrâd-Bâhrâm
va Hîrad Bâhram-î Mar*d*ân-shâ*d*, Mit*ra*-aîyyâr-î,
Bâhram-panâh va Bâhrâm-panâh-î Mit*ra*-aîyyâr,
Falân-zâ*d* va Zâ*d*-sparham-î Âtû*r*-mâhân,
Nûk-mâhân va Dîn-Bâhrâm va Bajûrg-âtû*r*
va Hîrâ*d*-mar*d* va Bêh-zâ*d*ô-î Mâh-bâzâe,[2]
Bâhrâm-panâh-î Mit*ra*-bandâ*d*.
Mâh Âtû*r* Aûha*r*mazd-î Âvân-bandâ*d* mûr*d*.[3]

Translation.

"2. In the name of God.

"*In* the year 378 of Yazdakard, the month Âvân and day Mitrô (24th November 1009), *there* have come to this place the co-religionists Yazdân-pânak and Mâh-aîyyâr, *sons* of Mitra-aîyyâr, Panj-bûkht and Padar-bûkht *sons* of Mâh-aîyyâr, Mardân-shâd *son* of Hîrâd-Bâhrâm and Hîrâd-Bâhrâm[4] *son* of Mardân-shâd, Mitra-aîyyâr *son* of Bâhrâm-panâh and Bâhrâm-panâh[4] *son* of Mitra-aîyyâr, Falân-zâd and Zâd-sparham *sons* of Âtûr-mâhân, Nûk-mâhân, Dîn-Bâhrâm, Bajûrg-âtûr, Hîrâd-mard, and Bêh-zâd *sons* of Mâh-bâzâe, *and* Bâhrâm-panâh *son* of Mitra-bandâd. *In* the month Âtûr[5] Aûharmazd *son* of Âvân-bandâd died."

The third inscription in point of time is that on the left-hand pilaster of the verandah, and is numbered with the Pahlavi cipher for "three" preceding the invocation in its first line (No. 2 of the accompanying plates). It is dated twelve years later than the preceding inscriptions, and contains a different list of names, in which only four of the names in the previous inscriptions occur. It is fairly legible, and may be read as follows:—

---

[1] This word is illegible, but is assumed to be the same as in the preceding inscription. The *za* in *yazatô*, like the *zd* in *yazdân* and *Aûharmazd*, and the *zda* in *yazdakardô* is written like *â* or *ha*, as it always is in Pahlavi MSS.; but this is merely a graphical variant, as these words are written with *za*, *zd*, and *zda* in Sasanian Pahlavi.

[2] The last syllable is circumflexed, but can hardly contain the letter d.

[3] The last letter is doubtful, and the word looks more like *mûrû*, but this would be unintelligible. This last line is evidently an addition to the inscription after the list of names was finished.

[4] Probably a son of the preceding man, who had been named after his grandfather, a custom still common among the Pârsis.

[5] That is, in the following month (9th Dec. to 8th Jan.). It might possibly be "*on* the *day* Mâh *of the month* Âtûr (20th Dec.)"; or it might be translated "Mâh-Âtûr *and* Aûharmazd *sons* of Avân-bandâd died," but the word "died" is doubtful. This last sentence seems to have been a later addition to the inscription.

No 2

Kanheri. Pehlavi Inscription

Govt. Photozincographic Office, Poona, 1880.

Transliteration.

3. Pavan shem-î yazdân.
Bidanâ Mitrô va yôm Dinô shnat 300 90-î Yazdakardô min Aîrân[1]
val denman *j*înâk yâtûnd hômand
Mâh-Frôbag va Mâh-aîyyâr
î Mitra-aîyyâr, Panj-bûkhtô-î
Mâh-aîyyâr, Mardân-shâd-î
Hîrâd-Bâhrâm, Bêh-zâd-î
Mitra-vindâd,[2] Jâvidân-bûdô-î
Bâhrâm-Gûshnaspô, Bajûrg-âtûr-î
Mâh-bâzâe, Mâh-aîyyâr va Bandêsh[3]
î Hîrâd-farukhô, va Mâh-bandâd-î
Gêhân-khash châsh[4]-nyôkhsh.

Translation.

"3. In the name of God.[5]

"*In* the month Mitrô and day Dînô *of* the year 390 of Yazdakard (30th October 1021) *there* have come from Irân[6] to this place Mâh-Frôbag and Mâh-aîyyâr[7] *sons* of Mitra-aîyyâr, Panj-bûkht[7] *son* of Mâh-aîyyâr, Mardân-shâd[7] *son* of Hîrâd-Bâhrâm, Bêh-zâd *son* of Mitra-vindâd, Jâvidân-bûd *son* of Bâhrâm-Gûshnasp, Bajûrg-âtûr[7] *son* of Mâh-bâzâe, Mâh-aîyyâr and Bandêsh *sons* of Hîrâd-farukhô, and Mâh-bandâd *son* of Gêhân-khash, the listener to instruction."[8]

It must have been during the visit mentioned in this third inscription that the few words were inscribed on the dâgoba (discovered by Dr. West),[9] for they mention the same year and one of the same names. This short inscription was correctly deciphered in 1866, as published in the *Zartoshti Abhiâs* No. 3, p. 164, and is as follows :—

Shnat 300
90-î Yazdaka(*rd*)
Shatra-îyâr
Mâh-Frôba(g).

"The year 390 of Yazdakard, Shatra-îyâr. Mâh-Frôbag."

Besides these four Pahlavi inscriptions at Kaṇheri there has been a fifth, of which only two or three detached letters are legible on another stone of the dâgoba, which is now in the Museum of the Bombay Branch of the Royal Asiatic Society. This inscription appears to have consisted of seven vertical lines on a

---

[1] These last two words are doubtful, *min* being nearly all cut away, and *Aîrân* hardly legible; they occupy the place of the doubtful word *hamdînkân* in the first two inscriptions.

[2] Possibly the same name as the Mitra-bandâḍ of the first two inscriptions.

[3] Or, perhaps, *Bôsth*.

[4] This word is doubtful, being partly broken away.

[5] The Pahlavi word is here in the plural number.

[6] The words "from Irân" are doubtful, being partly cut away to form a mortice in the rock for attaching wood-work.

[7] These four names also occur in the former lists in Nos. 1 and 2.

[8] This last phrase is doubtful, and it is possible that the list of names is incomplete in this inscription, as it is in that on the other pilaster.

[9] See *Jour. Bom. B. R. As. Soc.*, vol. VI., p. 119, and plate iii, fig. 21.

flat space between two groups of sculpture; but the surface of the stone is so much decayed, that the letters legible are only just sufficient to show that the words have been Pahlavi.

4.—Coins.

During the excavations in making a path round the upper contour of the great reservoir at Vihâr in Salsette, in January 1855, upwards of a thousand copper coins were dug up in an earthenware pot. They were much corroded, but of some of the best of them drawings were made by the Messrs. West. As no notice has been published of these, it may not be uninteresting to have a reproduction of the drawings preserved, which is done in the accompanying plate. Three of them are distinctly Muhammadan, and not of a very early type. Only about half a dozen were of this coinage, and most of the others bear a cross on one side with a point between each of the arms; and on the obverse is a small figure like a Maltese cross with a point on each side of it, over which is a line bent down at each end, and the remainder of the field is occupied by a symbol—the intent of which is very doubtful—between two sets of four points. A sixth has a rude outline of a cross on one side of it, the other being plain. Other pieces of copper of similar sizes were quite smooth.

10.—CAVE AT AMBIVALE.

The cave is about half a mile from the village of Ambivale near Jambrug, north from Karjat, under Kotaligadh, and to the east of it. It is cut in a long low hill forming the concave side of a curve in the bank of the river. The cave overlooks the river, being about 20 feet above it, sloping rock leading up to it from the water. It consists of a large square hall, about 42 feet by 39 feet and 10 feet high, having four cells off each of three sides (12 cells in all). Around these same three sides runs a low bench similar to the bench in Cave 35 at Kaṇheri and in No. III at Nâsik. Two doorways, a central and a side one to the right, lead into a verandah, 31′ long by about 5′ 10″ deep, the eaves of which are supported by 3′ 9″ of return of wall at either end and by four pillars. Between each pair of pillars (except the central pair—where the entrance is,) and the end pillars and pilasters is a low seat, with a parapet wall running along the outer side and forming a back to the seat. The outside of the parapet wall was ornamented in the same style as Cave III. at Nâsik, with festoons and rosettes, but is so damaged that little now remains.

The pillars are of the same pattern as those of Nâsik—pot capitals with flat tiles surmounting them, but roughly finished. The shafts, springing from the seats, have no bases. The central pair of pillars have octagonal shafts, the remaining two are 16-sided.

The doorways have had modern carved doors inserted at a late date, and with some built basements with carved figures on them in six of the cells at the back. The cave has thus been converted into a Brahmanical temple. A Jogi, recently dead, occupied the cave, the consequence being that the surface of the rock in the hall and verandah has been thoroughly coated with soot.

On the second pillar of verandah, on the left of entrance, is a Pâli inscription in one vertical line, reading downwards.[1]

---

[1] There are some remains of letters on each of the centre pair of pillars, though indistinct.

Coins found at Vehar

(Natural Size)

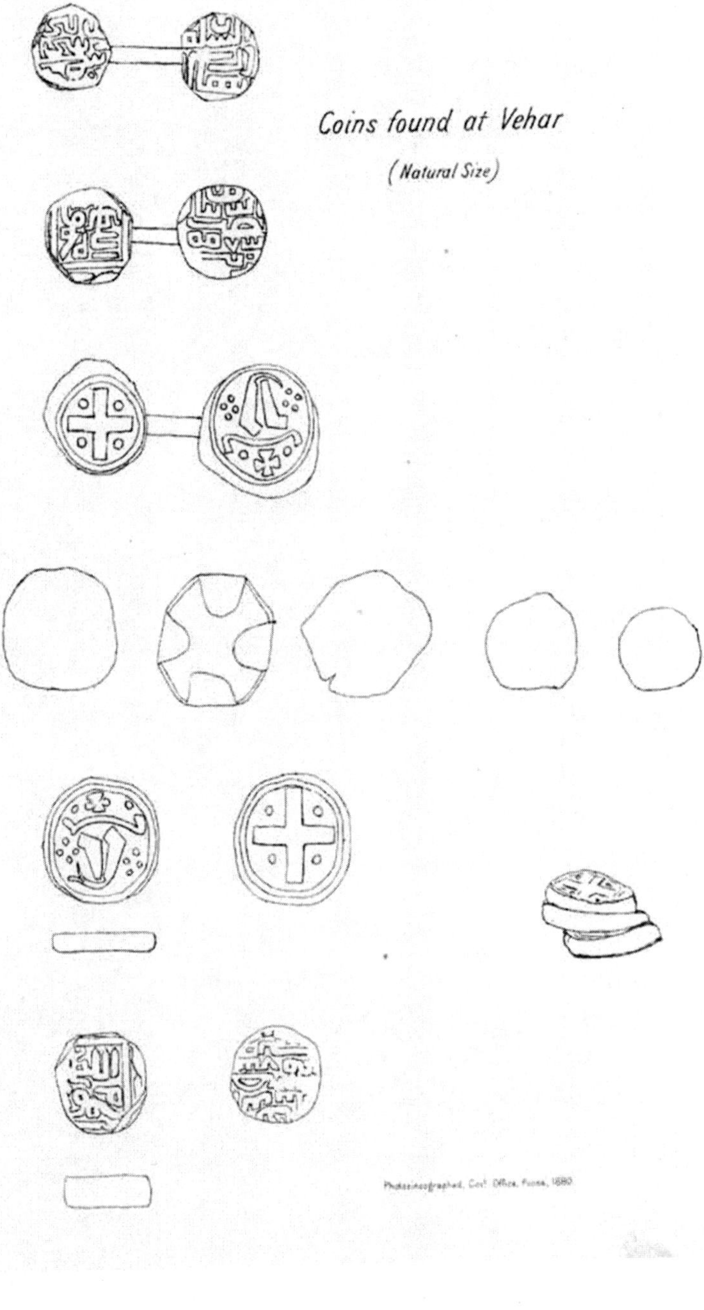

Photozincographed, Govt. Office, Poona, 1880

AJANTÂ FRESCOES FROM CAVE X

1. From left wall

Govt. Photozincographic Office, Poona, 1879

2. From right wall

11.—INSCRIPTIONS IN THE AJANTA CAVES.

The Ajaṇṭâ Caves and their paintings were treated in considerable detail in No. 9. of these papers,[1] and some specimens were there given of the remaining fragments of the oldest wall-paintings from Cave X.

Since writing the *Notes*, however, I have come upon two wood engravings in the *Illustrated London News* of 8th September 1849, representing, on a very small scale, two of the large copies made by the late Major Gill, and so unfortunately destroyed by fire at the Sydenham Crystal Palace in 1866. They represent portions of these old paintings as they existed more than thirty years ago. These woodcuts are not executed with much minuteness of detail; they represent, however, the grouping of the figures in a portion of the painting on each wall of this cave. The first, from the left wall, is that from which most of the copies given in the *Notes* were taken, and shows that nearly forty years ago it had become a mere series of fragments.

The second represents part of a scene from the right wall, which has since become almost black, and has been scribbled all over by native visitors. It may perhaps be possible even yet, however, to recover a portion of these interesting paintings; but in the meantime it seems desirable to preserve such records as we possess of them, and with this view the accompanying lithograph from these woodcuts is here given. Almost at the first glance we may recognise this as a representation of the famous *Chhadanta Jâtaka.*[2] The head of the Chhadanta elephant appears in the extreme left of the drawing, under his favourite Banian tree; the hunter Sonuttara appears among the rocks of the ridge named Suvarṇa in the *kâshâya* dress of a mendicant, and further to the right he is seen carrying the tusks to Subhadrâ, the consort of the king of Banâras. To the right of this, he and a companion are again represented supplicating or listening to the king with the queen at his right hand; and lastly, the queen is represented seated, in deep grief for the murder and dying of a broken heart, while the king stands before her addressing her.

The larger inscriptions are unfortunately so damaged as to render satisfactory translations impossible. Transcriptions of all, so far as they are legible, have been made by Paṇḍit Bhagwânlâl Indraji, and are here given with tentative translations and remarks on them.

Rock Inscription No. 1.

The oldest is that on the left side of the arch on the front of the Chaitya Cave No. X. It is in Prâkṛit, and the characters are of a very early form of those used throughout the Western India Cave Inscriptions.

वासिठिपुतस कट
हादिनो घरमुख
दानं

---

[1] *Notes on the Bauddha Rock-Temples of Ajaṇṭâ*, Plates VIII. to XI., and pp. 50, 51.

[2] Julien, *Mém. sur. les Cont. Occ.*, tom. I, p. 360; Cunningham's *Bharhut*, p. 62; M. Coomâra Swamy's *Daṭhâvaṇsa*, c. iii, 31, p. 50.

Sanskrit.

वासिष्ठीपुत्रस्य कटा		वासिष्ठीपुत्रस्य कट-
हो दत्तः गृहमुख-	*Or*	ह्रादिनो गृहमुख-
दानम्		दानम्

"A Kaṭahâ and the gift of a cave-façade by Vâsiṭhiputa."

Kaṭahâ may be the Sanskṛit *kaṭâha*, 'a bambu lattice-work' or 'partition of bambu work,' in Gujarâti *kûḍa* or *kaḍo*. Hence it may be inferred that the cave had some wooden lattice-work in the great arch over the doorway and lower façade, (which was probably of brick[1]) and both were gifts of Vâsiṭhiputa.

Vâsiṭhiputa or Vâsishṭhîputra might be supposed to be the well-known Vâsishṭhîputra Puḍumâvi of the Nâsik inscriptions, but from the character of the letters, compared with those of the inscriptions of that king, this would seem to be earlier by two centuries. Then we find no title, such as Râño, applied to him, as in other inscriptions. And the usage of naming sons from their mothers is shown from other inscriptions to have been common to other families besides that of the Ândhrabhṛitya dynasty. Thus at Pitalkhorâ, we have the royal physician Vachhiputa; at Bhâjâ, Kosikiputa; at Kuḍâ, Kochhiputa, &c. He seems, therefore, to have been a private person, and if so, we may translate thus:—

"The gift of a cave-façade by Vâsiṭhiputa Kaṭahadi."

Kaṭahadi might then be regarded as either a family name or one derived from his native place, Katahaḍa, Sans. Katahrada.

Inscription No. 2.

On the back wall of Cave No. XII, on the left side of the door of the right end cell—

ठानको देयधंम
घनामदडस वणिज[स]
सउवनरको सउपा[सयो]

Sanskrit.

स्थानकं देयधर्मः
घनामदडस्य वणिजः
सोपवरकं सउपा[श्रयम्]

"The meritorious gift of a dwelling with cells and hall by the merchant Ghanâmadaḍa."

Remarks.

The letters of this inscription are not very clear, the language is Prâkṛit and at the end of the last line are the syllables *saupâ*. It may have been intended to engrave *saupâsayo*, but these syllables as they stand convey no meaning.

Sthânaka is 'a dwelling.' The residence of the priests of the Dhundiyâ sect of Jainas is still called *sthânaka*. It may have been applied to the *layanas* of early times. The *uvavarakas*, Sans. *apavarakas*, are the cells which surround the hall, and the *upâsaya*, Sans. *upâśraya*, is the central hall,—the whole together constituting a *sthânaka*.

---

[1] See *Notes*, ut sup., p. 50.

Ghanâmadaḍa resembles a local name probably corrupted from Sans. *Ganapadra*, and if so, the record may mean the gift of a merchant residing at Ghanâmadaḍa: it is, however, very seldom to find such a record without the name of the donor.

Inscription No. 3.

This is on the left end wall outside the verandah in Cave XVI. The language is Sanskṛit, and the composition is in verse. It is written in 27 lines. The letters are in the same square style as in the Śivanî Copper-plates, and which was current in the Chhatisgarh district and the country around the Benagaṅgâ about the 5th and 6th century. It is much weatherworn, especially towards the left side where it is most exposed. The following is a transcription of all the letters that are legible, made from a careful examination. Though the translation cannot, from the nature of the case, be very satisfactory, still some information may be gleaned from it.

It records the gift of a dwelling for monks by the son of a minister named Hastibhoja; his name is effaced, but it was perhaps Varâhadeva, which occurs in the 21st line. The donor was minister to king Harisheṇa, and his father Hastibhoja was minister to Devaseṇa, the father of Harisheṇa. The inscription supplies the following list of kings :—

1. Vindhyaśakti.
2. Pravarasena.
3. (Rudra ?)sena.
4. ....
5. Devasena.
6. Harisheṇa.

From the broken state of the inscription it is not clear whether Pravarasena was a son of Vindhyaśakti, or, as is probable, of a member of the Vindhyaśakti family. Of his son only *-sena* is legible, preceded by a faintly traceable form like *-dra*, so that the name may have been Bhadrasena, Chandrasena, Indrasena, Rudrasena, &c. The expression "Kuntalendra"—king of Kuntala—occurring in connection with him shows that he had something to do with the king of that country. Later on Kuntala is included in his dominions. His son's name in lost: he began to reign as a minor. His son was Devasena; and his was Harisheṇa. Besides this inscription we have two copper-plate grants of this Vâkâṭaka dynasty which seems to have had a somewhat extensive sway: one of these is the Śivanî grant translated (but not very accurately) by Mr. Prinsep, and the other found in a ploughed field at Chamak, 7 or 8 miles south of Ilichpur, some 11 or 12 years ago, and a transcript of which is given in the *Notes*, No. 9 (p. 54).

[१] उदीर्ण्णलोकत्रयदोषवान्हेनिर्व्वापनो.................................. ....
.....................प्रणम्य पूर्व्वां प्रवक्ष्ये क्षितिपानुपूर्व्वी[म्] [॥]

[२] महाविमर्देष्वाभिवृद्धशक्तिः क्रुद्धस्सुरैरप्यनिवार्य्य[वीर्य्यः] [।] ....
............रणदानशक्तिः द्विज ✕ प्रकाशो भुवि विन्ध्यशक्तिः [॥]

[३] पुरन्दरोपेन्द्रसमप्रभावः स्वबाहुवीर्य्यार्ज्जितस[र्व्वलोकः] [।] ....
...................[यशों]शुकानां बभूव वाकाटकवंशकेतुः [॥]

[४] रणे[षु] हर्म्युत्थितरेणुजालसञ्छादितार्क..[।]...
...........................नरातीन्कृत्वा[भि]वादप्रवणाञ्चकार [॥]

[५] [विनि]र्ज्जितारि[स्सुर]राजकार्य्यश्चकारपुण्येषु परं प्रय[त्नं] [।]........................[।]
.. ..नरेंद्रमौलिविन्यस्तमणिकिरणलीढक्रमाम्बुजः

[६] प्रवरसेनस्तस्य पुत्रोभूद्विकसन्नवेन्दीवरेक्षणराविमयूख ....
....................[रुद्र? सेनः] प्रवरसेनस्य जितसर्व्वेतेनस्सुतोभवत्

[७] पार्त्थिवेन्द्रस्य [प्रशशास]धर्म्मेण मेदिनीम् कुन्तलेंद्राबे..
...............प्रवरसेनस्य पुत्रोभूत्प्रवरोर्ज्जितोदारशासनप्रवर[:] [।]

[८] .... [॥] तस्यात्मज ✕ कामत......
...........[।].........मवाप्य राज्यमष्टाब्दकोय ✕ प्रशशास सम्यक् [॥]

[९] तस्यात्मजोभून्नरदेव.......................................भुवि देवसेन[:।] यस्योपभोगैर्ललितै-
र्विपावनैर्नृदेवराजस्य ....भूः [॥]पुण्यानुभावात्क्षितिपस्य

[१०] ....[।]..............यगुणाधिवासो ....
कोशो भुवि हस्तिभोजः[॥]इस्य.................. ✕ पृथुपीनवक्षास्सरोरुहाक्ष ✕ क्षपि

[११] ....[।]..........................दिग्गन्धहस्तिप्रतिमो बभूव[॥]
हितो विनीतः प्रणयप......मनोनुकूलानुविधानवर्त्ती [।] निरत्ययं

[१२] [शा]सन.....................................सकश्च[॥] तथैव लोकस्य हिताशय-
त्वात्सुखेन सम्यक्परिपालनाय [।][पितेव] मातेव सखेव नित्यं प्रियोभिगम्यश्च बभूव

[१३] [नित्यं] [॥].....................................[।]स्वस्यस्समावेश्य स तत्र राजा ससर्ज्ज
भोगेषु यथेष्टचे[ष्टाम्?] [॥] अथ तस्य सुतो बभू-

[१४] [व राजा] समलाम्भोरुह ....[।] हरिरेष हर[:] स्मरेव कान्तिर्हरिषेणो
हरिविक्रमप्रतापः [॥] सकुन्तलावन्तिकलिङ्गकोसलत्रिकूटलाटान्ध्र-

[१५] ....[।]..........................स्वनिर्देश............[॥]प्रथितो-
भुवि हस्तिभोजसूनुस्साचिवस्तस्य महीपतेर्ब्बभूव [।] सकलक्षिति

[१६] ....[॥]........................जेष्टः स्थिरधीरचेतास्त्यागक्षमौदार्य्यगुणैरु-
पेतः [।] धर्म्मेण धर्म्मप्रवणश्शशास देशं यशःपुण्यगुणांशु

[१७] ..... [॥]............ .. ..प्रवि पुण्योपचयं परं चकार [।] यत ऊर्द्ध्व-
मदस्सहायधर्म्मा परितो लोकगुरौ चकार कारम् [॥] आयुर्व्वयोवित्त[सु]खानि

[१८] ....लानि [।]उद्दिश्य मातापितरावुदारं न्यवी-
विशद्वेश्म यतीन्द्र [सेव्यं] [॥] [सज]लाम्बुद...........रुद्धिताग्रे भुजगेन्द्राध्युषिते मही-
धरेन्द्रे [।]

[१९] ....श्रीपतिना शरानिकुञ्जे [॥] गवाक्षनिर्य्यू-
हसुवीथिवेदिकासुरेन्द्रकन्याप्रतिमाद्यलङ्कृतम् [॥]मनोहरस्तम्भविभङ्ग

[२०] ....रचैत्यमन्दिरं [॥] म.........तलस्तीभाविष्टं विस
..........नमनोभिरामं [॥] व.........म्बाम्बुमहानिधानं नागेन्द्रवेश्मादिभिर-

[२१] प्यलंकृतं [।]..................समीरण...[॥]ग्री-
ष्मार्कस्य च किरणोपतापतसं सर्व्वर्तुप्रथितगुणोपभोगयोग्यम् [।]

[२२] ....सुरेन्द्रमन्दिराणां रुचिमन्मन्दरकन्द[रानुरूपं][॥] ....
..................सुखौ यथेप्सितः [।] असमप्रतिरोचने गिरौ विक[च]

[२३] ....श्रमान्तकः [॥]...................................[।]........
......................यस्य जनेन नाम प्रीतिप्रसादविकचप्रणयेन चक्रे [॥] चेतः

[२४] ....लयनं सुरेन्द्र मौलिप्रभोपचित.............................हायं [।] निवेद्य
उद्धाय.....................र्थ्यं सबन्धुवर्गस्स वराहदेवः [॥] नृदेवसौख्यान्यनुभूय

[२५] ....शास्ता सुगतप्रशस्तः [॥] सान्द्राम्भोदभुजङ्गभोग ....
........तमाराम..................श्मनशिलालकपिलैर्य्यावत्करैर्भास्करः [।] तावच्छि-

[२६] ....सेव्यतामन्तर्म्मण्डपरत्नमेतदमलं रत्नत्रयोद्भावित[म्]
[॥] विविधलयनसानुस्सेव्यमानो महद्भिर्गिरिरय-

[२७] ....म्यः [।] जगदपि च समस्तं व्यस्तदोषप्रहाण-
म्विशतु पदमशोकं निर्व्वैरं शान्तमार्य्यं [॥]

Translation.

"...... extinguisher of the increasing fire of the sins of the three worlds ....having bowed (*to him*) I describe the early succession of kings.

"Vindhyaśakti, whose valour increased in great battles, whose strength in his anger cannot be overcome by the gods,...........mighty in alms and in wars. Who was twice-born (*dvija* or *kshatri*), distinguished,—such was (*he*) on the earth. (*He*) who was majestic, like Indra and Vishṇu, who had won the whole earth by the vigour of his own arms........and who was a standard of the web of glory to the dynasty of Vâkâṭaka. Who covered the sun by the dust cloud caused by (*the prancing of*) his steeds in the battlefield......... Having made his enemies......... caused them bowed down and humbled. He who had quelled his foes, and whose deeds are like Indra's, toiled in meritorious acts.....................

His son was Pravarasena whose lotus-like feet were kissed by the rays from the jewels in the coronets of kings, whose eyes are like the fresh opening lotus and the rays of the sun ....Pravarasena's son was (Rudra ?)sena the conqueror of all enemies, who justly (*ruled*) the earth of the king of kings. King of Kuntala................

"(*He*) the son of Praṿarasena, exalted by highest excellence, by power, by generosity in punishing..............

"His son.........having obtained power when eight years of age, ruled excellently.

"His son Devasena became in the world.........of men and gods. By his lovely and purifying enjoyments.........of king of men and gods. Through the meritorious acts of this king......... Hastibhoja (*became his minister*) on this earth, who was the dwelling of good qualities and treasury of...........

"Who had a broad and firm breast and lotus eyes..............who resembled the *Gandhahasti* [1] of the quarters; he was a well-wisher, modest,.........and who acted in accordance with the dictates of his heart; whose punishments are not destructive. Again, he being desirous of good, and from his capability to protect the people in the best and happiest way, he became popular and daily accessible by the people as a (*father*,) mother and friend...........This king having installed (*him*) and being at ease, he began to enjoy himself according to his heart's desire.

"Afterwards this (*king's*) son was king Harishena, whose (*eyes*) were like the wet lotus...... the destroyer of miseries (*Hari*), the attractor of (*men's*) minds (*Hara*), beautiful like Kâma (*Cupid*), of glorious deeds and majesty like Indra's, (*lord of the countries*) including Kuntala,[2] Avanti,[3] Kalinga,[4] Kosala,[5] Trikûṭa,[6] Lâṭa,[7] Andhra[8]............ ....

"...Son of Hastibhoja well known in the world, became minister to this king; the whole world......................who was a senior, of staid and tranquil mind, endowed with the qualities of almsgiving, mercy, and generosity, and possessed of a sense of justice, ruled the country uprightly......

"To whom merit is a help for the other world because he acquired a heap of merits and made a prison round Lôkaguru (*the teacher of the world—Buddha*). Life, age, wealth, happiness............constructed a magnificent dwelling fit for the abode of the chiefs of monks, in honour of (*his*) mother and father, in the chief of mountains inhabited by the king of serpents, whose fronts are covered with clouds filled with water..................

"(*The dwelling*) ornamented with windows, doors, splendid verandahs, railings, and images of Devakanyâs (goddesses) and delightfully arranged pillars...... with Chaitya-Mandira[9] ....

"A large reservoir of water and (*adorned*) by the abode of the chief of serpents and others[10] ....Warmed in summer by the heat of the sun, and fit for enjoyment at all seasons......(*as*) the dwelling of Indra and the bright caves of Mandara..........in the mountain to which none is equal in greatness .... (*he*) made with love, pleasure, and expansive modesty .... a cave brilliant with the radiance of the crown of Indra .... This Varâhadeva, praised among the Sugatas, having given (*the cave*) into possession of the Sangha, having enjoyed comforts of men and gods, with

---

[1] The elephants of smell, so called because it was fabled that ordinary elephants were terrified by the mere smell of these.

[2] Part of Kânnaḍâ, somewhere about Anagundi or Hampe.

[3] Western Mâlwâ, round Ujjain.

[4] The country between Oḍesa and the Krishṇâ.

[5] Usually Audha, but here perhaps the district about Chhatisgarh in Central India.

[6] Junnar in the Pûṇâ Zilla and adjacent districts.

[7] Bharoch district.

[8] The Tailanga country: the name of the chief seat of power is probably lost in the lacuna.

[9] This is no longer found: it may have been structural and outside.—J. B.

[10] *Nâgendraveśma* is the recess for the image of the Nâga. This without doubt refers to the figure of Nâgendra in the staircase leading down from the front of the cave. (See *Notes*, p. 57.)—J. B.

his relations .... enjoy this pure jewel-like dwelling, declared by Ratnatraya, while (*the earth rests*) on the body of the serpent as the dense clouds and .... while it shines by the yellow rays of the sun as red arsenic. This mountain having various summits and caves inhabited by great ....

"Again, may the whole world attain the state of tranquillity, excellence, freedom from evil, and sorrow, and various sins."

Inscription No. 4.

This is on the side wall outside the verandah in Cave No. XVII, and like the last has also suffered much from the weather. This inscription is in 29 lines, and is in Sanskṛit verse, each line containing one śloka.

This inscription furnishes the following names of kings :—

1. Dhratarâshṭra.
2. Harisâmba.
3. Saurisâmba.
4. Upendragupta.
5. (Agaja ? or) Kâcha.
6. Bhikshudâsa.
7. Nîladâsa.
8. Kâcha II.
9. Kṛishṇadâsa.

There was perhaps one name more, preceding that of Dhratarâshṭra, who is said to have been the son of some king. Whether Harisâmba was the son or brother of the preceding king is not clear. Saurisâmba is apparently the son of Harisâmba, but we know nothing of the relation of Upendragupta to his predecessor; so also the relation of Bhikshudâsa to Upendragupta is lost. Kṛishṇadâsa had two sons whose names, where they first occur, are obliterated, as is that of his wife. Later on Ravisâmba occurs as the name of one of them, and from the fragmentary phrases it appears that the elder murdered his brother, but afterwards repented. This is followed by the account of the construction of the Vihâra by the king or his minister, while Harisheṇa was ruling—almost certainly one of the Vâkâṭakas to whom this Asamaka family may have been subordinate.

The characters in this inscription bear a close resemblance to those of the Valabhî and early Châlukya copperplate grants. From the style of alphabet and the tenor of the inscriptions it would seem then that Caves Nos. XVI, XVII, XVIII and the Chaitya-Cave No. XXVI, belong all to very nearly the same date.

Transcript.

[१] ....मावर्नि, प्रणम्य विद्यात्रयपारगं मुनीम् [।]
विहारदातुर्व्यवदातकर्म्मणो गुणाभिधानोपनय ⁑ करिष्यते [१॥]

[२] ....नेश, लब्धात्मभावस्य नराधिपस्य [।]
धृवातपत्रस्य बभूव पुत्रास्सितातपत्रो धृतराष्ट्रसंज्ञः [२॥]

[३] ....स्यराज्ञो, हरिसाम्बोम्बुरुहेन्दुकान्तवक्रः [।]
नृपतेस्तनयो बभूव तस्याप्यमलश्रीः क्षितिपालशौरिसाम्बः [३॥]

[४] ....नेश पृथुकीर्तिद्युतिमानुपेन्द्रगुप्तः [।]
समभूद[गज]स्सुतोाथ तस्य क्षितिप ⁑ काच इति प्रकाशनामा [४॥]

[५] ....[द्रु]वि कीर्तिन्यसनाय भिक्षुदासः [।]
प्रथितो भुवि नीलदासनामा नृपतिस्तस्य सुतो नराधिपस्य [५॥]

[६]..........................प्रथित ⁑ काच इति प्रदीप्तकीर्तिः [।]
नृपतेरथ तस्य कृष्णदासः कुलवंशद्युतिवर्द्धनो बभुव [६॥]

[७] ....प्तनया चन्द्रकरावदातवेषा [।]
अभ[व]त्परिपूर्ण्णचन्द्रवक्त्रा विनयाचारविभुषणा ... चन्द्रा [७॥]

[८] ....,...........द्योतकरीमवाप [।]
तस्यान्च तस्याम्नुदहायताक्षावुत्तप्तचामीकरकान्तरूपी [८॥]

[९] ....[प्रद्यु]म्नसाम्बप्रतिमौ कुमारौ [।]
एकाधिपअप्रथमावतारं दध्रे द्वितीयो रविसाम्बसंज्ञाम् [९॥]

[१०] ....अश्मकादि [।]
......नुताभ्यामतिभूय भूयसा रराजतुश्चन्द्रदिवाकराविव [१०॥]

[११] ....[।]
विवृद्धसौहार्द[यश]प्रतानयोस्सदानुकूल्येन सुखं विनन्हतोः [११॥]

[१२] ....,.........रप्यानिवार्य्य शासनः [।]
पुराकृतोद्भावितभीमविक्रमः कनीयासि प्रा [...........] ताशनिः [१२॥]

[१३] ....धैर्य्यादि...........याधिराजः [।]
आचिंत्यसंज्ञः सचिवस्तत ⁑ परं व्यवीवृधत्पुण्यमहामहीरुहम् [१३॥]

[१४] ....,...........नु[याततोष]म् [।]
भूयश्श्रुतत्यागदयाप्रमोदमैत्रीक्षमावीर्य्यधियस्सिषेवे [१४॥]

[१५] ....नरेन्द्रान् [।]
प्रशस्तवृत्तान्सुविशुद्धवृत्तो वृत्तेन सम्यक् क्षुभितोनुचक्रे [१५॥]

[१६] ....चकार [।]
अ.........र्थिकस्यार्थिजनस्तवैव कीर्त्तिकृतार्थः प्रथयाम्बभूव [१६॥]

[१७] ....विप्लुताक्षान् [।]
अमूमुचद्वित्तविसर्गशक्त्या पुत्राभिचेष्टान्करुणाभिमृष्टः [१७॥]

[१८] ....येन पुत्रवत् [।]
अनूचिवां सोपि हि यस्य इद्गतां विन्दन्नृवध्याशयशुद्धिसम्पदम् [१८॥]

[१९] ....,...........कराणि सद्यः [।]
सर्व्वज्ञभावप्रणिधानसिद्धिः सत्याभिधानाभिभवादपेयुः [१९॥]

[२०] ....म्भारचयांधियोगः [।]
यशोम्बुभिश्चन्द्रमरीचिशुभ्रैर्जगत्समग्रं समलंचकार [२०॥]

[२१] ....,...........वदनारविन्दचन्द्रे [।]
परिपाल्याति क्षितीन्द्रचन्द्रे हरिषेणे हितकारिणि प्रजानाम् [२१॥]

[२२] ....,............त्यद्भुतपुण्यराशिः [।]
......भुवस्तूपविहारभूषा दानोदयैश्चार्थिजनप्रमोदम् [२२॥]

[२३] ....[नानिलनादवाद्भिः] [।]
................शरयाभद्दाद्भिः.................मविसद्मपादे [२३॥]

[२४] ....गाम्भीर्यगुणैरुपेतम् [।]
निवेशितान्तर्मुनिराजचैत्यमेकाश्मकं मण्डपरत्नमेतत् [२४॥]

[२५] ....ष्टिं विपुलां विसृज्य [।]
अचीकरच्चैत्यमिहानकल्पमल्पात्मभिः कल्पनयाप्यशक्यम् [२५॥]

[२६] ....शे नयनाभिरामम् [।]
न्यवीविशत्स्वादुलघुप्रसन्नशीतं प्रकामाम्बुमहानिधानम् [२६॥]

[२७] ....नेत्रमनोभिरामम् [।]
अन्यांगदेशेस्य दिशि प्रतीच्यामचीकरद्गन्धकुटीपुद्दाराम् [२७॥]

[२८] ....,......द्वितायोद्यतसर्वकर्मणः [।]
मुनीन्द्रनाथप्रणिधानसिद्धये भवन्त्वभीष्टा भुवि सर्व्वसम्पदः [२८॥]

[२९] ....सप्रणयेन मण्डपः [।]
करोतु तावत्कुशलोदयं सतां निहन्ति यावद्रविरंशुभिस्तमः [२९॥]

Translation.

" ......Making obeisance to the Muni who completely attained to the three sciences, I will set forth a description of the qualities of the donor of the vihâra, whose deeds are pure...to the king regarding all as equal to himself and who has the royal umbrella over his head, was a son by name Dhratarâshṭra of the white umbrella..................This king's (*son*) was Harisâmba, whose face was as the lotus and the moon. Again king Saurisâmba, of pure lustre, was this king's (*son*)............Upendragupta of great fame and beauty. Then his son was king (*Agaja*)[1] whose well-known name was Kâcha..... ....(*was*) Bhikshudâsa for spreading renown in the world. The king known in the earth by the name of Nîladâsa (*was*) the son of this king.................... Kâcha, renowned and famous. Then Kṛishṇadâsa was this king's son who was an increaser of the splendour of his dynasty .... was (*his wife*) who was gentle, whose dress was white as the moonbeams, whose face was like the full moon, and who was adorned by modesty and good behaviour.............. to this king by her were born two sons .... equal to Pradyumna and Sâmba, whose large eyes were lotus-like and whose beauty was as red burning gold. The first born, first to enjoy independent power (*Ekâdhipati*), and the second assumed the name of Ravisâmba[2] ....Asmaka and others......by frequently overcoming, they two were glorious as the sun and the moon .... of those, the creepers of whose glory in friendship have spread, and who conduct

---

[1] The word may also be read *Avana* instead of *Agaja*, which means 'a protector,' and if this reading be correct it cannot be a proper name; and the whole may mean that his "son was a protector (*of the world*) whose well-known name was Kâcha "

[2] It would seem that correctly either Ravisâmba should be a title, or Ekâdhipatya is a proper name, which however seems unlikely.

themselves always in happiness and mutual agreement.........................but he whose punishment is unrevokable and whose wicked actions grow from the deeds of his former life, (*was as*) a thunderbolt to the younger..... .... patience, &c.,......great king......after this the minister named Achintya (?) throve, a great tree of merits,........and again possessed knowledge of the sacred books, generosity, mercy, kindliness, friendship, benevolence, valour, and good sense, ... and being greatly ashamed conducted himself as men of renowned behaviour..................... who is successful in glory, became famous .... he who is filled with mercy, and by his generous disposition released those whose eyes are wet, and whose behaviour is filial, ... (*the minister*) who, although he knew that the king has acquired in his heart a conscience purified from murderous tendencies, did not disclose .... who acquired knowledge, by faith in, and meditation on, the omniscient (*Buddha*)................ by the waters of (*his*) glory, white as the beams of the moon, he much beautified the whole world.........when Harisheṇa—who was (*as*) a moon to the face of......... and a moon among kings, and a well-wisher of his subjects,—was ruling.......................................the heap of whose merits is extraordinary (*making*) the needy glad by the gift of a stûpa, a vihâra, and ornaments (?).................................of winds .... this jewel of a monolithic temple, which is majestic, and contains within a Chaitya of the Munirâja (*Buddha*)[1] ....made here an incomparable Chaitya, expending profusely upon it, such that the poor cannot even grasp in imagination...............................made a large reservoir charming to the eyes, of tasteful, clear, pleasant, and cold water..............................delightsome to the eyes and mind; on the other side of it, towards the west, made a splendid *Gandhakuṭi* (temple)[2] ....may the whole wealth of those whose actions are ready (?) for the benefit of the world, be for the attainment of the meditation on Munîndranâtha (*Buddha*) .... with courteousness may this temple increase comforts to the sages until the sun's rays destroy the darkness."

Inscription No. 5.

This occurs on the pilaster at the left end of the verandah in Cave XXII. Much of it is broken away, only a few letters in each of the eleven lines are now left. The language is Sanskṛit prose, and the letters are similar to those of the inscription in Cave XVI.

[दियधर्म्मो]यं मण्डप
.........प्रपौत्रस्य कृ
.........पौत्रस्याचार्येन्द्र
.......स्य धर्म्महग..........[पु]
त्रस्य जयता.........

---

[1] As there is no *dâgoba* or *Chaitya* in Cave XVII, it seems that the word *Chaitya* was used by the Buddhists, as it still is by the Jainas, for an image of Buddha.

[2] The *Gandhakuṭi* was perhaps the small Cave No. XVIII. The name is applied only to a temple containing images, and not to a monastic abode. The image in Cave XVIII must have been moveable.

स्य कुलाप्रि......[वर]
मोपासकस्य......
...न्चामिकस्यै... [यद]
[त्र]पुण्यं तद्भवतु मातापितृ
[पूर्वं]गमानां स[कलसत्वाना]
मनुत्तरज्ञानावाप्त[ये]

"The meritorious gift of a maṇḍapa by Jayata.........of......family, a great Upâsaka, great-grandson of ....grandson of............ of Âchârya Indra... ....son of Dharmahaga..............may the merit of this be for excellent knowledge to all sentient beings, beginning with father and mother."

INSCRIPTION No. 6.

On the front of the Chaitya-cave No. XXVI, over the right side door (see *Notes*, p. 83, and Plate XXI). It consists of 27 lines in Sanskṛit verse, and with the exception of flaws in the first and in some of the lower lines, it is fairly legible. The alphabet is similar to that used in the early Châlukya and Valabhî copper-plates, and if not of the same date as that on Cave XVII, is but little later.

Transcript.

[१] जयति लोकहितावहितोद्यतो...हिसुखान्तकरः परमार्थवि[त्] [।] त्रिविधानिर्म्मलसर्वगुणोदयो
मु[षितभीः?] करुणामलचन्द्रिकः[॥ १ ॥]

[२] पुनरपि[1]मरणादि येन सम्यक्शिवमजरामरधर्म्मता च लब्धा शिवमभयमनाल्पयं गतोपि प्रशमपुरं
जगतां करोति चार्त्थं [॥ २ ॥]

[३] ततो नमस्कारगुणाभिधानं भवत्यवन्ध्यं विपुलं महार्थं प्रदत्तमेकं कुसुमं च यत्र स्वर्गापवर्गाख्य-
फलस्य हेतुः [॥ ३ ॥]

[४] अत इह विदुषा तथागतेषु प्रथितगुणाधिकलोकवत्सलेषु कृतमनुसरता ननेन कार्य्या त्ववक-
रुणाहृदयेष्वती-

[५] वभक्तिः [॥ ४ ॥] देवा निरस्तविजयास्तविपत्तिकत्वाच्छापेन शंभुरपि काचरलोचनोभूत् कृष्णो
वशोपि वशमापतितोन्तकस्य तस्माज्जयन्ति

[६] सुगता भयविप्रमुक्ताः [॥ ५ ॥] स्थविराचलेन मुनिना शासनमद्भावयकृतज्ञेन[2] कृतकृत्येनापि[3]
सता शैलगृहं कारितं शास्तुः [॥ ६ ॥]

[७] प्रागेव बोधिसत्वैर्भवसुखकामैश्च मोक्षकामैश्च संविद्यमानविभवैः कथन्न कार्य्या भवेत्कीर्तिः [॥ ७ ॥]
यावत्कीर्तिर्ल्लोके तावत्स्वर्गे-

[८] षु मोदति च देही चन्द्रार्क्ककालकल्पा कार्य्या कीर्तिर्म्महीध्रेषु [॥ ८ ॥] अनेकजन्मांतरबद्धसौहृदं
स्थिरं कृतज्ञं सुधियं विपश्चितम्

---

[1] Read ° वि. [2] Read मुद्भावयत्कृ°. [3] Read ° कृतकृत्य°.

[९] सुरासुराचार्य्यमतेषु कोविदं महानुभावाश्मकराजमंत्रिणम् [॥ ९ ॥] लोकद्वमेकान्तसमन्तभद्रं
सर्व्वार्त्थिनामर्त्थकरं सुवाचं गुणोन्नतं प्रश्रय·

[१०] नम्रमूर्तिं ख्यातिं गतं सच्चरितैः पृथिव्यां [॥ १० ॥] दण्डसाध्यानि कार्य्याणि न्यायामैकरसा-
न्यपि यस्साधयति साम्नैव नृपतेर्म्मन्त्रिपुङ्गवः[1] [॥ ११ ॥] इत्थं

[११] भूतोस्य पुत्रोपि देवराजो धुरन्धरः पितर्य्युपरते येन पदमुन्नामितं गुणैः [॥ १२ ॥] तं भवि-
राजमुद्दिश्य मातापितरमेव च भिक्षुणा बुद्धभद्रेण

[१२] कारितः सुगतालयः [॥ १३ ॥] आगम्य धर्म्मदत्तञ्च भिक्षं सच्छिष्यमेव च भद्रबन्धुमिदं वेश्म
ताभ्यां निष्पादितं च मे [॥१४ ॥] यदत्र पुण्यं तत्तेषां

[१३] जगतां च भवत्विदं सर्व्वामलगुणध्यातमहाबोधिफलाप्तये [॥ १५ ॥] यो बुद्धशासनगतिं समनु·
प्रव्रजातो भिक्षुर्व्वयस्यभिनवेभिजनोपपन्नः

[१४] बहुव्रतः शीलविशुद्धचेता लोकस्य मोक्षाय कृताधिकारः [॥ १६ ॥] न संसारापन्नं शुभमपितु
किञ्चिच्छुभकरं विपाको दिव्यो

[१५]...त्य.........चनियमा...........लोकार्त्थाय प्रसृत...............पुण्यमहतां विपाको
धीराणां भवति सुखभोगाय

[१६] जगताम्...........बलभिर्म्मानाण्डजव्याहृते गोलाङ्गूलीननादपूरितदरे प्राग्भावि........

[१७] योगीश्वराध्यासिते वेश्मेदं न.........जनकभूत्यै प्रतिष्ठापितं पूर्व्वापि चेयं तेनैव द्रिढ्या-[2]
चार्येण सौगतिम् लोकचिन्तामुपादाय........

Translation.

"He (*Buddha*) is victorious, ready and attentive to the good of the people, the destroyer of.........comforts, indued with spiritual knowledge, in whom all the three pure virtues have grown up, who has .... whose pure splendour is mercy, (2.) by whom release from frequent deaths, comforts, and power of not growing old, and of immortality, have been obtained, and who, though he is deceased and gone to happy and fearless and houseless final emancipation[3] (*yet*) does good to the world. (3.) For this cause, saluting him and reciting his virtues is fruitful and of great and abundant advantage, and where even the gift of a flower is the cause of the fruit called heaven and final beatitude.[4]

"(4.) Therefore, a learned person, who follows the practice of those before him should here worship the Tathâgatas (*Buddhas*), whose hearts are soft through mercy and who are greatly popular among people by their well-known virtues.

"(5.) Devas from being subject to miseries are devoid of success. Also Śambhu, from the curse, was of trembling eyes. Krishṇa, though unwilling,

---

[1] Read °र्म्मन्त्रिपुङ्गवः°. [2] Read दृढ्या°.

[3] Literally, "who, though he is gone to the city of quiescence, happy and without danger, and where there is no need for a house."

[4] The northern or Mahâyâna Buddhists hold that if Buddha had lost all influence, it would be useless worshipping him or remembering his deeds. The Hinayâna sect say that worshipping and meditating on him of itself purifies the heart and leads to the desired end without any influence exerted on Buddha's part. The doctrine in the inscription is that of the Mahâyânas.

became subject to the will of Yama. The Sugatas, therefore, because altogether free from fears, are victorious.

"(6.) Even Sthavirâchala Muni who was grateful, of accomplished desires, and virtuous, made for Buddha a stone dwelling, glorifying religion. (7.) Why should the Bodhisattvas, who are desirous of worldly happiness as well as of final release and are possessed of prosperity, not previously have acquired fame? (8.) A human being enjoys heaven so long as his fame in the world lasts; (*so*) fame that may endure as long as the sun and moon, must be acquired in the mountains.

"(9.) [*In honour of that Bhavirâja*] who has been in friendship with him through several transmigrations, who is steady, grateful, wise, learned, proficient in the Sura and Asura teaching of the Âchâryas, minister of the magnanimous king Asmaka, (10.) clever in worldly business, exceedingly fortunate every way, fulfiller of the desires of all the needy, a sweet speaker, exalted by virtues, gentle in modesty, much praised in the world for good behaviour: (11.) and who, as the excellent minister of the king, accomplishes merely by conciliation what is attained (*usually*) by punishments and by exertions only. (12.) His son Devarâja, a leader, was equal to him, and on the demise of his father exalted his dignity by his high qualities. (13.) In honour of that Bhavirâja, and in honour of his father and mother, Bhikshu Buddhabhadra has caused a temple to be built to Buddha.

"(14.) Having recourse to Bhikshu Dharmadatta and (*his*) good disciple Bhadrabandhu, I constructed this temple through them.[1] (15.) May whatever merit is therein be for the attainment by these and by the world of the fruit of great Bodhi desired by all of pure qualities.

"(16.) He who on attaining the knowledge of the religion of Buddha is surrounded by relatives, and whose heart has been purified by the observance of many religious abstinences and by moral conduct, and has made the final release of people his duty, became a Bhikshu in his youth. (17.) Again the smallest virtue resulting in good cannot be accomplished while engaged in worldly affairs. The result of the actions of sages who are exalted by virtue tends to the enjoyment of happiness by the people.

"This temple is established for the welfare (*of people, in a hill?*), tuneful with the notes of various birds, and whose caves are filled with the sounds of cow-tails (*chauris*).............and which is inhabited by the Yogîśvaras.................The same aggrieved Achârya having taken over the anxiety of the people regarding the Sugata.................................."

INSCRIPTION No. 7.

On a plinth under the feet of a tall standing figure of Buddha, to the left of the façade of Cave XXVI.

[१] देयधर्म्मोयं शाक्यभिक्षोर्भदन्तगुणाकरस्य यदत्रपुण्यं तद्भवतु मातापितरं पूर्व्वङ्गमं कृत्वा

[२] सर्व्वसत्वेभ्य अनुत्तर ज्ञान आप्तये

Translation.

"The Śâkya Bhikshu, the Bhadanta Guṇâkara's meritorious gift, may whatever merit is in this be for the attainment of supreme knowledge by all sentient beings, mother and father being first."

---

[1] It would seem from this that the donor Buddhabhadra was not resident near, but entrusted the work to these devotees.

INSCRIPTION No. 8.

On the plinth under a similar figure on the opposite side of the façade. This is injured by the breaking away of the stone, leaving only the beginnings of the three lines.

[१] ॐ देयधर्मो[य......................]
[२] यदत्रपुण्यं [तद्भवतु मातापितरं पूर्व्वङ्गमं कृत्वा ?]
[३] सर्वसत्वानाम[नुत्तर ज्ञानावाप्तये ?]

Translation.

"The meritorious gift of.................
attainment of supreme knowledge.....................
all sentient beings, mother and father................"

INSCRIPTION No. 9.

On the wall of the rightside aisle under a small figure of Buddha:

[१] देयधर्मोयं शाक्य-
[२] भिक्षुसंघमित्रस्य

Translation.

"The meritorious gift of the Śâkyabhikshu Sanghamitra."

PAINTED INSCRIPTIONS IN THE AJANṬA CAVES.

Inscriptions written on the paintings are found in six of the caves,—Nos. II, IX, X, XVI, XVII, and XXII—most of them more or less mutilated.

PAINTED INSCRIPTIONS IN CAVE No. II.

No. 1.

There are no inscriptions in Cave No. I, but in No. II. besides fragments of a pretty long one in small letters on a dark green ground in the left hand cell outside the verandah there are two or three inside. No. 1 is on the lotus throne of a painted figure of a seated Buddha on the back wall of the hall.[1] The letters of this inscription are as late as the 6th or 7th century.

[१] देय[धर्म्मोयं] शाक्यभिक्षोर्भदन्त ... [बुद्ध]गुप्तस्य यदत्र पु[ण्यं]
[२] ....[स]र्वसत्व ....

"The meritorious gift of the Śâkya Bhikshu the reverend Buddhagupta: may whatever merit...................of sentient beings."

No. 2.

No. 2 is on the right hand of the shrine door among many figures of Buddhas.[2] It is much effaced and not very distinctly written, so that a trans-

---

[1] See *Notes*, p. 34. The execution of the painting is somewhat different from that on the right side wall of the cave, but it is hard to say whether this is due to the artist or to its being of somewhat later date.—J. B.

[2] *Notes*, p. 35.

Ajantâ Painted Inscriptions

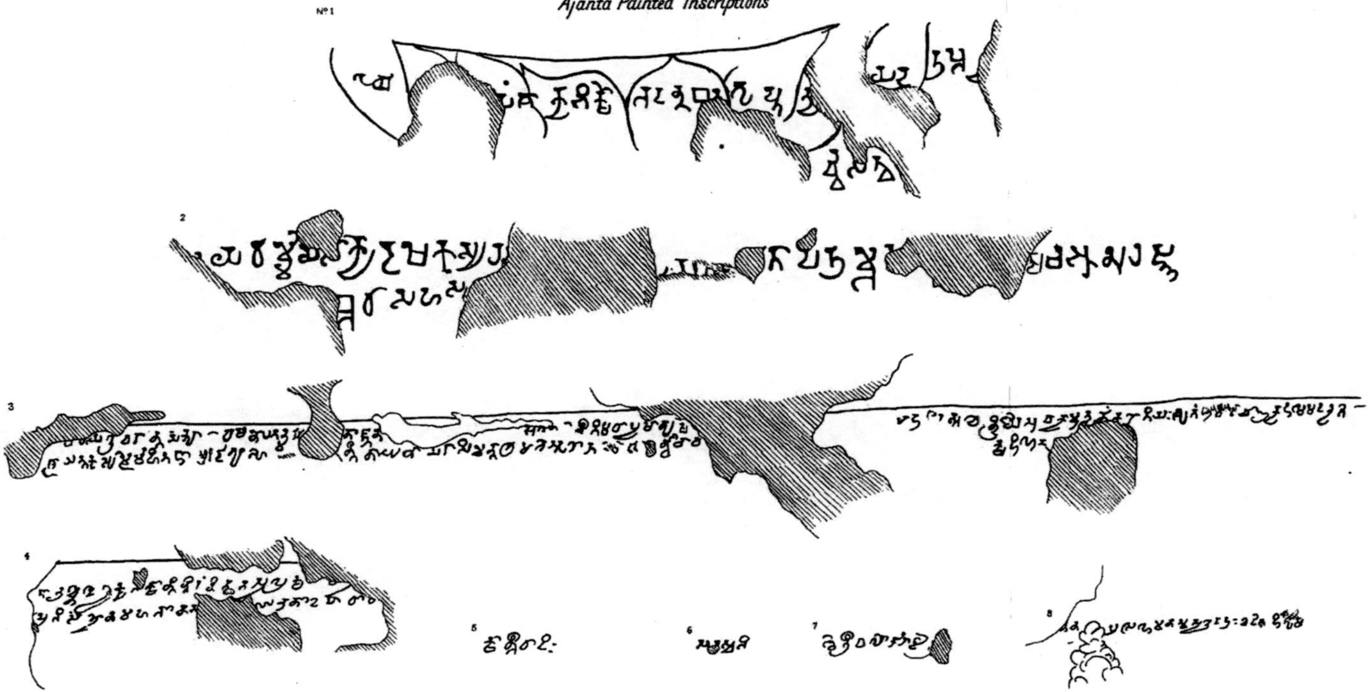

Scale ⅙ the original.

lation is impracticable. It begins with the usual donative phrase *deya-dharmoyam*, and probably recorded the presentation of the painted figures. It concludes with the common formula, "May whatever merit, &c."

[१] देयधर्म्मोयं साक्यो उपकस्य ....[मा]तापितृम्म......च अनु[त्त]रज्ञा-

[२] ....बुधा सह सं.........

Besides this there is a line written among the Buddhas, but the letters are so mutilated and indistinct as almost to defy copying.

Nos. 3 to 8 are on the back and right hand wall of a chamber outside Cave II. to the left. They are descriptive of the subjects of the paintings on which they have been written, but unfortunately the paintings are as much destroyed as the inscriptions.

No. 3.

क्षान्तिवादि:[1]

On the back wall to the right of a door in it, a man is represented seated on a stool (*bhadrâsana*) in a plain dress indicative of a Sâdhu or Brâhmaṇ; his head is destroyed; under his seat is No. 3 in letters of about the 6th century, in which we read the word *kshântivâdiḥ*—'a discourse on forbearance.'[2]

No. 4.

Facing him is another seated figure, and below is a belt of green colour on which is No. 4 in two lines, so mutilated as to be untranslateable—possibly it related to the *kshânti* philosophy.

[१] .... न यत्र वरान्तसंकु .. धेषणा तन्म..... नाज्ञान ....
सुताहि नीतिमवाप्य मानुष.............................पाद्र.. स्तचेन्द्रियै सुवाक्य-
मुत्पन्नं करोति य: शुभं .... चा.. क्यहमेमदं न्यते

[२] ....शायन्तकुसुमैर्भिहितहा ... दागुसे ....न्तिताय नापरा सिमन्ताग्रे
मतेस्स...त......न्वाचा व.................................. ..क्षाहिण ......
....

Below this is a Brâhmaṇa or Pâsupata, seated on a stool in plain dress and with a Rudrâksha rosary about his neck. Opposite him is another male figure and between them is a woman seated, with her hands joined towards the former, whilst she speaks to the latter of the two.

No. 5.

Below these figures is inscription No. 5, also so destroyed as to be illegible,—but perhaps relating to the same subject.

[१]...................नात्वच्छेदित्यक्षतक्षान्तिाचिरनिर्वृतस्य क्षेप............

[२]...................पतिसंन्यानमहतां नस........ णात्र नादेवाधार............

---

[1] Read दी

[2] *Kshântivâdin* was the name of Gautama Buddha in one of his previous births. The *kshântis* are the states produced by continued meditation on the four verities: see Vassilief, p. 140.

Below this again has been a royal figure surrounded by attendants, but the merest fragments are left of the scene.

The painting on the right side of this same room has also been almost entirely destroyed.

No. 6.

Among the fragments left are parts of a cow, over which is written the inscription No. 6 consisting of the name—*Sarasuti*, in letters of the same age as the others.

सरसुति

Sarasuti is a Prâkṛit form of "Sarasvati," the goddess of learning.

No. 7.

On the same wall near the front corner, has been a figure of a king seated on a throne, which bears the inscription No. 7 :—

चैत्रिवलोर्कराजा (?)

"King Chaitri of Valorka."

Vallura is met with in the Ghaṭotkacha inscription, and may be a form of Valorka.

No. 8.

Above this is the broken inscription No. 8 which possibly expressed some religious tenet :—

[१]..........................नान प्रसेहे मन: स्वस्यात्रैव दु:खादि गाहि..................

Painted Inscriptions in Cave No. IX.

Fragments of inscriptions on the paintings of this cave are numerous, but all in a more or less dilapidated condition. As many as sixteen have been noticed, but of some only a letter or two have been left. Five of the most legible have been given on the accompanying plate.

No. 9.

This is on the front wall of the Chaitya Cave No. IX, inside, over the door and close to the head of a Bhikshu :—

[दियधर्म्मो]यं शा[क्यभिक्षो]

स्सङ्घप्रि[यस्य]

........माता

....

"The meritorious gift of the Śâkya Bhikshu Sanghapriya."

The letter *ya* has been supplied. The characters are similar to those of the 6th century, and the portion of the painting on which it is, is of a correspondingly modern date, but it overlies part of a picture in a much earlier style of painting.

No. 9

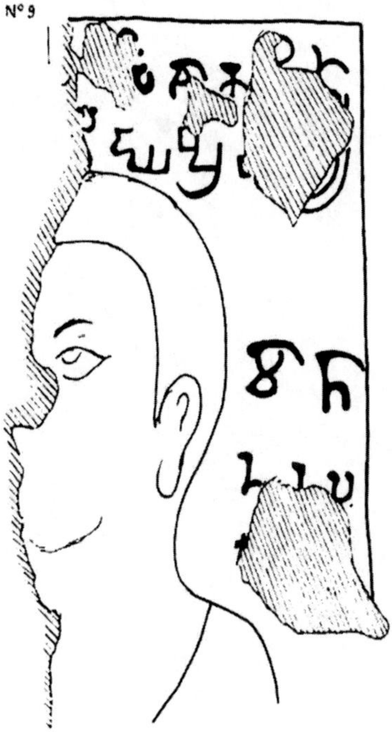

10

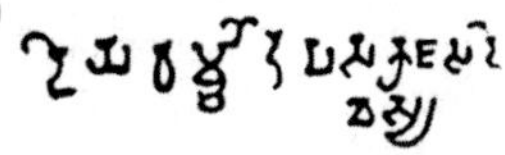

11

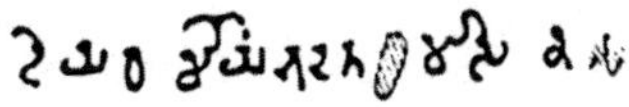

12

13

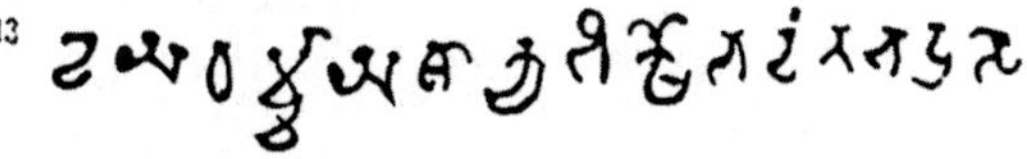

Scale ⅓ the original

No. 10.

On the first pillar on the left side of the aisle, under a painted figure of a standing Buddha. The letters are of the 6th century:—

देयधम्मों उपासकजसदे-
वस्य

"The meritorious gift of the Upâsaka Jasadeva."

There are three other fragments on different sides of this same pillar; two of them are over umbrellas, and one on the petals of a lotus. All are apparently of the same general character.

No. 11.

On an architrave or jamb attached to the first pillar on the left side of the cave, under the throne of a seated figure of Buddha. It is in somewhat earlier letters than the preceding:—

देयधर्मोयं भदन्त[ध]र्मसेन[स्य]

"The meritorious gift of the reverend Dharmasena."

On a broken pillar, the fourth from the front, on the same side of the cave, is a fragment in one line and a half. On the third standing pillar is another, also mutilated. And on the fifth standing (8th) pillar is another, on an umbrella, a line and half in length.

No. 12.

On the back wall of the cave under a painted dâgoba or Chaitya. This inscription is so damaged as to be illegible, but it affords specimens of the letters which apparently belong to about the 5th century, the period to which the painting on which it occurs may belong.[1] The inscription as usual begins with *Deya dahama*,—the second word misspelt as it sometimes is in these inscriptions. The letter *bha*, may perhaps indicate that the donor was a "Bhadanta."

देयद्धर्म्मभ............स्य म.........

There are also two other fragments on this same wall.

No. 13.

On the 9th pillar (6th *standing* one) on the left side, under a standing figure of Buddha:—

देयधर्म्मोयं शाक्यभिक्षोर्भदन्तभद्रसे[नस्य?]

"The meritorious gift of the Śâkya Bhikshu, the Bhadanta Bhadra-sena."

On the first standing pillar, on the right side, are about eight letters of another; and at the feet of a standing Buddha are traces of two or three letters. On the next are large fragments of two lines. On the entablature over this pillar, are fragments of an inscription in four lines.

---

[1] See *Notes*, pp. 47, 48, 49.

Inscriptions in Cave No. X.

Fragments of about twenty inscriptions have been found in this cave, most of them on the pillars, and having reference to the painted figures of Buddha with which they have been covered. Of several only a few bits of letters remain.

No. 14.

This is on the left wall, opposite the third column, just over a portion of the very early painting in this cave, and evidently belongs to the same age.[1] It is painted in dark brown letters on a light ground. The characters belong to the same age as the carved inscriptions elsewhere of the time of Sâtakarṇi, as on the Amarâvati tope, &c. Unfortunately only a fragment is left of what it must originally have been.

भगवस यतिपुवदे[ब]...तयातिपातिस यस ....

Sanskrit.

भागवतो यतिपूर्वदेवस्य...यतिपते: ....

"Of Bhagava (Buddha) first *deva* of Yatis......master of Yatis."

No. 15.

On the same wall, opposite the space between the fifth and sixth pillars, above the old painting and just below a portion of the later painting consisting of figures of Buddha in orange colour. It is in three lines on a thin white ground. The letters are of about the 6th century, but it is much defaced:—

आचार्य..............सचिवस्य
देयधर्म्मो यदत्रपुण्यं तद्भवतु सर्व्वस-
त्वानांदु ˣₓ खमोचा ....

"The meritorious gift...............Âchârya of.........Sachiva: may whatever merit is in this be for the (*release*) from miseries of all sentient creatures."

There was another inscription, also on a thin white ground on the same wall, but it has faded entirely.

No. 16.

This is on the 6th pillar—4th standing one,—on the right side of the cave, about 5 feet up, at the feet of a standing figure of Buddha, in three short lines in white, on a reddish ground. The letters resemble those of about the 5th century:—

देयधर्म्मोयं शाक्य-
भिक्षोर्भदंत द्राढ-
धर्म्मस्य

"This meritorious gift of the Śâkya Bhikshu, the reverend Draḍhadharma."

The name is written as Drâḍhadharma—apparently by mistake.

---

[1] See *Notes*, p. 51.

Nº 14

15

16

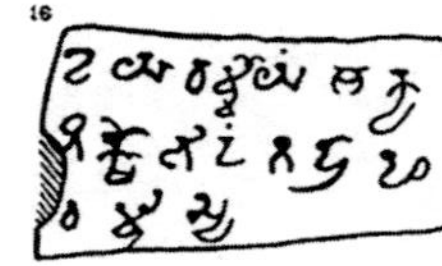

17

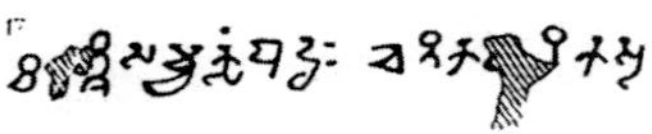

18

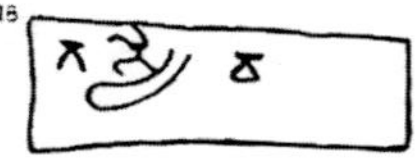

19

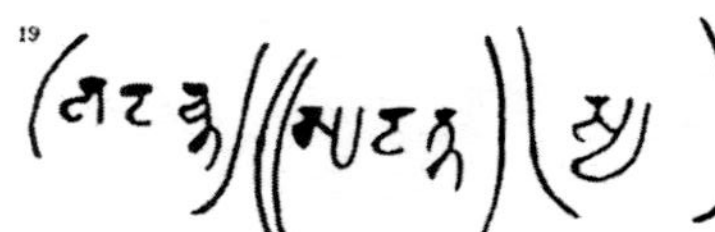

20

Scale ⅓ the original

Ajantâ Painted Inscriptions Cave No. X.

No. 21

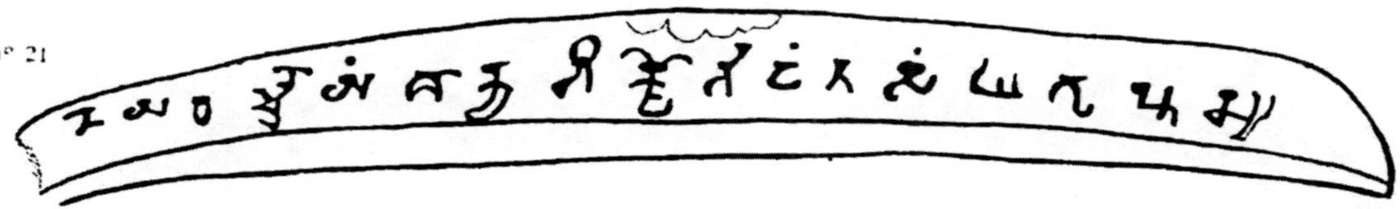

22

Scale ⅔ the original

Photozincographed Govt. Office, Poona, 1880

No. 17.

On the front of the 7th pillar (5th standing one), on the right side of the nave, at about 4½ feet from the earth painted on a green ground below a figure of a standing Buddha.

विपश्शि सम्यक्संबुद्धः चेतिक[य]रिकस्य

" Vipaśśi, the perfectly wise. (*Gift*) of Chetikayarik."

By Vipaśśi is probably to be understood the name of the Buddha represented: the name, however, should be written with *ssi*.

On the 7th standing pillar on the same side over an umbrella is another in two lines and perhaps a letter or two of a third.

On the first standing pillar, on the left of the nave, are parts of an inscription in one line; and on the petals of a lotus is another in two lines, in a later character than the others. On the third is a fragment of a small one in two lines.

No. 18.

On the ninth pillar on the left side of the nave there have been two inscriptions under figures of Buddha on adjoining sides; one of these is destroyed, but it probably contained the name of the donor. Under the other Buddha we read—

तस्यै व

" Of the same."

No. 19.

On the 8th pillar (3rd standing) on the left side of the cave, on the lotus under the feet of a standing Buddha—

भदन्त सुदत्तस्य

" Of the reverend Sudatta."

No. 20.

On another side of the same pillar, also on a lotus, under a seated Buddha, with a kneeling figure on each side the lotus stalk, but the inscription mutilated—

[भद]न्त सुदत्तस्य

" Of the reverend Sudatta."

On the 4th standing pillar, left side, are very faint traces of two,—one surrounded by a black border, over the nimbus of a Buddha; the other on an umbrella over a Buddha, on another side of the pillar.

No. 21.

On the 10th pillar (the 5th standing one) on the same side, on the umbrella, over a standing figure of Buddha—

देयधर्म्मोयं शाक्यभिक्षोर्भदंतसंघगुप्तस्य

"This meritorious gift of the Sâkya Bhikshu the Bhadanta Sanghagupta."

On the 6th standing pillar, on the left side, are a few letters of another on an umbrella.

No. 22.

On the 5th pillar on the right side, below a standing figure of Buddha :—

देयद्धर्म्मोंयं भदन्तशीलभद्रस्य माता

पितरमुदि[श्य]

"This meritorious gift of the Bhadanta Śilabhadra, in honour of father and mother."

No. 23.

On the 10th pillar (6th standing one) on the right side near the feet of a figure of Buddha :—

मातापि

तरमुद्दि[श्य]

सर्व्व...........

देयध[र्म्मोयं शाक्यभिक्षोर्भ]दन्तकेशवस्य

"This meritorions gift of the Sâkya Bhikshu the Bhadanta Keśava in honour of mother, father, and all.............."

No. 24.

On the 17th pillar (10th standing one), on the left side, below a seated figure of Buddha, in three pretty long lines, but much defaced. The alphabet is apparently in characters of about the 5th or 6th century. In the beginning is a verse on the importance of making images of Buddha.

....न्द्रिया भासुर[दी]क्षयस्ते

.......................कारयंतीह जिनस्य बिंबं

[दियध]र्म्मोयं शाक्यभिक्षोराचार्यभदन्तबुद्धसेनस्य.

".................. whoever makes an image of Jina (*Buddha*) they...........of senses and of good lustre.....................this meritorions gift of the Sâkya Bhikshu Âchârya the Bhadanta Budhasena."

On the next pillar there is also an inscription of two short lines. On the wall of the right aisle, under the 4th, 5th, and 6th ribs, are a few letters of an inscription in larger characters. Under the 20th rib is a single line. And under the 24th and 25th ribs are some fragments of another in two lines.

Painted Inscriptions in Cave No. XVI.

These are below three figures of seated Buddhas on the left wall of the hall.[1] The characters used in these inscriptions belong to about the 6th century.

[1] See *Notes*, p. 59, No. vii.

No. 23

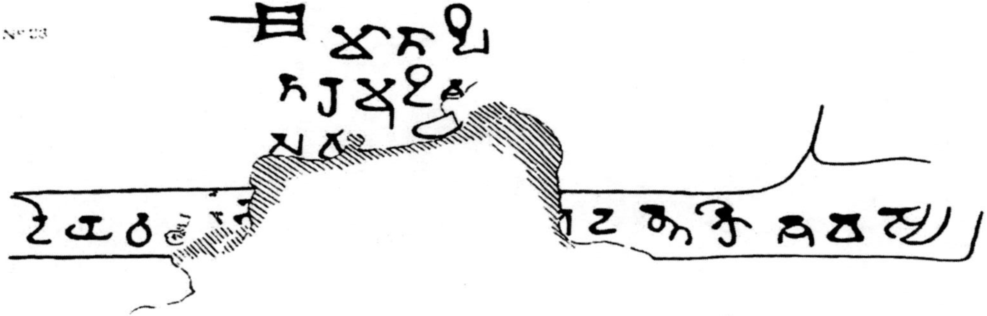

24

Scale ⅓ the original

Photozincographed at the Government Offices, Poona, 1881.

No. 25

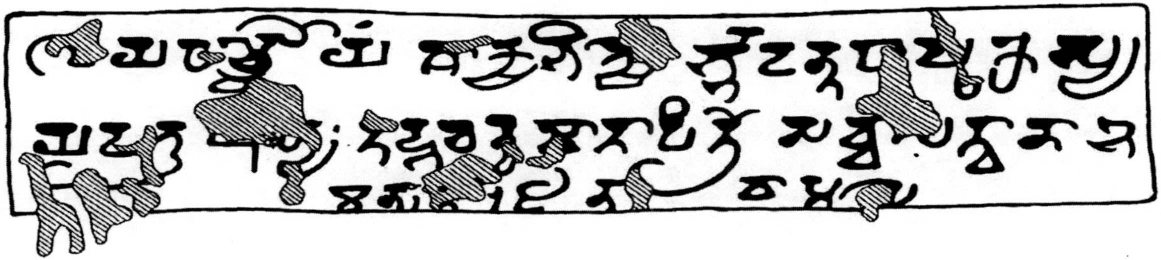

26

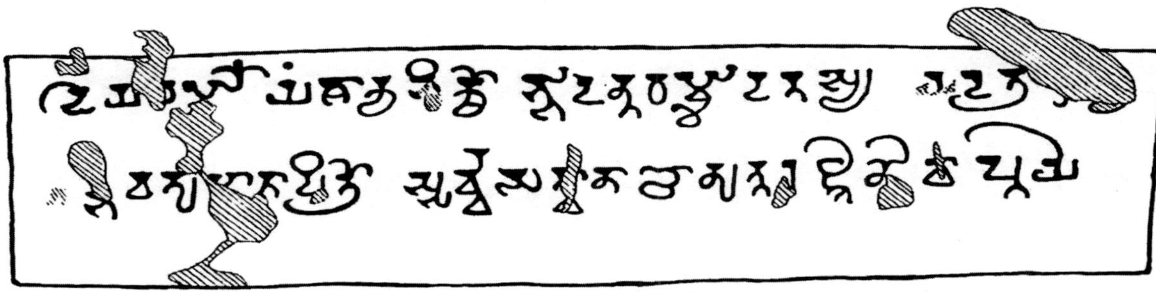

Photozincographed Govt. Office Poona, 1880

Scale ⅔ the original

No. 27

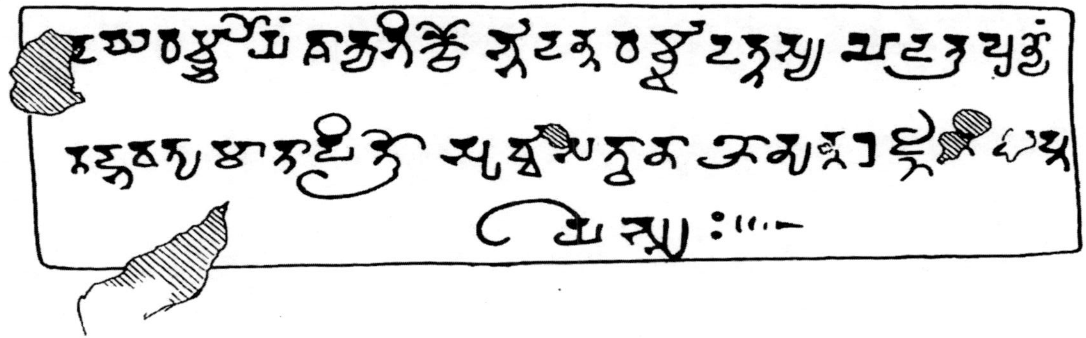

Cave No. XVII.

28

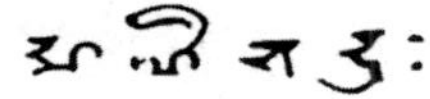

29

Scale. ⅓ the original.

No. 25.

देयधर्म्मोयं शाक्यभिक्षोर्भ्भदन्त दापुकस्य
यदत्रपुण्यं तद्भवतु मातापित्रो[:] सर्व्वसत्वानाञ्चा-
नु[त्त]रज्ञानावाप्तये

"The meritorious gift of the Śâkya Bhikshu the Bhadanta Dâpuka. May whatever merit may be in this, be for the attainment of the highest knowledge by mother and father and all sentient beings."

The symbol at the beginning of the 3rd line, which is written from under the 6th syllable of the second line and not from the extreme left side of area must be a mark of continuation like those used in some of the *Tâḍpatra* books of the Jainas.

No. 26.

देयधर्म्मोयं शाक्यभिक्षोर्भ्भदन्त धर्म्मदत्तस्य यदत्र [पुण्यं]
तद्भवतु मातापित्रोस्सर्व्वसत्वानाञ्चानुत्तरज्ञानावाप्तये

"The meritorious gift of the Śâkya Bhikshu the Bhadanta Dharmadatta. May whatever merit is in this be for the attainment of supreme knowledge by mother, father and all sentient creatures."

No. 27.

देयधर्म्मोयं शाक्यभिक्षोर्भ्भदन्तधर्म्मदत्तस्य यदत्रपुण्यं
तद्भवतु मातापित्रोस्सर्व्वसत्वानाञ्चानुत्तरज्ञानावाप्त-
येस्तु

"The meritorious gift of the Śâkya Bhikshu the Bhadanta Dharmadatta. May whatever merit is in this be for the attainment of supreme knowledge by mother and father and all sentient beings."

PAINTED INSCRIPTIONS IN CAVE NO. XVII.

No. 28.

Below a figure of a Yaksha in the left end of the verandah (*Notes*, p. 62). The letters employed in this are of the style in use in Eastern India about the 6th century.

माणिभद्रः

"Mâṇibhadra."

Mâṇibhadra is the name of a Yaksha well known among the later Buddhists and Jainas.

No. 29.

On some painted figures in the right end of the front aisle of the hall (*Notes*, pp. 75, 76,) being names on the figures relating to the *Sibi Jâtaka*. The letters closely resemble those of the rock inscription No. 3, of the Vâkâṭakas :—

शिबिराजा	शिबिराजा	इन्द्र	शिबिराजा	इन्द्रः
"King Sibi.	King Sibi.	Indra.	King Sibi.	Indraḥ."

PAINTED INSCRIPTION IN CAVE NO. XXII.

No. 30.

This is below eight figures of Buddhas painted on the left side of the shrine (see *Notes*, p. 81).

[१] विपश्वी [५] कनकमुनि
[२] शिखी [६] काश्यप:
[३] विश्वभू [७] शाक्यमुनि
[४] .... [८] मैत्रेय

[९] देय धम्मोयं शाक्यभिक्षो मषरशैल..
...नी सुस्य मातापितृ......त्रन्य .. सर्व्वसत्वानामनुत्तरज्ञानवाप्तये

[१०] सौरूप्यसौभाग्यगुणोपपन्ना गुणेन्द्रियैर्भास्वरदिप्तयष्टे भवन्ति ते नयनाभिरामा
ये कारयंतीह जिनस्य विंबं

"Vipaśvi. Śikhi. Viśvabhu...............Kanakamuni. Kâśyapa. Śâkyamuni. Maitreya.

"The meritorious gift of the Śâkya Bhikshu Masharśaila..........mother and father.........for the attainment of supreme knowledge by all sentient creatures.

"Whoever makes an image of Jina (*Buddha*) becomes complete in beatitude, auspiciousness, and good qualities, and his splendour is brilliant through virtues, and physical organs, and is delightsome to the eyes."

12.—GHATOTKACHA INSCRIPTION.

This inscription is cut on the left end of the back wall of the verandah of the large Buddhist cave near Gulwâḍâ, a few miles from Ajaṇṭâ. It was originally a very long one but has been much destroyed by the decay of the stone, especially below the tenth line. It is in Sanskrit ślokas, and the lines are made to follow the verses. The letters agree closely with those of Ajaṇṭâ Rock Inscription No. 3 (p. 69).

[१] मुनिर्मुनीनाममरोमराणां गुरुर्ग्गुरूणां प्रवरो वराणां [।]
जयत्यनाभोगनिवुद्दवुद्धिर्बुद्धाभिधानो निधिरद्भुतानां [॥]

[२] धर्म्मस्ततो धर्म्मविदा प्रणीतस्तथा गणश्चाग्र्यतमो गणानां [।]
भवन्ति यस्मिन्निहिता सुपात्रे कारापकारास्तनयाप्युदारा [॥]

[३] अस्ति प्रकाशो दिशि दक्षिणस्यां वल्लूरनाम्नां द्विजसत्तमानां [।]
आत्रह्मणस्संभृतपुण्यकीर्त्तिर्व्वंशो महीयान्महितो महद्भिः [॥]

[४] तस्मिन्नभूदाहतलक्षणानां द्विजन्मनां प्राथमकल्पकानाम् [।]
भृग्वत्रिगर्ग्गाङ्गिरसां समानो द्विजर्षभो यज्ञ... प्रकाशः [॥]

N° 30

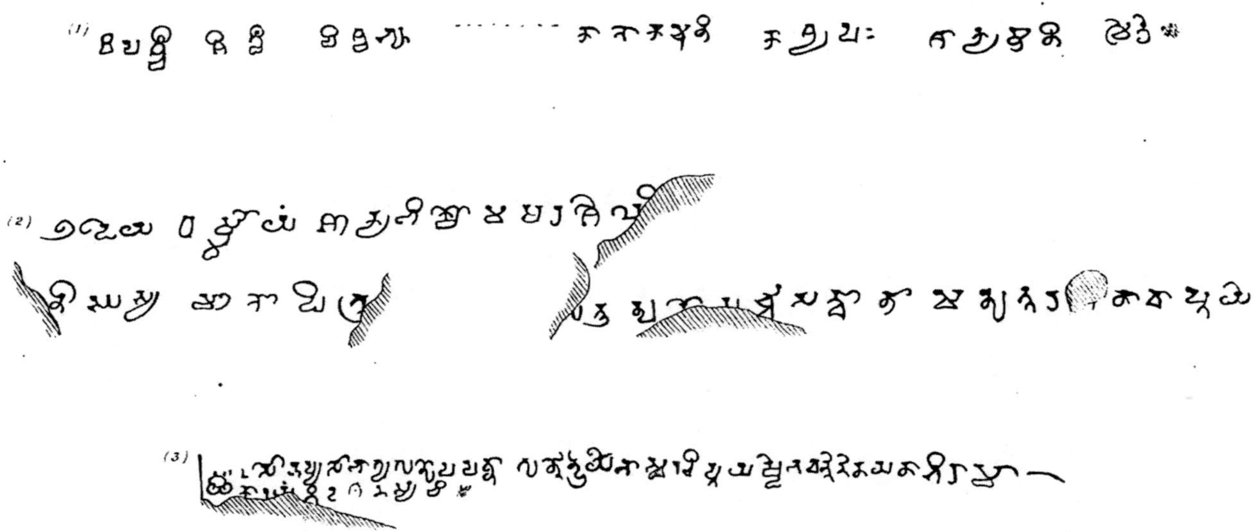

Scale ⅔ the original.

[५] तदात्मजो देव इवास देव[:] कृती गृहस्थो नयवान्क्रियावान् [।]
सरानकं राष्ट्रमुपेत्य यस्मिन्धर्म्याः क्रियाः पार्थ इव प्रचक्रे [॥]

[६] सोमस्ततः सोम इवापरोभूत्सब्राह्मणः क्षत्रियवंशजासु [।]
[श्रुतिस्मृतिभ्यां] विहितार्थकारी द्वयीसु भार्यासु मनो दधार [॥]

[७] स क्षत्रियायां कुलशीलवत्यामुत्पादयामास नरेंद्रचिन्हं [।]
सुतं सुरूपं रविनामधेयं कृताधिपत्यं मल्ये समग्रे [॥]

[८] द्विजासु चान्यासु सुतानुदारान्स [सोमः] वेदेषु समाप्तकामान् [।]
वल्लूरनाम्ना दिशि दक्षिणस्यामद्यापि येषाम्वसतिर्द्विजानां [॥]

[९] रवेः सुतोभूत्प्रवराभिधानः श्री[रा]मनामाथ बभूव तस्मात् [।]
तदात्मजः कि‍र्त्तिरभूत्सकीर्तिर्ब्बभूव तस्मादथ ह[स्तिभोजः] [॥]

[१०] वाकाटके राजति देवसेने गु[णैषिकोशो] भावि हस्तिभोजः [।]
[अद्यापि] ... स्याभिम ... य .... ना .... [॥]

[११] धीरेषु धीमत्सु सहोत्थितेषु .... गुणान्वितेषु [।]
............कार्य्यं नृपतेर्यदे...... ....स्य [॥]

[१२] यस्यासनार्द्धं पुरुषाक्ष......मत्संसदि.................. [।]
...............विवृ.................... ....[॥]

[१३] अय देवराज ....[।]
......................................[॥]

[१४] शशिकरधवलानि..........................
[१५] अथ गृणशतसंभुतो ....
[१६] तस्यात्मजेषु बहुषु ....
[१७] फलमाखिलपिल ....
[१८] सम्यग्विभा ....

Translation.

1\. "The treasure of marvels called Buddha is victorious, who is the sage of sages, god of gods, teacher of teachers, best of the good, whose genius results from unproductive actions.

2\. "From him virtue declared by the skilled in religion (*arises*) as also the assembly (*gaṇa-sangha*), the foremost of assemblies (*gaṇa*) (*originates*), and even an ungrateful and unjust prison (?)[1] dedicated to his virtuous person, becomes the bestower of good.

3\. "In the southern country there was a renowned and great family of the best of Brâhmaṇs named Vallûra which has earned deserved glory since the time commencing from Brahmâ, and which is adored by the great.

4\. "In this (*family*) was Yajña........prakâśa the best of Brâhmaṇs equal to the Brâhmaṇs of ancient times (*as*) Bhṛigu, Atri, Gargga, Angiras, noted for good qualities.

---

[1] A similar expression occurs in the Ajaṇṭâ inscription No. 3. The allusion is obscure.

5. "His son was Deva equal to a Deva (*god*), who was wise, a householder, just, a performer of religious rites. Having obtained possession of the countries of several princes, like Arjuna he performed religious rites therein.

6. "After him came Soma, equal to Soma (*the moon*), a Brâhmaṇ, the performer of acts mentioned in Śruti and Smṛiti; he set his heart on two wives born in Kshatriya families.

7. "He had born by his Kshatriya wife, of high family and chastity, a beautiful son named Ravi bearing the mark of a king, and who obtained rule over the whole Malaya country.

8. "He (*Soma*) had, by other Brâhmaṇî (*wives*), sons who were generous, and had attained their desires in the Vedas, the residence of which Brâhmaṇs is still Vallûra in the southern country.

9. "The son of Ravi was by name Pravara; to him was born the illustrious Râma by name. His son was the famed Kîrtti, and his was Hastibhoja.

10. "When the Vâkâṭaka Devasena lived, Hastibhoja, the store (?) of people of good qualities, in this world, till now..................

11.—18. "In men of patience, wise, advanced together.........men of good qualities ....which action of the king....................... half of whose seat.................................After this Devarâja....................... ....white as the rays of the moon.. then filled with a hundred qualities...................................In many of his sons....................................the whole consequence........................ ....well ...."

Remark.

The Hastibhoja of this inscription is probably the same as is named in the 3rd Ajaṇṭâ inscription (p. 69). He is here made the contemporary of Devasena. This supplies us with the ancestry of the minister Hastibhoja:—

1. Yajña......prakâśa.
2. Deva.
3. Soma.
4. Ravi, born of a Kshatriya.
5. Pravara.
6. Râma.
7. Kîrtti.
8. Hastibhoja, after whose name the inscription is much defaced.

There is, however, a Devarâja mentioned who may be the same as in the 6th Ajaṇṭâ inscription (p. 77), and if so we should then add—

9. Varahâdeva.
10. Bhavirâja.
11. Devarâja.

It would follow from this that this cave is of somewhat later date than Ajaṇṭâ Caves Nos. XVI, XVII, and XXVI.[1]

---

[1] This is borne out also by its architecture.

ELURÂ.

PANEL IN TÎN ṬHÂL.

J. Burgess. Photozincographed, Govt. Office, Poona, 1879. Jayrao Raghoba delt.

13.—INSCRIPTIONS IN THE ROCK-TEMPLES OF ELURA.

The inscriptions at Elurâ are very few and mostly so dilapidated as to be disappointing. Beginning from the south end of the series, at the Bauddha Caves, we take them in order as they come.

(1).—VIŚVAKARMA CAVE.

In the Buddhist Chaitya known as the Viśvakarma Cave, on the balcony above the porch, is the Mantra of the Mahâyâna sect—

Ye dharma hetu prabhavâ hetuṅ teshaṁ tathâgato hyavadatteshâṁ cha yo nirodha evaṁ vâdi mahâśramaṇa[ḥ].

It is written at the end of every MS. in Nepâl, but does not occur in India perhaps before the 5th century; the earliest yet known being on a dâgoba at Kaṇheri and one given from a slab *Jour. Asiat. Soc. Beng.*[1] of rather later date. This is in characters of perhaps of the 8th or 9th century.

In the Tîn Ṭhâl, the last of the Bauddha Caves at Elurâ, there is a panel, repeated in several places, and in each instance divided into nine compartments each sculptured with a separate figure. In the centre is Buddha, seated in the *jñâna mudrâ* or attitude of meditation, his hands placed over one another with the palms up, and resting on the upturned soles of his feet. He squats upon a *padmâsana* or lotus seat. On each side of him is an attendant with a *chauri* or fly-flap. In the compartments right and left of the central one, and also seated on *padmâsanas*, are Padmapâṇi and Vajrapâṇi, recognisable by their positions with respect to Buddha as well as by the frontal emblems of a Buddha and a dâgoba, and the cognizances of a lotus and the *vajra*. The three figures in the upper line are perhaps Sâmanta Bhadra, Viśvapâṇi, and Ratnapâṇi—though the second bears the sword,[2] one of the symbols of Manjuśri. Of the three in the lower row, that on the right has the book borne on a flower, the special emblem of Manjuśri, who holds the place of Sarasvatî in the Bauddha mythology. The one on the left, in this row, bears a flag (*dhvaja*), and he and the next must be also Bodhisattvas,—such as Dharmapâṇi, Manipâṇi, Karmapâṇi, &c. It will be observed that the attitudes of the eight figures surrounding the central one vary: the legs in the 1st, 2nd, 6th, 7th and 8th are in the same positions,—the right knee being raised; in the 1st, 6th and 7th, the right hand is open, as if these figures were in the act of speaking; the 2nd and 8th have the fingers of the hand closed upon the knee; again the 3rd, 4th and 9th have the right knee flat on the seat and the hand leaning on it, while the left hand in each of these supports the cognizance. The symmetry of this arrangement is evidently studied. The same figures appear as supporters or attendants on the figures of Buddha in the shrines in the Do Ṭhâl and Tîn Ṭhâl (see plate).

---

[1] *J. A. S. B.*, vol. IV, pp. 133, 211, 286, 713; vol. V, p. 658; vol. X, p. 95; *Asiat. Res.*, vol. V, p. 131.

[2] The sword borne on a lotus is also one of the distinguishing marks or cognizances of the Siṁhanâtha Lôkêśvara Bodhisattva of the modern Nepalese Buddhists. This sword is called *Chandrahâsa Khaḍaga* (see *Notes*, No. 9, p. 101). Both the sword and book, together with the bow and arrow, are borne by the six-armed figure found at the temple of Sambhunâtha and figured as Lokanâtha by Mr. Hodgson in *Trans. R. As. Soc.*, vol. II, p. 255, pl. iv, fig. *g*.

On some of the pillars of the Tîn Ṭhâl are rudely cut inscriptions in characters of about the fourteenth century, probably the work of visitors.

(2).—DÂS'A AVATÂRA.

On the west side of a maṇḍapa in front of the Dâśa Avatâra temple is a long Devanâgarî inscription, but faintly cut, and very much chipped. About half of the first two lines is lost, and indeed few letters are not injured. With much care the Paṇḍit painted what was intelligible and then made the following transcript. A photograph was also taken. The language is in Sanskṛit verse and the letters of about A.D. 700-750. It is in 14 long lines and contains 29¾ ślokas of different metres :—

Transcript.

[१] ॐनमः। शिवाय

अर्द्धाकृष्टे गरिष्टे धनुषि शिशुतया जानुलग्नं कुमारं
वामार्द्धेनापनेतुं झटिति विघटिते गाढबन्धेपि मुष्टौ
यातः पाया ...... सन्नादपि [दह्यति पुरे ?]........
[सृ]ष्टः त्स्रुष्टामराति त्रितयपुरवर................[१]
....

[२] भसन्तुष्टा वियुक्ता नया
सैमेत्युक्तवती हरं रहसि वः पायान्नगेन्द्रात्मजा [२]
[स्व]स्कृत यत्न ...... पि निर्म्मलं परेणजाप्यं नलिनीं करोत्यलं
प्रकटमाकृष्ट .... पयोबिन्दुरिवायुधङ्कुरः [३]
स्थिरात्मकः [सद्गुण] ....
............................क... स्य ... नां सजनो ......[४]
....

[३] ये कीर्त्तिताः क्षितिभुजः कविभिः पुराणाः
तानेव संस्मरति वेत्यधुनापि लोक-
स्तस्यान्वयस्य कविरेष तनोति कीर्तिं [५]
समग्रजगतीतला .... पालनैकोचितं
प्र[कामचतु]रार्णवप्रमथनार्जितःश्रीपतिं
न वेत्ति खलु कः क्षितौ प्रकटराष्ट्रकूटान्वयं [६]
.... तपय .... द्वैर्यवन्तः
कर्त्तारः प्रार्थितार्थः प्रणयिजन ....
....

[४] प्र[थित]टयुचमूविक्रमाणामरीणां
झंकारः कौञ्जरीणां समदकटतटश्लाघिनीनां घटानां [७]

तस्मिदुग्धाम्बु[वीची]द्यु[ति]धवलयशश्चान्द्रिकोद्भासिताशो
योषिच्चक्रस्य ....रणदधन्मत्तमातंगगामी
स्वामी वर्ण्णाश्रमाणां प्रशमितसकलव्यापदानन्ददा[ता]
...... भास्व ....तपसां विद्विषां दन्तिवर्म्मा [८]
सुदुस्त्यजा येन सतापि भूभृता स .. ..त्र
विवेकिनाश्चर्य
[५] मसज्जनाय यं दयालुना सज्जनवृत्तशालिना [९]
आलेख्यार्पितमूर्त्तयः स्वभवनेष्वद्यापि यस्य द्विषः
पश्यन्तः किमु युद्धमुद्धतरुषाश्चित्रस्यमानन्तनोः
तन्नामस्मरणागत............मात्वन्येपि नष्टशृयः[2]
प्रेक्ष्यंते पार्थिकैः शुचेव विविधास्तेनैव निर्मूलिताः [१०]
तस्यातत्मज...............देवराज... ....कमलायताक्षः
क्षुण्णारिपक्षवनितानयनान्तवान्ततोयान्वितक्षितिमरक्षयदीन्द्रराजः [११]
यस्मिन्क्षोणी
[६] मखण्डां कृतभयमुनतां रक्षति क्षुण्णदुष्टे
संपन्नैः सार्व्वसिष्टे ×× प्रवरकृतयु[ग ?] क्ष्मापतीन्याययुक्त्या
यज्ञै............[भक्ताः].........विबुधानांजिरे............
कश्चिन्नाभूत्सशोकं कलिकलुषमतिर्न्नैव नाप्यल्पवित्तः [१२]
विकासि यस्य क्षणदास्वविक्षतं शशाङ्कधामव्यपदे[शका]री
करो[ति]संप्रत्यपि निर्म्मलं जगत्प्रसन्नदिग्मण्डलमण्डनं यशः [१३]
दुर्व्वारोदारचक्रः पृथुतरकटकः क्ष्माभृदुन्मूलनेन
ख्यातः शंखाङ्कपाणि
[७] र्व्वलिविनयमहाविक्रमावाप्तलक्ष्मीः
क्षोणीभारावतारी विषममहिपतेस्तस्य सूनुर्नृपोभूत्
मान्यो गोविन्दराजो हरिरिव हरिणाक्षीजनप्रार्थनीयः॥ [१४]
यस्यामलै[ः]प्रणतभूपतिवच्छलस्य[3]
रामाभिरामचरितस्य सहस्रसंख्यैः
आनन्दभिर्गुणशतै[ः]प्रसृतैर्दिगान्तं
व्याप्तं जगत्करशतैरिव शीतरश्मेः [१५]
तस्मा.........जन्मारिपुजनतिमिराकाण्डचण्डांशु......
मेषः पुण्यैः प्रजानां सुगतसमकृपः कल्पवृक्षानुकारी
भीतापन्नार्त्तिहारी
[८] कलिकलुषजुषा............मकारी
राजश्रीकर्क्कराजः खर...र [खुराक्षेप?] निःशेषितारिः [१६]
यस्यारूढस्य नक्तं नियतनृपजनास्थानदानापकान्तं

---

[1] Read तस्मिन्दु.° [2] Read श्रियः. [3] Read °त्सलस्य.

रम्यं हर्म्यस्यपृष्टं प्रवरतरमणिश्रेणीसिंहासनांकं
वारस्त्रीहारतारद्युतितरलमहारत्नरोचिश्शिखाभिः
कामं ध्वस्तेन्धकारे न सितकरकरै ....यैः ॥ [१७]
दुःप्रापवांछितमनोरथसंविधान
निर्नाशितार्थिबुधसार्थमनोभितापः
यः कल्पपादपमपीन्दुसितोरुकीर्त्ति
[९] रानन्दिभिर्गुणशतैरधरीचकार ॥ [१८]
तस्याभूद्भुवनप्रकाममहिमा भग्नारिवीरोन्नतिः
क्षिप्तः क्षुद्ररजः प्रजापरिभवव्यापत्तिविच्छित्तिकृत्
माद्यद्दिक्करिकुम्भभित्तिविलसत्कीर्त्तिप्रतीतायतं
.........द्वाजिरणार्ज्जितजयः श्रीरीन्द्रराजः सुतः ॥ [१९]
यो माच्छर्यमनार्यकार्यविमुखः प्रोच्छार्यधैर्योदधिं
धृत्वा सज्जनवृत्तमेष सुकृतैः.........ग्रहीत्
यस्याद्यापि गुणैः शशाङ्कशुचिभिर्धामापरं तत्समं
भ्राम्यद्भिर्भ्भवे ऽखिले
[१०] नुशरदं हंसच्छलेनाप्यते ॥ [२०]
वर्ण्णाश्रमानशेषं तनयस्तस्य स्ववर्त्म ....न्यसितुं
श्रीदन्तिदुर्ग्गराजस्सकलमहीपालनायोभूत् [२२]
यस्य हरेरिव चरितं नातिक्रान्तैर्नभाविभिः कैश्चित्
शक्यमनुकर्त्तुममलं नरपतिभिर्न्नापि सांप्रतिकैः ॥ [२२]
दण्डेनैव जिगाय वल्लभबलं यः सन्धुभूपाधिपं
काञ्चीशं सकलिङ्गकोसलपतिं श्रीशैलदेशेश्वरं
शेशान्मालवलाटटंकनृपतीनन्यांश्च नीत्वा वशं
यः श्रीवल्लभ
[११] तामवाप चरणं न्यस्य द्विषां मस्तके ॥ [२३]
शौर्येणाश्रशयिष्ट यः प्रथनकं तेजास्विना मारुतिं
त्यागेनांशुमदात्मजं रणनयैर्द्रोणं गुरुं प्रज्ञया
रूपेणाप्रतिमेन मन्मथमथ स्थेम्ना सुवर्ण्णाचलं
लावण्येन शशाङ्कमुज्वलयशः शुभ्रीकृतो [यं] यथः [२४]
देवं ....सबरपरिकरं भीमसेनानुयातं
प्रव्हैर्भूपेन्द्रवृन्दैः परिवृतमभयैरुग्रसेनो जितारिः
व्यापद्युद्धर्न्नुमेकं प्रसभपरकरिध्वंससंस्कारदक्षो
बीभच्छुर्द्दुष्टनागो

[1] Read मात्सर्य. [2] Read प्रोत्सार्य. [3] Read बीभत्सु.

[१२] जयिनमिवपरं श्रीमहाराजशर्व्वः ॥ [२५]

दत्तं येनोज्जयिन्यामपि नृपतिमहादानमाश्चर्यभूतं
न्याय्यं संचिन्त्यदीप्तद्युतिबहुकनकं रत्नमुक्तावतंसं
माणिक्याकीर्ण्णमन्यं दिवसमविरततृप्तदीनार्थिसार्थं
कर्त्तुं क्रिडामपूर्व्वामपरनृपतिभिः स्वप्नकाल्प्यनाप्यां ॥ [२६]
धौरेयं तु प्रकृष्टं सकलवसुमतीभारधारि[त्व]योग्यं
दृष्ट्वैवं श्लाघनीयं रघुनघुषनृगेष्वप्यदृष्टं य ......
त्सर्व्वं द्वीपाधिपत्यं परमविज[यिन]

[१३] मादरैश्वार्यसारं

प्रीतः प्रादात्सयस्मै मुषितकलिमुदे राजासिंघाय[1] वेधा ॥ [२७]
यस्माद्दुःखं द्विषंतः सुमहदुपचितिं प्रापुरिष्टा विशिष्टा-
श्चित्रं चित्तेन वित्तं चिरमभिलषितं यत्तदेवार्थिसार्थाः
भृत्यास्सद्भोगयोगं भयविधुरधियः प्राणिनस्त्राशनाशं
वृद्धिं धर्म्यस्य विप्राः सुखमभिरुचितं बन्धुमित्राप्तवर्गाः ॥ [२८]
यस्याखंडितविक्रमस्य कटकेनाक्रम्य तीरक्षितिं
सौधेस्मिकृतगुर्ज्जरेन्द्ररचिते रम्ये......तैस्तस्थुषः
स्नान्तीभि......ताङ्गरागसुरभि

[१४] प्रोत्कंपिपद्माकरं

धारितृष्वापि पुष्करेष्वापि..............नाभिश्चिरं ॥ [२९]
यस्यास्तोदयशैलसानुवनजेषूत्कंपिकर्णोत्पला[:]
सार्द्धं कामिजनैर्लवंगसुमनोगन्धान्धमुक्तालिषु
व्याकीर्णेषु लतागृहेष्वविरलः कर्पूररेणूत्करै

A connected translation would be almost impossible, but the contents are as follows :—

(Śl. 1, 2). It opens with an address to Śiva and Pârvatî; (3) contained probably an address to Sarasvatî; (4, destroyed) but probably in it the poet announced his subject; (5) he says what had been told by poets of former kings was remembered and known, so he is led to celebrate the fame of this dynasty; (6, the 1st *charaṇa* is wanting—perhaps forgotten:) he writes of the Râshṭrakûṭas: Who in the world does not know of them? the only dynasty fit to protect the earth; who conquer Vishṇu in the churning of the four oceans; (7, much damaged,) relates to the râjas of the past, who were liberal to those they loved and who asked of them: who were terrible to the crowds of elephants of the armies of their powerful enemies; (8) account of Dantivarman, whose glory like the waves of the milky ocean lightened the whole horizon, &c; (11—13) his son Indrarâja is celebrated; (14) this Viśam Mahipati Indrarâja's son was Govindrâja; (15) Govind's praises; (16) his son was Karkarâja; (17, 18) his praises; (19) his son was Indrarâja; (20) his

[1] Read सिंहाय.

praises; (21) Dantidurga was his son; (22) he is praised; (23) placing his feet on the necks of his enemies, and Vallabha having become tributary was overcome, and Sandhubhupa[1], Kanchi, Kalinga, Kośala, Śri Śailadeśa, and besides, the Mâlwâ, Lâṭa, Tauka râjas were subjugated, whence he took the name of Śrivallabha; (24) continues his praises; (25) contains the name of Mahârâja Śarva, who was probably a brother or a friend to the king, for he is described as connected with the king as Arjuna (Bibhatsu) with Yudhishṭhira (Jayin). (26) At Ujjain he gave great presents to râjas and much money to the poor; (27, 28) his praises are continued; (29) the second part of this is obscure,—he approached with his army and staid at this temple; a Gurjara râja is mentioned, apparently in connection with it: his fame is then celebrated. The inscription, however, is unfinished and stops before ending the 30th verse.

This inscription then carries the Râshṭrakûṭa dynasty back two generations previous to those mentioned in other inscriptions.[2] The kings here named are—

1. Dantivarma	...	...	cir. A.D.	600
2. Indrarâja	...	...	„	630
3. Govinda I.[3]	...	...	„	660
4. Karka	...	...	„	685
5. Indra	...	...	„	710
6. Dantidurga	...	...	„	725-755

(3).—KAILÂSA.

On the ceiling and architraves of the front porch of the great monolithic temple of Kailâsa there are some remains of painting of three different ages. The lowest of these is perhaps of about the 8th century or when the temple was finished, and done on a ground similar to that used at Ajaṇṭâ. An elephant, a human figure, &c., can be distinguished, of good execution.

At a later date this has been covered over with a coating of lime and painted upon with figures of the gods, and on the architraves is a battle scene. On the south side are two armies; in the one to the left are a horse and then two elephants; over one are the letters *-lurumghu*(or *thu* ?), and behind are horsemen, &c. The man on the horse has a spear; in the army to the right is, first an elephant bearing a spearman, who is about to slay the horseman, and a man is represented falling down. Above the elephant, painted in modern Devanâgarî characters, we read—

Svasti Śrî Pramârirâû

and over the horseman—

Malagaha.

Behind Pramârirâû's[4] elephant are footmen in mail, bearing spears and round shields, their hair tied with a band, and all with large earrings—as the Arab

[1] The letters are much injured, and Sandhubhupa may be read Sandhukûpa, and *yaśrîvallabhatâmarâpa*, may perhaps be *prithvîvallabhatâmarâpa*.

[2] See *Ind. Ant.*, vol. V, p. 144; vol. VI, pp. 60-72; or *Arch. Reports*, vol. III, pp. 31ff.

[3] For the Râshṭrakûṭas after Govinda, see *Arch. Surv. West. Ind.*, vol. III, p. 32; or *Ind. Ant.*, vol. VI, pp. 59—72.

[4] Kṛishṇadeva Pramâra, the fifth predecessor of Bhôja Râja of Dhâra, reigned about 890-900 A.D., and Kṛishṇarâjadeva Akalavarsha of the Râshṭrakûṭa dynasty ruled about 945 A.D. (*Ind. Ant.*, vol. VI, p. 51; *Report Arch. Sur. W. India*, vol. III, p. 32); but neither of these could have come into contact with the Muhammadans.

writers remarked of the Râshṭrakûṭas; behind are horsemen with swords and shields.

On the west side, a râja is represented seated with a *chhatra* held over him; to the left some people are paying respects to him, and to the right are two bearded men seated with *chhatras*. Over the râja is written—

Svasti Kannuradêvarâya,

and over the men—

-raraṇa(or ? *la*)

the rest is lost.

This Kannuradêva is probably Krishṇadêva or Kannaradêva II of the Nikumbhavaṁśa who ruled at Pâtna, probably as feudatories of the Devagiri râjas. Kaṇhar fort, near Pâtna, possibly takes its name from the same prince who flourished about 1150 A. D.

On the north side is a fight; from the left an army advances, in which is, first, an elephant bearing a râja, and behind him come men with drawn bows and arrows and others with sword and shield: the râja's name, however, is lost. On the right, many men with sword and shield advance rapidly all with the sword arm stretched out, and pierced with arrows; all have beards and large eyes and may be intended for Muhammadans; over them is painted the word *Mahamaraloku* (or *Masamaraloku*).

On the base of the pilaster on the north or left side of the entrance to the hall is a short inscription in three lines of Canarese, which reads—

Gaṁgapagaḷa maga
Vagayaṁṇana ba-
raha | *Śaka* 1312 *Śrî*

It is thus translated by Mr. J. F. Fleet:—

"The writing of Vagayaṇṇa, the son of Gaṅgapa. Śaka 1312. Śrî!"

In Kailâsa there is a rock-cut inscription on the pilaster to the right of a figure of Lakshmî facing the visitor in entering the court, and under a figure of a four-armed *gaṇa*. There was one also on the left, but it is abraded so that only two letters are left; that on the right is also partly destroyed, but seems to read—

rāḍhē[*ku*]*labhadraṅkarasya*
Śrî jalaki(*nde* ?)
dadhichaḍḍa(*ṇḍa*)......

The 3rd letter is injured and the 7th is read doubtfully *-ṅka*, so also is the last letter in the 2nd line: the last letter legible in the 3rd line seems to be *dda*, but it is very faint and may be *ṇda* or even *dau*. Any interpretation must be doubtful, but it seems probable the reading is—

Raḍhekula Bhadraṅkurasya
Śrî jalakrîdau
dadhichaṇḍa......

"(*The gift*) *of* Lakshmî sporting in water and Udadhichaṇḍa (a *gaṇa* of Śiva), by Bhadrâṅkura of the Râdhe family."

The value of the inscription however is, that the alphabet belongs to the date of the temple, and corresponds to that in use in Râshṭrakûṭa inscriptions of the time of Dantidurga, early in the 8th century, and thus confirms the date assigned to Kailâsa on architectural grounds.

Beside a *liṅga* on the right side of the porch are some four letters in the southern form of alphabet and of about the same age. On the other side is a painted inscription of Śaka 1384, below a *liṅga*, worshipped by Mârkaṇḍêya, and was probably written when the painting was renewed and the *liṅga* restored, after the last iconoclastic invasion of the Musalmâns. On the *padmâsana* of Lakshmî at the entrance, is a carved inscription :—

Saṁvatu 1385 *Kârtika vadi* 8............

Probably the date here is also in the Śaka era, to which the characters agree, thus bringing it to the same time as the above date of restoration.

The first of the small temples on the platform behind the great shrine and to the right was dedicated to the Mâtṛis, whose seven seats are arranged along the back, with Kârtikasvâmi's or Śiva's at the left end and one for Gaṇapati and Bhṛingi at the right wall; a small figure was found of Vaishṇavî in excavating the area below. The next temple was for Chanda—whose place it is,—and has a pedestal for one image. Chanda is usually represented nude, in a state of lustful excitement, two or four-handed, with triśula, and jug or ḍamaru, jaṭâ head-dress, and Śiva's third eye; the refuse of the offerings in a Śaiva temple are thrown to him.

The third small temple is for Pârvatî, whose shrine ought always to be just behind Śiva's; the fourth, on the north-east, is for Bhairava or Rudra; and the fifth—on the north, was for Gaṇeśa.

(4).—RÂMEŚVARA.

In Râmeśvara, on a pillar by the side of the entrance, is carved—

Śri Nâgadêvana

the name of some visitor from the south, in characters of the 7th or 8th century.

(5).—THE JAINA CAVES.

Among the Jaina Caves in the northern spur of the hill, the Chhota Kailâsa,—as it is called, from its being a monolithic temple like the great Brahmanical shrine,—has never been finished. During the excavation of a part of the earth with which the court and hall is filled, some images were discovered, all more or less mutilated. On one of these wanting the head is an inscription dated Śaka 1169 (A.D. 1247) recording the dedication of the image by a native of Vardhanâpura.

In the lower hall of the Indra Sabhâ on the front of a square pillar is a colossal figure of a Tîrthaṁkara with a short inscription in the Kâyastha or old Nâgarî character, and attributed by Mr. J. F. Fleet to the 9th or 10 century. It reads—

Śrî Nâgavarmma kri(kṛi)tâ pratimâ.

"The image made by Śrî Nâgavarmâ."

At the left or west end of the front aisle is a chapel with colossal Digambara Tîrthaṁkaras on each side the entrance, and under the one on the north or right side is an inscription in three short lines in rather older like characters than the last. It reads—

Śrî Sohila Brahma-
chârinaḥ Śântibhaṭṭâ-
raka pratimeyaṁ.

"This is the image of Śântibhaṭṭâraka (*made by*) Sohila, a Brahmachâriṇa.[1]"

There are also in the hall on the left of the court of the Indra Sabhâ some fragments of inscriptions in old Canarese characters which Mr. Fleet ascribes, from the form of the alphabet, to about 750 to 850 A.D.

(6).—PÂRŚVANÂTHA.

On the northern spur of the hill in which the Elurâ Caves are, is a large image of Pârśvanâtha, the 23rd Jaina Tîrthaṁkara. It is in the usual squatting position on a *sinhâsana* or throne, and measures 9 feet from knee to knee, and 16 feet from the snake-hoods, which form a canopy over it, to the base of the throne, which has a wheel in front. Right and left are worshippers—among whom are represented Śiva and Pârvatî. Over this figure a structural building was erected early last century.

On the cushion on which the image is represented as sitting, is carved the following inscription dated in 1234-5 A. D. It was copied by me in 1877, and has been translated by Dr. Bühler.

Inscription.

[1] स्वस्तिश्री शाके ११५६ जयसवछरे[2] [फाल्गुण सुधत्रीतिआवुवे][3]
श्रीर्द्धनापुर[4] ⁻ा जभा ⁻ – जाने राणुगि:।
तत्पुत्रो म्हाल्लुगि: स्वर्ण्णा वल्लभो जगतोप्यभूत् ॥ १ ॥
ताभ्यं[5] वभूवुश्चत्वर:[6] पुत्राश्चक्रेश्वरादय: ।
मुख्यश्चक्रेश्वरस्तेषु दाधर्म[7]गुणोत्तर : ॥ २ ॥
[2] चैत्यं श्रीपार्श्वनायस्य गिरौ वारणसेविते[8] ।
चक्रेश्वरोसृजद्दाना[9]द्धृताहुतौ च कर्मणां ॥ ३ ॥
वहूनि विंवानि जिनेश्वराणं[10] महाति[11] तेनैव विरच्य सर्वत: ।
श्रीचारणाद्रिर्गमित: सुतीर्थतां कैलासभूभृद्भरतेन यद्वत् ॥ ४ ॥
[3] धर्म्मैकमूर्ति: स्थिरशुद्धदृष्टिर्हृद्यो सती[12]वल्लभकल्पवृक्ष:।
उत्पद्यते निर्मलधर्मपालश्चक्रेश्वर: पञ्चमचक्रपाणि: ॥ ५ ॥
शुभंभवतु ॥
फाल्गुण त्रितीयां वुधे

Translation.

"Hail! in the year 1156 of the famous Śaka era, in the year (*of the Bṛihaspati cycle*) called Jaya. In Śrî (*Va*)radhanâpura was born Râṇugi......his son (*was*) Gâlugi (*whose*) wife (*was*) Svarṇâ (*dear*) also to the world.

---

[1] A so-called Paṇḍit of the Digambaras.—J. B.

[2] Read संवत्सरे. [3] These words are added above the line.

[4] श्रीवर्द्धनापुर according to the inscription of 1169 and the metre. [5] Read ताभ्यां. [6] Read चत्वार:

[7] Read दानधर्म, required by metre and sense. [8] Read चारणसेविते. (See verse 4.)

[9] Read द्दाना घृता, doubtful. Bhagwânlâl suggests ०द्दात्रीछता इंत्रोव० [10] Read जिनेश्वराणाम्.

[11] Read महान्ति. [12] हृद्यासती, doubtful. Bhagwânlâl Indraji reads दीनो सती.

"2. From those two sprang four sons, Chakreśvara and the rest. Chakreśvara was chief among them, excelling through the virtue of liberality.

"3. He gave, on the hill that is frequented by Châraṇas, a monument of Pârśvanâtha, and by (*this act of*) liberality (*he made*) an oblation of his *karma* [1]!

"4. Many huge images of the lordly Jinas he made, and converted the Châraṇâdri thereby into a holy *tirtha*, just as Bharata (*made*) Mount Kailâsa (*a tirtha*).

"5. The unique image of faith, of firm and pure convictions, kind, constant to his faithful wife, resembling the tree of paradise (*in liberality*), Chakreśvara becomes a protector of the pure faith, a fifth Vâsudeva. *Quod felix faustumque sit!* Phâlguṇa 3, Wednesday."

14.—BANAVASI PALI INSCRIPTION.

In the court of the great temple of Banavâsi in Canara, I found the following Pâli inscription on the two edges of a large slate slab on which was carved a five-hooded cobra. The first line is on the left margin of the slab from top to bottom, and the second line and the half are on the right side margin,—a letter being broken away at the beginning of the full line, perhaps two more a little way down [2] and some at the end.

The following is Paṇḍit Bhagwânlâl Indraji's reading and translation:—

[१] सिधं रञो हारितिपुतस विण्हुकडडुटुकुलानंद सातकणिस वससताय सवछरं १२ हेमंतान पखं ७ दिवस १ महाभूविय महाराज [बालि]काय जिवपुत

[२] [भा]जाय सकुमा[राय] सिवखंदनागसिरिय देयधंम नागो तडागं विहारो च एथ [!] कमतिको अमचो खदसातिस नयंतकस अचरियस [पुतस]

[३] दमोरकस सिसेन णटकेन नागो कतो

Sanskrit.

[१] सिद्धं राज्ञो हारितीपुत्रस्य विण्णुकटड्डुट्टकुलानंदशातकार्णिनो वर्षशतेभ्यः संवत्सरः १२ हैमंतानां पक्षः ७ दिवसः १ महाभोज्या महाराजबालिकाया जीवपुत्र

[२] भार्यायाः सकुमारायाः शिवस्कन्दानगश्रिया देयधर्मो नागो तडाकं विहारश्च। अत्र कर्मत्रयं आमात्यस्कन्दस्वातिनः। नयंतकस्याचार्यस्य पुत्रस्य

[३] दमोरकस्य शिष्येण णटकेन नागः कृतः॥

Translation.

"To the Perfect! In the year 12 of the century the king (*being*) Hâritiputa Sâtakaṇi, the cherisher of the Vehnukaḍaḍuṭu(?) family, the 7th fortnight of the winter months, 1st day, the meritorious gift of the Mahâbhuvî (Mahâbhojî) the king's daughter, Sivakhandanâgasiri, wife of Jîvaputa, with her son—of a Nâga, a tank and a vihâra. These three works by the prime minister Khadasâti. Naṭaka, the disciple of Damoraka and son of the Âchârya Jayantaka, made the Nâga."

---

[1] That is, destroyed his *karma*, which bound him to the *Saṁsâra*.

[2] The letters in the second line transliterated as °*ya saku*° and *Sivakhadanâ*° may be also read somewhat differently.—J. B.

Remark.

The letters of this inscription seem to belong to the second century, and resemble those of the inscriptions of Yajña Sri Sâtakarṇi; it may be a little later, but not earlier. Who this Hâritîputra was we cannot say; he has the title of Sâtakarṇi, which, though associated with the Ândhrabhṛitya dynasty, may have prevailed also in other families. It is a title for a warrior. The "century" of the date, if it means a cycle of a hundred years, has not been previously met with in the Peninsula of India,[1] though used in Kâśmîr. As in Rudrâdaman's inscription we have the 72nd year, not of his reign, but the numeral of the current year; so here the date is in that of the current year of the century. Until we find other inscriptions connected with or throwing light on this we need not say more about it.

Vehṇukaḍa, Sans. Vishṇukaṭa, probably was the name of a place, to which the Ḍuṭu family belonged.[2]

15.—SILAHARA GRANT OF MARASIMHA.

It is well known that the late Mr. Wathen, Secretary to the Government of Bombay, collected a considerable number of copper-plate grants, which he translated in the early volumes of the *Royal Asiatic Society's Journal*. Some of the grants are still in possession of the Bombay Branch of the Royal Asiatic Society, though even of these some plates seem to have been lost; thus, of Wathen's Grant No. 10 (*Journal Royal Asiatic Society*, Vol. II, p. 388, and Vol. V, p. 183), only the second plate is now in the Society's Museum; and of his No. 1 (*Journal Royal Asiatic Society*, Vol. I, p. 379, and Vol. III, p. 94), the third plate has disappeared within the last eight or ten years. How many may have been lost entirely we have no means of knowing.

Mr. Wathen published no fac-similes,—indeed no real fac-similes of Indian inscriptions had been published before his death,—and, though a good scholar, he sometimes fell into mistakes and mislections. It is exceedingly desirable, then, that we should have fac-similes of his inscriptions, and indeed of all old inscriptions translated in the first-half of the century, to submit to the examination of the greatly advanced scholarship of the present time.

Mr. Wathen seems to have taken ink impressions of many, if not of all, of his plates, and left numerous copies of these with the Society. The paper has now, after a lapse of forty years, become very rotten, and will scarcely bear handling. From among these old impressions, however, I picked out a few, and succeeded in mounting them. They are all "reverses," and can only be read by looking *through* the paper, or holding them up before a looking-glass; but this can be remedied in photo-lithography, and I have thought it worth while to have the accompanying plates, forming a complete grant, taken from these impressions, in order to preserve it, the original plates being lost.

---

[1] Albiruni, in speaking of the Lokakâla, says the natives of India reckon by centuries, and leaving out the number of the century, call the year of it the 'Saṁvatsara of the century.'—J. B.

[2] An article containing my somewhat different reading and translation will be published in the *Indian Antiquary*.—G. Bühler.

They contain a Śilâhâra grant of Mârasiṁha, dated Śaka 980. Wathen's account of them was published in the *Journal Royal Asiatic Society*, Vol. II, p. 384, and Vol. IV, p. 281.

Mr. J. F. Fleet, C.S., has supplied me with the following transliteration and analysis of this grant. He will publish a full translation at some future date.

Transcription.

First Plate.

[1.] Jayatu jagat-[t*]raya-nâthaḥ | sakaḷa-kaḷâ-jñâna-dhâna-nêtra-tritayaḥ | phaṇi-pati-

[2.] vibhûshaṇ-âṅgaḥ | kapiḷa-jaṭâ-jûṭa-maṇḍanas(ś)=Saṁ(Śaṁ)bhuḥ || Svasti Śrî-Śiyaḷâ-

[3.] ra[1]-vaṁśa-tiḷakô Jîmûtavâh-ânvaya-prastâra-prabhavaḥ | suvarṇṇa-Garuḍa-vyâḷôḷa-lî-

[4.] ḷâ-dhvajô | vistîrṇṇ-ârṇṇava-mêkhaḷ-âvani-vadhû-kântô mahî-maṇḍaḷa-prastutyô | Ma-

[5.] leyaṁka[2]-sarppanṛipati[ḥ*] śrî-râja-vidyâdharaḥ || Ari-bhûbhṛich-chakra-vakras=Tagara-nagara-

[6.] bhûpâḷakas=ti(tî)vra-têjâḥ | sthira-vâkyaś=śauryya-śâḷî nara-vara-vara-Pannâḷ-durgg-âdri-sim-

[7.] haḥ | sphurit-ôdyat-kî[r*]tti-kânta-kshiti-mahita-mahâmâṇḍaḷik-âdhinâthaḥ | dharaṇî-ra-

[8.] ksha-kshama[ḥ*] Śrî-Jatiga-narapatis=tasya sûnu[ḥ*] prachaṇḍaḥ || Ari-baḷa-sarppaḥ pâ[r*]tthiva-Pu-

[9.] randaraḥ khachara-vaṁśa-chûḍâratnaḥ | kharakara-sama-prabhaḥ saṁgara-raṅga-praṇayi-

[10.] mâṇḍaḷika-nidhânaḥ || Gaṁjâm=agram=udîryya vairi-nikarasy=âtmîya-tîvr-âsi-

[11.] nâ | bhuṁjaṁ(jaṁs=) ta(=ta)t-Karahâṭa-Kûṇḍi-vishayaṁ svâṁgîkṛitaṁ sarvva-|[3] Mairiṁjâ-dêsa(śa)m=u-

[12.] dagra-Koṁkaṇa-mahâ-dêsa(śa)ṁ nija-trâsanâd=bhaṁjaṁ(jan=) ni(=ni)tya- | m=udâra-vîra-nṛipati[ḥ*] Śrî-Goṁka-râ-

[13.] j-ôttamaḥ || Tasy=ânujâtô nṛipa-nîti-vidyaḥ | hâsyaṁ na krid-gaṇḍa-guṇê raṇê vâ |

[14.] lâsyaṁ vidhânê nṛipa-Gûhalâṁkaḥ | Śasyâśrayasyâ krama-pûjan-êpṭaḥ(shṭaḥ) || Ripu-baḷa-

[15.] sarppa maṇḍaḷika-Bhairava | vâraṇa-vâji-sâdhan-âdhipa | nija-vaśya-taṁtra | nava-râjya-

[16.] samuddharaṇ=âri-vargga-nipkṛi(shkṛi)pa | nṛipa-thî(dhî)ra sat-Kî(ki)ligiḷ-âchaḷa-durgga-samagra | bhûri-bhûmi-

[17.] pa tava sâhas-âṁkam=ari-râja-manô-rujam=ugra-paurushaṁ || Pûrvvâ(rvvô)kta-Goṁka-râ-

---

[1] This form of the name must be an adaptation of *Śiḷâra*, to suit the metre of this particular verse. The usual form, *Śiḷâhâra*, occurs in line 27.

[2] This serpent king, Maleyaṅka, is not mentioned in any other Śiḷâhâra inscription known to me.

[3] The punctuation of this inscription is very indifferent. The marks are frequently put, as here, in the wrong place and in the middle of a word.

SILAHARA GRANT OF MARASIMHA.— ŚAKA 980

Ia

SILAHARA GRANT OF MARASIMHA _ ŚAKA 980

I.

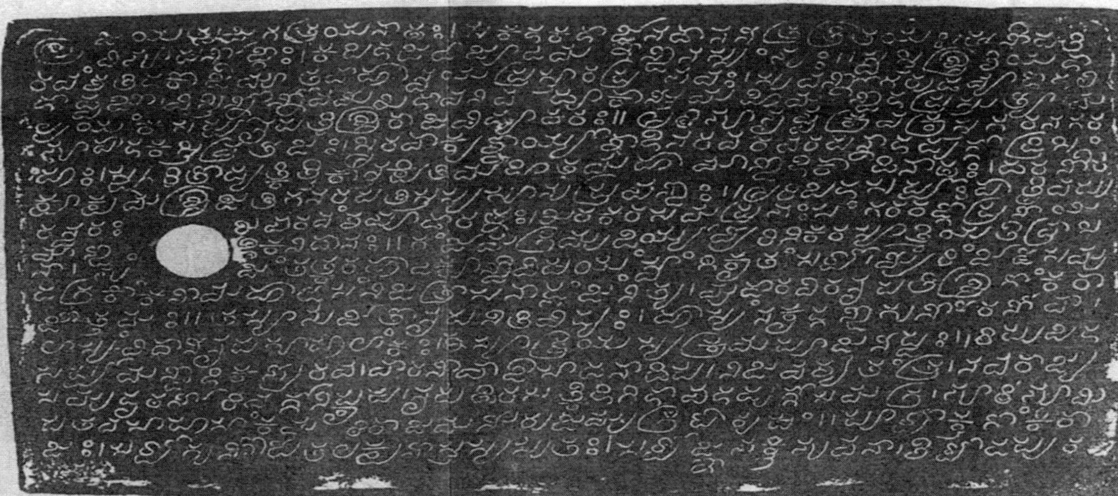

Photozincographed, Govt. Office, Poona, [illegible]

SILAHARA GRANT OF MARASIMHA _ ŚAKA 960

IIb.

SILAHARA GRANT OF MARASIMHA_ ŚAKA 980

IIa.

[18.] jaḥ | sarvva-guṇ-ôpêta-lakshaṇas=tasya sutaḥ | Sarvvajña-bhakti-bhuvan-â- | -śîrvvâda-pura-

Second Plate (first side).

[19.] ssarô mahâ-mahimaḥ || Baḷavad-vidvishṭa-sainya-kshaya-kara-paripûrṇṇ-âsi-hastaṁ | daridr-â-

[20.] khiḷa-dîn-ânâtha-vandi-prakara-mudakar-ôddâna-hastaṁ | Surêṁdr-âchaḷa-lîḷ-âkâra-dêvâyata-

[21.] na-kara-lasad-dharmma-hastaṁ | mah-ôrvvîtaḷa-bhâr-ôddhâra-hastaṁ | tribhuvana-tiḷakaṁ Mâ-

[22.] rasiṁh-âgrahastaṁ || Mâr-âkâra-śarîraḥ | vîr-âri-madândha-gandhaśi(si)ndhura-siṁhaḥ | śûra-pra-

[23.] tâpa-niḷayaḥ | sâra-guṇ-audâra-Mârasiṁha-nṛipaḥ || Rêma(va)ntô Vatsarâjô vara-turaga-cha-

[24.] y-ârûḍa(ḍha)-rêkhâ-viśuddhau | Bhîmô bhîma-pratâpê | nija-bhuja-vijayî râja-nîti-pravîṇaḥ | Kâ-

[25.] mô rûpa-prasannê dhavaḷa-vimaḷa-digvartti-kîrtti-pratânaḥ | Râ'm-âdy-âdikshitipa-charitô Mâra-

[26.] siṁh-âvanîśaḥ || Samadhigatapaṁchamahâśabda-mahâmaṇḍaḷêśvara | Tagara-pura-

[27.] var-âdhîśvara | Śrî-Śiḷâhâra-narêṁdra | Jîmûtavâhan-ânvaya-prasûta | suva-

[28.] rṇṇa-Garuḍa-dhvaja | maṛuvaṁka[2]-sarppa | Goṁkan=aṁkakâṛa | Gûhêyana siṁhaṁ(ha) |

[29.] ripu-maṇḍaḷika-Bhairava | vidvishṭa-gaja-kaṇṭhîrava | iḍuvar=âditya | rûpa-Nârâyaṇa | Kaliyu-

[30.] ga-Vikramâditya | turaga-Rêvanta | kâminî-Kâmadêva | Śrî-Mahâlakshmi(kshmî)-labdha-vara-prasâd-âdi-sa-

[31.] masta-râjâvaḷî-samaḷaṁkṛita-mahâmaṇḍaḷika-Śrî-Mârasiṁhadêvaḥ | nija-râjadhâni-Śrî-Khiḷi-

[32.] giḷa-durggê | sukha-saṁkathâ-vinôdêna râjyaṁ kurvvaṇ(rvvaṁs)=ta(ti)pṭha(shṭha)[3]ty=avasarê || Śrî-Siṁha-sparś-ârjjita-

[33.] pâśupat-âgama-kṛit-âbhinava-bhuvan-ârgghy- | -âvâsita-Mudunîrô Lemeliś-ârppita-santati-prakâśa-

[34.] munîśaḥ || Dûrô duranta-duritâ- | -d=ârâdhyas=sakaḷa-bhuvana-manujânâṁ | dhîras=tapaḥ-prabhâvê |

[35.] mâr-âstra-jayî vimukta-saṁsâraḥ || Brahmâ kalâsu | bâḷa-Brahma-suchârî Mahêśva-

Second Plate (second side).

[36.] r-âṁghri-dhyânaḥ | jihma-rahitas=su-marggî | Brahmêśvarapaṇḍitô munir=jjayatu || Tadîy-â-

[37.] gra-śipya(shya)s=samast-âgama-jñaḥ | mada-krôdha-lôbh-âdi-dôsha-pradûraḥ | sudṛishṭas=suvṛi-

[38.] ttas=sudharmma-pradi(dî)paḥ | padârttha-pravîṇô mumukshu-pradhânaḥ || Śrî-Maleyâḷô dêvaḥ |

---

[1] The metre changes here from *Sragdharâ* to *Mandâkrântâ*.

[2] *Sc., mare-vokka.* The meaning is either "as venomous as a snake in its place of shelter," or "as venomous as a snake to any one who intrudes on its place of shelter."

[3] Some letter or other seems to have been engraved and then cancelled here.

[39.] tasya mahâ-śipya(shya)-jana-pati-stutyaḥ | śrîman-Miriṁja-nagarasy=â- | -sy-âmbuja-maṇḍanô mumu-

[40.] kshu-nidhiḥ || Karmm-ârât-îbha-kuṁbha-prahara-japa-nakh-ânîka-durvvâra-siṁhaḥ | dharmm-âṁbhôja-prakâ-

[41.] śat-kara-pariṇata-siddhânta-nity-ôday-ârkkaḥ | kûrmmâdhâna-praśast-âcharaṇa-karaṇa-pâd-âmbuj-â-

[42.] sêva-bhṛiṁgaḥ | ni[ṛ*]mmôhô nishkaḷaṁkô niratiśaya-tapa[ḥ*]-śrî-yutaś=Chikkadêvaḥ || Dâna-dha-

[43.] rmma-tapaś-śîḷa- | -brahmacharyya-vrat-âdishu | Chikkadêva-samô n=âsti | na bhutô na bha-

[44.] vishyati || Sa(śa)ka-nṛipa-kâḷ-âtîta-saṁvatsara-śatêshu | asî(śî)ty-adhika-nava-śatêshv=aṁ-

[45.] kêshu[1] | pravarttatayiti[2] Viḷaṁbi-saṁvatsarê | Pausha-mâsasya śuddha-pakshê | saptamyâṁ

[46.] Bṛihaspati-vârê | udagayana-parvvaṇi | pâdau prakshâlya | dhârâ-pûrvvakaṁ cha | śa(sa)hasra-trita-

[47.] ya-Miriṁja-dêś-âbhyantarê | Sirivoḷala-chaturvviṁśati-madhyê | Kṛishṇâvêrṇṇâ-nadî-dakshiṇa-taṭê |

[48.] pûrvva-dakshiṇa-paśchima-tridiśâ-bhâga-samâvâsita- | -Kannavâḍa- | -Hâḍalivâḍa-Gâḷikuṭṭi |

[49.] êtêshâṁ pârśvava[r*]tti-grâmâṇâṁ madhyê | chatur-âghâṭa-samêta- | -saṁsthitaḥ Kuṁṭavâḍa-

[50.] nâma-grâmaḥ | Têna Śrî-râjaputrêṇa | tasmai divya-tapasvinê | taṁ grâmaṁ dattavân

[51.] bhaktyâ | yat-sâmyaṁ tat-samastakaṁ || Miriṁjâ-pura-bâhiryyô-(ṛyyê) | Śivâyatana-paṁcha-

[52.] kaṁ | Mârasiṁha-mahîśêna | kṛitavat ki[r*]tti-śâsanaṁ || Tad-âyatana-saṁbandhaḥ | tad-grâ-

Third Plate.

[53.] mas=tatra tâpasaḥ | pûrvv-âśrayêbhavêd=dhi(vi)praḥ | ity=âśraya- | -sya naishṭhi-

[54.] kaḥ || Khâraṁkharyyô(ryyê) su-śauchê japa-niyama-samâdhâna-saṁpanna-śîḷê | mô(mau)-

[55.] n-ânushṭhâna-yuktê śama-dama-niḷayê brahmacharyyô(ryyê) su-dhe(dhai)ryyô(ryyê) |

[56.] svâdhyâya-dhyâna-dhânê Hara-charaṇa-yajê tatva-vitvê(ttvê) su-yôgê | ni-

[57.] tyaṁ saṁdhyâs=tav=ê(ai)tat-pariṇata-munayas=tatra nishṭhaṁti n=ânyê || Parama-

[58.] śrî-kâminî-kêtanam=amaḷa-vacha[ḥ*]-śrî-ram-âvâsa- | -m=ugr-âcharaṇa-bhrâ-

[59.] jat-tapa[ḥ*]-śrî-viluḷita-vara-kânt-âḷayaṁ | nitya-śa(sa)tr-âkara-dâna-śrî-satî-

[60.] saṁpadam=akhiḷa-yaśa[ḥ*]-śrî-vadhû-nîda(ḍa)m=itthaṁkara-śôbhâ-pûta-paṁ-

---

[1] The repetition of the date in figures, however, is omitted.

[2] *Sc., pravarttati*, for *pravarttamânê.*

SILAHARA GRANT OF MARASIṀHA — ŚAKA 980

III.

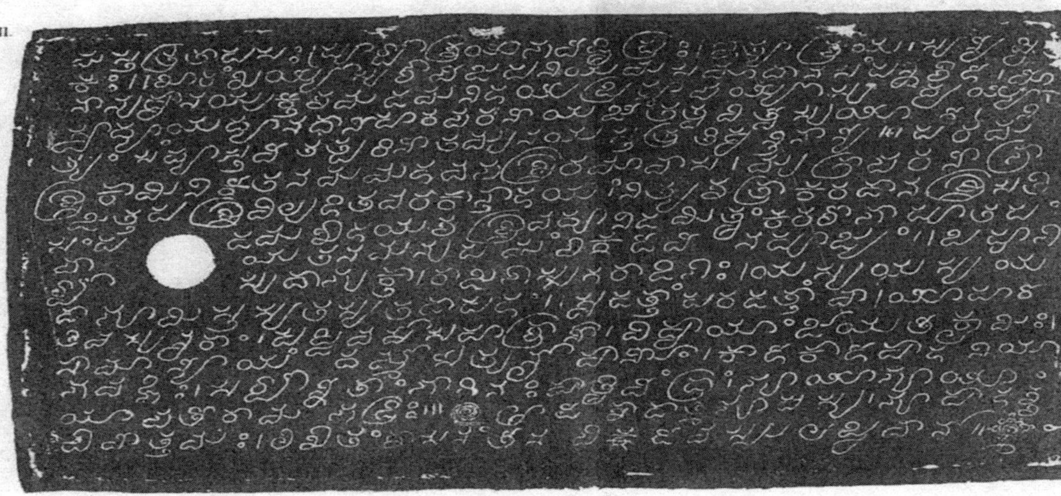

SILAHARA GRANT OF MARASIMHA.— ŚAKA 980

IIIb.

[61.] châyatanam=anupamaṁ Chikkadêvêna pûjyaṁ || Bahubhi-
[62.] r=vvâ(vva)sudhâ bhuktâ | râjabhis=Sagar-âdibhiḥ | yasya yasya ya-
[63.] dâ bhûmis=tasya tasya tadâ pa(pha)laṁ || Sva-dattâṁ para-dattâṁ vâ | yô harê-
[64.] ti(ta) vasundharâṁ | shashṭi-varshâ(rsha)-sahaśrâ(srâ)ṇi vishṭhâyâṁ jâyatê krimiḥ ||
[65.] Sâmânyô=yaṁ dharmma-sêtur=nṛishâ(pâ)ṇâṁ | kâḷê kâḷê pâḷanîyâ(yô)
[66.] bhavadbhiḥ | sarvvânn(n)=êtâṁ(tân) bhâgi(vi)naḥ pâ[r*]tthivêṁdrâṁ(drân) | bhûyô bhûyô
[67.] yâchatê Râmabhadriḥ(draḥ) || Âdêśâd=âtma-bhûpasya | bhûpâḷaśśa(sa)-
[68.] chiv-ôttamaḥ | likhitaṁ śâsanaṁ têna | Chikkadêvas=su(sa) labdhavân ||

Analysis.

After giving the Śiḷâhâra genealogy from Jatiga down to the *Mahâmaṇḍalêśvara* Mârasiṁha, this inscription proceeds to record that,—in Saka 930, the Vilambi *saṁvatsara*, on Thursday, the seventh day of the bright fortnight of Pausha, at the time of the sun's commencing his progress to the north,—Mârasiṁha, while reigning at his capital of Khiḷigiḷadurga or Kiḷigiḷadurga,[1] bestowed upon a priest named Chikkadêva the village of Kuṇṭavâḍa,[2] situated on the south bank of the river Krishnâvêrṇâ, in the centre of the villages of Kannavâḍa[3] and Hâḍalivâḍa[4] and Gâḷikuṭṭi,[5] in the Sirivoḷal[6] Twenty-four, which was in the Miriñja[7] district of the (Kûṇḍi) Three-thousand.

16.—THREE INSCRIPTIONS

FROM THE CABINET OF THE AMERICAN ORIENTAL SOCIETY, NEWHAVEN, U.S.

The accompanying plates are photo-lithographed from rubbings kindly sent me by Professor Addison Van Name, the Treasurer and Librarian of the American Oriental Society, Newhaven. The stones on which the inscriptions are engraved were presented to the Society by Dr. Fitz-Edward Hall about 20 years ago.

---

[1] It occurs spelt in both ways in this inscription. I cannot identify the place.

[2] The 'Kootwar' of the maps.

[3] The 'Kunwar' of the maps.

[4] Probably the modern 'Ghalwar' of the maps.

[5] I cannot identify this place, unless it is represented by the modern 'Dowlee' of the maps.

[6] The Sanskrit form of this name would be Śrîpura. It is the modern Śirôḷ,—the 'Sheerool' of the maps,—in lat. 16° 44′ N., and long. 74° 40′ E. The other places are close by.

[7] The modern Miraj.

The first and largest was procured by him in 1857, at Bhera-Ghâṭ on the Narmadâ about six miles west of the village of Tewar, where also the second was found, and which is about six miles west from Jabalpur. "The larger stone" he says, "had been brought as serviceable building material to the side of a temple which was in course of erection. When rescued it was on the point of being buried, face downward, in one the walls. Had its threatened fate been realized, quite possibly it would not have been spoken of in print for several centuries." This stone "is 33½ inches broad by 22½ inches high. It is a plain block of greenstone (aphanite containing a little carbonate of lime) of a soft texture, and easily cut. The inscription upon it is of 29 lines—the last one of them indented about 4 inches—which cover its whole surface excepting a narrow and unornamented margin. It is engraved with great care, and with no little skill and nicety of execution, and is in almost perfect preservation, so that its characters are, for the most part, as regular, elegant, and legible as the best manuscript." Dr. Hall remarks that "it seems to have been aimed, in the manuscription of this memorial, to make it as formidable in aspect as practicable. To this end few occasions are left unimproved of doubling consonants where the grammar permits their duplication, and of yoking the final letters of words to the initials of those that succeed. For example we have अर्ज्जुन, कीर्त्यां, and even निधिर्न्नै and गर्ब्भे; as also किम्वा, which is an error. Equally unauthorized is सिन्ह, which is everywhere put for सिंह. The dental न is, in two instances, combined laterally with र, and likewise in several places, with the dental and palatal sibilants; for the sake of conjunction, the *anusvâra* is changed to न, before a sibilant in stanzas 6 and 35. In the last verse of the 29th stanza the स of सार्धं is repeated, although the *visarga* of the preceding word is retained. But on the other hand the sibilants are nowhere confounded: व and ब have different symbols; and they are employed, generally, with just discrimination. The deviations, in this article, from accuracy, like several of the peculiarities above noticed, may have been the fault of the engraver. Thus वुद्धि is once substituted for बुद्धि, वन्धुर for बन्धुर, वहुमाय for बहुमाय, वाल for बाल, and वाष्प for बाष्प. From the 11th stanza we learn that the *juvâmûlîya* and its क were once written ᳵका; and from the 12th stanza that the shape of the *upadhmânîya* and its प (प्र) was ᳶप्र." Whether in the middle or end of a word "the *anusvâra* is more often turned into a conjunct nasal; and a consonant or the first consonant of a group is doubled under a ˆ, the only exceptions to this latter rule being र्घ र्थ, र्ध, र्श, र्स, in all cases of their occurrence; and also, in a single instance र्म. As regards the diphthongs *e*, *ai*, *o*, *au*, the inscription follows, with total indifference, the ordinary Devanâgarî method of writing them, or that which is usual in the Bengâlî. The sign of omission (ऽ) is not employed on the stone nor are the verses of its text numbered; but the marks of interpunction, (।) after a half-verse, (॥) after a verse, are introduced with entire regularity. At the end of a half-verse stands always म् and not *anusvâra*: in two cases, however, (10*a*, 28*b*) the *virâma* is omitted. Of other omissions, we have, verse 2*a*, ाकुरा: for ािकुरा:—this is at a place where a few syllables (viz. धर्म्मैवर्म्मा) have been erased and re-cut. Another like case of correction occurs just before in the same line (viz. वुमुदस्याकिश), and a third near the end of the 9th line of the inscription, or at the end of 12*a*, affecting the syllables" which read जगन्त्रय: "The correctness of this reading, however, is not entirely certain. The त्र,

I. INSCRIPTION OF ALHANADÊVÎ _ THE YEAR 907.

From the Cabinet of the American Oriental Society, New Haven, U.S.

From an ink impression by Prof. E. van Name

Scale ½ the original

Govt. Photozincographic Office, Poona, 1880.

indeed, admits of no question; the ग is less clear, but yet is altogether probable; for the next syllable the stone gives only the double *vv*," not *rvv* as read by Hall, "omitting the superposed *r* (˗) which causes the reduplication; and the following character is entirely illegible, but cannot possibly we think be स्तृ: (as read by Hall), its lower part, which alone remains unobliterated, is clearly (*r*), and not (*ṛ*); above it might stand almost any single letter, but not a double one; for that there is no room, nor could a स have been cut without leaving distinct traces on the unbroken part of the stone. We know not what to conjecture, if not ग्र:, ग्रह is sometimes found used in the sense of 'possession' by a passion; the clause might then mean 'Murala ceased to be possessed of arrogance.' In the following *pâda* the stone reads distinctly चकपे for चकमे. This is probably Mahîdhara's error; but, if the metre did not forbid, we might regard it as a misreading for चकंपे, 'trembled'; perhaps the word was in the cutter's mind. Of the first syllable in the same line and *pâda* only the upper part of the right hand lines are left: the consonant must be क; but it might be combined with *r* and with any vowel excepting *i*," but we presume the reading कङ्ग: proposed by Dr. Hall to be the correct one. At the beginning of verse 6 "the reading is रूपैरनेकैर्, 'with manifold forms.' In verse 10, the last syllable of the first half-verse, which comes at the end of a line, is much broken: what is left seems to us to point out distinctly, as the original reading, ता instead of वा (as read by Hall): this would change the meaning of the word from active to passive. In verse 17*b* finally the stone has जनिप (जानिपु?) for जनिष्ट."[1]

The inscription has been translated and commented on by Dr. Hall.

Transliteration.

(1). Oṁ namaḥ Śivâya ‖ Kalyâṇitâmavikalâṁ bhavatâṁ tanôtu bhâle kalânidhikalâ śaśiśekharasya | êkaiva yâ pramathasârthagatâṁ dvitîyâ buddhim(ṁ) pradoshavirahe'pi karôti nityam ‖ [1]

(2). Kiṁ mâlâh kumudasya kiṁ śaśikalâḥ kiṁ dharmmyakarmmâ(ṁ)-kurâḥ kim(ṁ) vâ kañchukikañchukâḥ kimathavâ bhûtyudramâ bhântyamî | itthaṁ nâkivitarkkitâḥ Śivasiraḥsañchârinâkâpagâriṅgadvalgutaraṅgabhan(ṅ)-gitatayaḥ puṇyapra-

(3). pâḥ pântu vaḥ ‖ [2] Bhûtam sad vibhu yad vibhâti bhuvanaṁ yadvi-bhṛamâd yaj jagannetrânandakaraṁ dharâśrayarasâdyanyatvahetuścha yat | yad gandhoddhuradhâma yach cha yajate śîtaṁ yadêkântataḥ sasparśaṁ yadarûpa-mêbhiravatâd yushmân śarîraiḥ

(4). Śivaḥ ‖ [3] Śaktihêtiparapritihêtuśchandrakacharchchataḥ | tâṇḍa-vâḍambaraḥ kuryân Nîlakaṇṭhaḥ priyâṇi vaḥ ‖ [4] Vighnaughasantamasasaṁ-haraṇâya śaktam(ṁ) muktaṁ kalaṅkakalayâ śakalaṁ sudhâṁśaḥ kundâvadâ-tataradantamishâd dadhâ-

(5). naḥ śrêyaḥ paraṁ diśatu vaḥ sadayaṁ dvipâsyaḥ ‖ [5] Rûpairanêkair-vvyavahârajâtam âtanvatî pâtu Sarasvatî vaḥ | yallêśal âlityalavâdapi syât saṁsatsu puṁsaṁ garimâ garîyân ‖ [6] Gôtre râtrikarasya bhûpati-

(6). rabhûd bibhrat sahasraṁ karân pratyêkaṁ trijaganmanôvinayane râtrindivaṁ jâgṛiviḥ | têjôbhirjjagatîbhṛitaṁ paribhavî nâmna'rjjunaḥ saṁs-mṛiter yasyâ'dyâ'pyadhigamyate vasu gataṁ nîtaṁ cha chauraiśchiram ‖ [7] Tasyâ-

[1] *Jour. Am. Or. Soc.*, vol. VI. pp. 499. 534 and 522.

(7). 'nvaye samabhavat prathitaḥ prithivyâ nâthaḥ kathâ'dbhutamâ'pi vrithâna yasya | Kokalladeva iti bibhradudârarûpaṁ nâma trilokasukhasañjananaikadhâma || [8] Nirjjityorjjitagarvvaparvvatabhritaḥ pratyarthiprithvî-

(8.) bhujaḥ prâptânantayaśâ babhûva nripatirGgâṅgeyadevastataḥ | prithvî yena vidhâya Merumatulaṁ kalpadrumeṇâ'rthinâṁ svarggâdûrdhvamadhaḥsthitâ'pi vibudhâdhâreyamâpâditâ || [9] Puṇyâmritena saṁsiktâ śuddhasattvapravardhi-

(9). tâ | yatkîrttivratatiḥ sarvvaṁ vyâpa brahmâṇḍamaṇḍapam(ṁ) || [10] Tenâ'jani mahîpâlah Karṇṇaḥ svarṇṇênakurvvatâ | pûrṇṇatrishṇârṇṇavânarthisârthânarthitakîrttinâ || [11] Pâṇḍyaśchaṇḍimatâm mumocha Muralastatyâja garvvagraha[1]

(10). Kaṅgaḥ saṅgatimâjagâma chakape[me] Vaṅgah kaliṅgaiḥ saha | Kiraḥ kîravadâsa pañjaragrihe Hûṇah praharshaṁ jahau yasmin râjani śauryavibhramabharaṁ bibhratyapûrvvaprabhe||[12] Asmadbharttriparâbhavena sakalâ-

(11). m bhuṅkte bhuvan yâmasau tâmetâṁ tanavâmahai tanutarâkârâmitîva striyaḥ | yatpratyarthimahîbhujâṁ nayanajairbbâshpaiḥ payôdhîn vyadhuḥ sphârân ratnamahôrmmibhiḥ punaramî saṁvarddhakâ(ścha)-

(12). krirê || [13] Champâraṇyavidâraṇôdratayaśaḥśubhrâṁśunâ bhâsayan âśâchakramavakrabhâvahridayaḥ kshmâpâlachuḍâmaṇiḥ | tasmâj janma samâsasâda viśadaṁ śrîmân Yaśaḥkarṇṇa ityaudâryâd dha(*niki*)[2]-

(13). chakâra vibudhân yaḥ prêkshya sarvvânapi || [14] Tasmâdaśeshaguṇaratnanidheragâdhâd bhûvallabhaḥ samabhavad Gayakarṇṇadêvaḥ | yasya pratâpatapano'pyarisundarîṇâṁ śokârṇṇavôdayanidânapadaṁ prapede || [15]

(14). Dyutijitaharitâlaḥ śîlatâkalpaśâlaḥ prithutaraguṇamâlaḥ śatruvarggaikakâlaḥ | vimalitaraṇabâlaḥ kântakîrttyâśaṭâlaḥ śitatarakaravâlaḥ so'bhavad bhûmipâlaḥ || [16] Asti

(15). prasiddhamiha Gôbhilaputragôtraṁ tatrâ'janishṭû(ṭa) nripatiḥ kila Haṁsapâlaḥ | śauryâvasajjitanirarggalasainyasaṁghanamrîkritâkhilamiladripuchakravâlaḥ || [17] Tasyâ'bhavat tanubhavaḥ pra-

(16). ṇamatsamastasâmantaśêkharaśirômaṇirañjitâṁhriḥ | śrî Vairisiṁhavasudhâdhipatirvviśuddhabuddhêrnnidhirnna paramarthijanasya chôchchaiḥ ||[18] Sa Vairisiṁho 'pyanayad ripûṇâṁ kulâni gambhîraguhâgri-

(17). hâṇi | svayaṁ cha teshâmadhiśayya chakre purâṇidûrâvajitâlakâni || [19] Tasmâdajâyata samastajanâbhinandyasaundaryaśauryabharabhaṅguritâhitaśriḥ | prithvîpatirvvijayasin(ṁ)ha iti

(18). pravarddhamânaḥ sadâ jagati yasya yaśaḥsudhâṁśuḥ || [20] Tasyâ 'bhavat Mâlavamaṇḍalâdhinâthôdayâdityasutâ surûpâ | Śriṅgâriṇî Śyâmaladêvyudâracharitrachintâmaṇirarchchitaśriḥ || [21]

(19). Mênâyâmiva Śaṅkarapraṇayinî kshôṇîbhritâm nâyakâd Vîriṇyâmiva Śubhrabhânuvanitâ Dakshât prajânâṁ srijaḥ | tasmâd-Alhaṇadêvyajâyata jagadrakshâkshamâd bhûpatêr etasyân(ṁ) nija-

(20). dîrghavan(ṁ)śaviśadaprem(ṅ)khatpatâkâkritiḥ || [22] Vivâhavidhimâdhâya Gayakarṇṇanareśvaraḥ [|] chakre prîtiṁ parâmasyâṁ Śivâyâmiva Śaṅkaraḥ || [23] Śriṅgâraśâlâ kalaśî kalânâṁ lâvaṇyamâlâ gu-

(21). ṇapaṇyabhûmiḥ | asûta putraṁ Gayakarṇṇabhûpâd asau narêśan(ṁ) Narasinhadêvam || [24] Asya śrî-Narasinhadêvanripateḥ prodyan yaśaśchandramâ digbhittirvvidadhâtu bandhurasudhâsambhâragarbhâ iva | bhûrbharttama-

---

[1] Hall reads गर्वस्पृहं here.

[2] The stone is damaged here : this is Hall's conjectural reading.

(22). vâpya chainamuchitaṁ prîtin(ṁ) tathâ prâpnuyât pûrvvêshân(ṁ) na yathâ manâgapi mahâkshôṇîbhṛitâṁ dhyâyati ‖ [25] Asyâ'nujo vijayatâṁ Jayasin(ṁ)hadêvaḥ Saumitrivat prathamaje'dbhutarûpasevaḥ yo meghanâdabahu-

(23). mâyamahâtikâyasainyaṁ dvishâmabhibhavannahaba prahastaḥ‖[26] Akârayan mandiramindumauler idaṁ maṭhenâ'dbhutabhûmikena । sahâ'munâ śrî-Narasiṁhadêvaprasûrasâv-Alhaṇadêvyudârâ ‖ [27] Vyâkhyânaśâ-

(24). lâmudyânamâlâmavikalâmamûm । akârayat svayaṁ Śambhuprâsâdâlîdvayan(ṁ) nijaiḥ ‖ [28] Dêvâyâ'smai Vaidyanâthâbhidhâya prâdâd dêvî Jâulî pattalâyâm । grâman(ṁ) nâmnâ nâma Uṇḍîti sarvvâdâyaiḥ ssâ-

(25). rddhaṁ châruchârchchâprasiddhyai ‖ [29] Narmmadâdakshiṇê kûle parvvatopatyakâśraye । tathâ'paramadâd grâman(ṁ) nâmnâ Makarapâṭakam ‖ [30] Lâṭânvayaḥ pâśupatastapasvî śrî-Rudrarâśirvvidhivad vyadhattam । sthânasya rakshâvi-

(26). dhimasya tâvad yâvan mimîte bhuvanâni Śambhuḥ ‖ [31] Maunyânvaye Bhârgga-Vavaitahavya-Sâvetasetipravaratrayâdye । Mahêśvarâkhyad Dharaṇîdharo'bhûn nâmnâ garimṇâ yaśasâ śriyâ cha ‖ [32] Komala-

(27). kântisaṭâlenochchaiḥsnehâtibhârabharitena । dîrghamanojñadaśena tribhuvanadîpâyitaṁ yena ‖ [33] Pṛithvîdharastasya sutaḥ samastagabhîraśâstrârṇṇavapâradṛiśvâ । praśastimetâmalikhad yadiyair ddi-

(28). ṅmaṇḍalî śishyagaṇairvvijigye ‖ [34] Etasyâ'varajastarkkaniśhṇâtâdbhutanaipuṇaḥ । praśastimakarodetâṁ sûriḥ Śaśidharâbhidhaḥ ‖ [35] Âsûtrayadidam sarvvaṁ Viśvakarmmavidhânavit । Piṭhêsamabhidhaḥ sûtra-

(29). dhâraḥ[pṛithvîṁ Pṛithuyarthâ‖ [36] Sûtradhârâgraṇi-Bâlasin(ṁ)hasûnurm-Mahîdharaḥ śilân(ṁ) tathâ'karôd varṇṇairnnabhastârakitaṁ yathâ ‖ [37] Saṁvat 907 Mârggasudi 11 ravau ।

Another copper-plate grant found many years ago at the village of Kumbhi,[1] on the Herun river, 35 miles N. E. from Jabalpur, and dated "Saṁ. 932," gives the genealogy of the Kalachuri or Kulachuri kings of Chedi or Ḍâhala as in this inscription but with some slight additions. With certain notes gathered from other sources, this genealogy stands thus :—

Yuvarâja Dêva, either the same as Lakshmaṇa Dêva or his son, and contemporary with Vâkpati Râjâ (cir. A. D. 974).[2]

Kokalla Dêva, his son, (mentioned in śl. 8 of this inscription) contemporary with Bhoja (cir. 1003-1058 A. D.).[3]

Gângeya Dêva, son (śll. 9, 10).

Karṇa Dêva, son, married Âvalladêvî, a Hûṇa (śl. 12,13); a great warrior. Bhîma Dêva of Gujarât (1022-1073 A.D.) marched against him.[4]

Yaśahkarṇa Dêva, son (śl. 14).

Gayâkarṇa Dêva, son (śll. 15-24), married Alhaṇa Dêvî, the daughter of Vijayasiṁha by Śyâmaladêvî, daughter of Udayâditya, son of Bhoja of Mâlava (cir. 1058-1080).

---

[1] *Jour. A. S. Beng.* vol. VIII, pp. 481ff., and vol. XXXI., pp. 111ff.

[2] *Asiat. Res.* vol. IX, p. 108; *J. A. S. B.* vol. XXX, p. 318, 321, 331; Bonthâdêvî "the glory of the family of the lords of Chêdi, the daughter of king Lakshmaṇa" was married to Vikramâditya, or Vijayâditya II., the Châlukya king (cir. 950-973 A. D.), and was the mother of Tailapa,—*Ind. Ant.* vol. VIII, p. 15; *J. A. S. B.* vol. XXXI, p. 114; and *Ind. Ant.* vol. VI, p. 48ff.

[3] *J. A. S. B.*, vol. XXX, p. 319.

[4] *Rás Málá*, vol. I, pp. 83, 90; *Ind. Ant.* vol. VI, p. 185; *Asiat. Res.* vol. IX, p. 103.

Narasiṁha Dêva, their son (śl. 25), in whose time this and the following grants were made, dated "Saṁvat 907 and 928."

Jayasiṁha Dêva, younger brother (śl. 26).

Vijayasiṁha, son, married Gosalâdêvî.

Ajayasiṁha Dêva, heir apparent in "Saṁ. 932."

It is evident that the era used in these and other[1] inscriptions of this dynasty is neither the Saka nor Vikrama Saṁvat; and Dr. Hall, after noting some of the coincidences, as that Udayâditya, the grandfather of Alhaṇadêvî, was the son of Bhoja, concludes that the year 850 of this Chêdi era must have fallen about A.D. 1100—making its initial epoch about A.D. 250. He then remarks that "the specifications attached to the dates 907 and 928 are, however, so full, that any one who chooses to undertake a somewhat tedious calculation is provided with data from which the first year of this, or of some other unaccustomed epoch, may be definitely determined."[2] If we take 26 years for a generation, the eight that precede Ajayasiṁha in "Saṁ. 932," will cover 208 years or bring us back to 724 for the accession of Yuvarâja, the contemporary of Vâkpati and probably of Tailapa (973-997 A.D.). This supports Hall's suggestion that the era began about A.D. 250. Kokalla's[3] and Gângeya's with part of Karṇa's reign would be covered by the long reign of Bhoja. Alhaṇadêvî's uncle Naravarma died in 1133 A.D. in her lifetime and most probably while her son Narasiṁha was a child, and so his accession would naturally fall about 1150-1160 A.D., or "Saṁ." 900-910, and this, his first inscription, is dated "Sunday, the 11th of Mârga Sudi, Saṁ. 907."

INSCRIPTION No. 2.

The second stone was found at the village of Tewar,—the Tripura of the *Purâṇas*. The stone on which it is cut "is of like character with the other, but has a more amygdaloidal structure, being full of little cavities which hold carbonate of lime. It is 12 inches broad and 7¼ inches high, and contains 8 lines. The characters are coarsely, irregularly, and inelegantly cut."[4] It is dated "in the year 928: Sunday, the 6th of Śrâvaṇa Sudi, asterism Haste."

Transcription.

(1.) Jñânâṁ(n)daṁ paramṁ brahma brahmâdisurasêvitaṁ | vaṁ(n)dema-
(2.) hi mahâdêvaṁ dêvadêvaṁ jagadgurum || SrimadGayâka-
(3.) rṇnanṛipasya sûnurnnarêśvaraḥ Śri-Narasiṁhadêvaḥ | jigyê dhari-
(4.) trîṁ anujo'sya samrâṭ jîyâch chiraṁ Śrî-Jayasiṁhadevaḥ ||
(5.) Vipro yo'stakanâmâ 'bhûdÂladêvastadâtmajaḥ |
(6.) Kês(ś)avaḥ kârayâmâsa prâsâdamamumais(ś)varam ||
(7.) Saṁvat 928 Śrâvaṇasudi 6 :: Ravau Haste ||
(8.) Nâyakakosa(śa)vasya gotraṁ Kâtyâyanaṁ sthânaṁ mâla- vako Sîkhagrâmaḥ||

[1] *Jour. As. Soc. Beng*, vol. XXX, pp. 317-ff; vol. XXXI, p. 103; *Jour. Am. Or. Soc.* vol. VI, p. 533; *Asiat. Res.* vol. IX, p. 108. We should like to know what has become of the Banâras copper-plate grant mentioned by Wilford: a good fac-simile of it would be interesting.

[2] *Jour. Am. Or. Soc.* vol. VI, p. 501; also p. 522.

[3] Akâlavarsha, the Râshṭrakûṭa (A.D. 835), married Mahâdêvî, the daughter of Kokalla of Chêdi (*Jour. R. A. Soc.* vol. III, p. 102; *J. B. B. R. A. S.* vol. IV, p. 101; *J. A. S. B.* vol. XXX, p. 319); but this must have been the earlier prince of the same name mentioned in the Jabalpur-stone removed from Bilharî (*J. A. S. B.*, vol. XXX, p. 318, &c.). Dr. Hall seems to have regarded them as the same person.

[4] The notes respecting these two grants are given here in considerable detail, because the *Journal of the American Oriental Society* is not always accessible in India.

2. INSCRIPTION OF THE TIME OF KING NARASIMHADÊVA—THE YEAR 928

Belonging to the American Oriental Society New Haven

From an ink impression by Prof. R. van Name *Scale ½ the original.* Govt. Photozincographic Office, Poona, 1880.

INSCRIPTION Nº 3 DATED SAMVAT 1275

Belonging to the American Oriental Society New Haven.

From a rubbing by Prof: R. van Name *Scale ¼ the original.* Photozincographed, Govt. Office, Poona, 1880.

Here again we have the names of the kings Gayâkarṇa, Narasiṁha Dêva, and the prince Jayasiṁha Dêva.

Inscription No. 3.

The third inscription was dug from the ruins of a temple in the village of Harsaudâ about 10½ miles from Chârwâ, in the district of Hoshaugâbâd. The stone measures 13½ inches in height by 13 inches in breadth, "besides a raised and rounded margin. It is thick and heavy, and shaped upon the back into some form of which the intent is not now recognizable. Its material is greenstone like that of the others, but much harder and tougher in quality." Dr. Hall published a revised Devanâgarî transcript and translation of this inscription in the *Journal of the Bengal Asiatic Society* (vol. XXVIII, pp. 1-8).

It will be remarked that it does not belong to the Chêdi dynasty, but to a Dêvapâla Dêva, of Dhârâ, not otherwise known to us. It is dated in Saṁvat 1275 (A.D. 1218-19), Chitrabhânu[1] Saṁvatsara.

Transcription.

(1). Oṁ namaḥ Śivâya || Sarvvakarmmasamârambhe girvvârṇairyyo namaskṛitaḥ || sa mayâ Pârvvatîputro Hêrambhaḥ prârthya-

(2). ti chiraṁ || 1 || Bhâratî bhavatâṁ bhûyâd vâgullâsavikâśadâ || jagajjâdyaṁ tamo'dhastât kurvvatî bhâ ravêriva || 2 ||

(3). Keśâḥ kañ(ṁ)jâlikâśâbhâhuṁ(ṅ)kârâri-Pinâkinaḥ | vivigogatayo dadyuḥ śaṁ vo(?)jâmbunagaukasaḥ || 3 ||

(4). Saṁvat paṁ(ñ)chasaptatyadhikadvâdaśaśatâṅ(ṁ)ke 1275 Mârggasudi 5 Sa(śa)nau svasti śrîmad-Dhârâyâṁ samastapraśastôpeta-

(5). samadhigatapaṁ(ñ)chamahâdâśabdâlaṁ(ṅ)kâravirâjamânaparamabhaṭṭârakamahârâjâdhirâjaparamêsvaraparamamâhêsvaraśrî-

(6). Litsvâryâprâsâdavaradalabdhapratâpaśrîma(d) - Dêvapâladevacharaṇânâṁ mahîpravarddhamânakalyâṇavijayarâjye sati

(7). || Adhike paṁ(ñ)chasaptatyâ dvâdaśâbdaśate Śake vatsare Chitrabhânau tu Mârggaṇi(śî)rsha śite dale || 4 || Paṁ(ñ)chamyâṁ(n)takasaṁ-

(8). yôge nakshatre Vishṇudaivate | yoge Harshaṇasajjñe tu tithyarddhe Dhâṭhidaivate || 5 || Srîmad-Uṁ(n)dapure sarvvamâsîd Dôsîti(ni)-

(9). pûrushaḥ || khyâtaḥ sarvvaguṇairllôke vilôke sammataḥ satâm || 6 || Tadaurasaḥ śuddhamatirbbabhuva śrî-Bilha-

(10). ṇo'naṁ(ṅ)gasamânamûrtiḥ || tasyâ"tmajo'bhûd vaṇijâṁ mahâtmâ śrî-Ḍhalanâmâ mahanîyakîrtiḥ || 7 ||

(11). Tasyâ'nujaḥ Kêśavanâmadheyo vaṇikpathe śuddhamatirjano ratiḥ || âsît sadâ dharmmaniketanaḥ sadâ

(12). bhûdevabhaktaḥ svajane'tiraktaḥ || 8 || Tenâ'kâri mano dharme Kêśavena sujanmanâ || naliṇidalanîrêṇa

---

[1] According to the usual reckoning in the Dekhan, this would be Bahudhânya, the 13th, but according to the Jyotishṭava rule, followed in Northern India, it is Chitrabhânu, the 16th of the cycle. The rules of the astronomical treatises also make it the 16th.—J.B.

(13). paśyatâ sadṛiśaṁ vapuḥ ‖ 9 ‖ Harshapurvvât purâ(d)dêśavibhâge lôkanaṁ(n)danaṁ | chakârâ"yatanaṁ Śaṁbhôraṁbhonidhi-
(14). śa(sa)maṁ saraḥ ‖ 10 ‖ Tatsannidhâne Hanumatkshetrapâlaganeśvarân | sṭhâpayâmâsa Krishṇâdin Nakuliśamath'Â
(15). 'mbakâm ‖ 11 ‖ Lôkânurâgatastyâgât viprasaṁ(n)tarpaṇât sadâ | devârchchanâgnihômâbhyâmarjjitaṁ sumahâ(ha)-
(16). d yaśaḥ ‖ 12 ‖ Lôke brûte Keśavaḥ satyavâkyaṁ matprâsâdaṁ yo nara(ḥ) paśyatîmaṁ ‖ taddôshaṁ ma bhûtale supra-
(17). siddhaṁ jânaṁ(n)tvete sajjanâḥ sarvvadaiva ‖ 13 ‖ Mahâjanânurâgêṇa śrêyo mama vitaṁ(n)vatâ ‖ kritâ sa(śa)-
(18). stâ praśastai(stô)yaṁ dhimata Devasarmmaṇâ ‖ 14 ‖ Śubhaṁ bhavatu lêkhakapâṭakayoḥ sarvadaiva ‖ Śivamastu ‖

Beneath the inscription in a rude figure of Śiva or perhaps of some other god and seven worshipping figures, at least three of them being females.[1]

17.—MODERN COPPER-PLATE GRANTS FROM KATHIAWAD.

Five copper-plates were sent me by the Darbâr of His Highness the Jâm of Nawânagar. They were in Gujarâti, and of so recent a date as not to require their being lithographed. The following are transcripts of them, prepared by the Paṇḍit. Three of the small ones are marked with the *kutar*.

First Copper-plate.

સ. જાડેજા વિક્રમસી વ
ચનાત મોજે કાટકોલા મધે બ
રમભોજ કરીને ભોમ પ્રાગ્જુ ર
ભોઢ વણિઆ પુંજાને કશનાર
પણ બુધે આપીછે ગામથી દખણા
ધી નદીથી આથમણી છે તે પુત્ર પુ
ત્રાદિક પાળે સહી સવત ૧૬૧૧ વર

ખે કારતક શુદ ૧૧	આત્ર સાખશ્રીસુ
સવંત ૧૭૧૧ માહા	રજની સાખ
વદ ૧ દિને જાડેજા	લણુ કાલીદાસ.
	ની સખ (૧)
પાતાજી નદીની વાડી	
	જાડેજા કપર
	જીની સાખ.

[1] Dr. Hall says only one female, but see the lithograph.

SECOND COPPER-PLATE.

લ. । જાડેજા સૂરાજી વચનાત મો
જે ઞ્રંઝરા મધ્યે ભુમીપ્રાજુ ૩ા બાટ વ
જીઆ પુંજાને શીકશનારપણુ (આ) પુછ આ-
પીછે. બારચથી ઉગમણી. વેલથી આથ
મણી. ઉગમણે વડ છે. વલતી વગત
પુનેાગતી કરીને આપી છ. તે પુત્ર પુ
ત્રાદિક પાલે. શવ. ૧૬૨૫. શ્રાવણુ વદ
૩૦) સોમ આવાપી છે ૪ પત્રા પરજીઆ કરા
વી દીધા છે સવંત ૧૭૨૧ માહા વદ ૧

૧ અત્ર સાખ શ્રી સૂ.
રજની સાખ.
૧ બાબા આલીની સા.
૧ બાટિઆ દાગાની.
૧ બાટિઆ રાજદેવ.
૧ લ. । કંસારા જીવા.

THIRD COPPER-PLATE.

લ. જાડેજા શ્રી ૫ પાતાજી વચનાત
મોજે કાટકોલા મધ્યે ભૂમી પ્રાજુ ૩
ગામથી આથમણી ને લાવડીથી ઉઅમ
ણી તથા દખણાધી તે મોટવડિઆ ગો
વંદજી ને શ્રી કૃશનારપણુ ભુવિ આ
પી છ પીડારૈજે નારાણુબલ કરીને
સંવત ૧૬૭૫ ના બાદરવા શુદ ૨ ધલ.
ખુ પરિઆદિક પાલે સહી.

સંવત ૧૭૧૧ માહા	આત્ર સાખ સુરજી
વદ ૧ દિને જાડેજા	૧ દેવડા મેઘરાજ
જા પાતાજી એ	જીની સાખ
કરાવી દીધા છ	૧ લં. । કંસારા

૧ જીવા

FOURTH COPPER-PLATE.

લખતંગ બાઇ શ્રી હીરજી વકારી જત જોગ શા
હુ ઇછારામ આતમારામને ધરમે ઠાકર મંદર ધરમ
ખાતે તુલસીને પાને જમી પરાજુ ૪ અંકે ચાર પાકી તે સરકાર
શ્રી જામસાઅબની આપેલ હતી તે તમારા નામનું લે
ખ કરીઆપું તે જમીની વગત રાઅમોગ (?) મારગને ઉગમ
ણુકાઠે ધારેચી કરીને ગજગુરને ઉતરાદે સેઢે બરાબર છે.

શ્રી ઠાકોરમંદરે તુલસીને પાને શ્રી કૃશનારપન આપી છ.
પરાજુ ૨ ભમરપરજ (?) નદીને કાંઠે ઝાડ નાખ્યું છે સામુ ખેતર છે જમલે
૨ ખેતરમાં કોએ સમસા કરે નહીં હીંદુને ગા મુસલમાનને સુ
અર સવંત ૧૮૫૯ ના વૈસાક સુદ ૪ વારરવી શ્રી સુરજની સાખ
પા. ૧ દેવાની સાખે ઇમડઢડ (૧) ની સાખ પા. ૧ કાનજી શાખ બખતંગ ઠા.૧
વરચદાશ મણ (?).

સહી.

FIFTH COPPER-PLATE.

Side 1.

લ. બાઇ શ્રી પ્રાગજી ભવાનાણી લખાવતંગ સાધુ ઇ
છા રાંમ આતમારામ જત જોગ મોજે જીરાગઢમાં ઠાકર
મંદર ચણાવ્યુ તેના ધરમમાં શ્રી કરશનારપનમાં જમી પર
જ ૩ તન પાકી આપી છે. તેની વગત મોજે વાડકાના મારગ
થી ઓતરાદી ને વેકરાથી ઉગમણી તે પડણીના મારગ સુધીવા
ડકાના બામણુના ખેતરથી આથમણુ શેઢે છે. વીઘા ૧૦૦ ને આં
દાદ મુસલમાન એ સુકર ને હીં (દુ) અખાજ છે (?)......સવંત ૧૮૬૩
વૈસાક સુદ ૨ શ્રી જગદીશ સાખ..
સાખ......ઓધાની સાખ ત.૧ ઠા.૧ મેઘજી સાખ.
બખતંગ ઠા.૧ રતુગોપાણી સહી

Side 2.

લ૦ બાઇ.શ્રી પચાંણું બાઈ ભવાનાણી. જત સાધુ ગંગારા-
મ ઇછારામને ખેતર ૧ મોજે મેઘપરના મારગથી ઓતરાદી
કોરે છે તે ખેતરની ધરતી પરાતુ ૧ પાકી શ્રીઠાકરમંદરમાં
કૃસનારપણુ આપી છે શા.૧ બાઇ આણંદબાઇ તથા જીવાણુ
તથા બાઇ જેસુબાઇ હયુ આપી છ. સ. ૧૯૦૯ ના જેઠ શુ
દ ૩ આપી છ અતર સાખ શ્રી સુરજની સાખ ગજીઆ
જીવાની સાખ. પટેલ રાઘવ સાખે કશીદરની સાખ લ.૧ મં
ભગવાનજી ખીમજી શ્રી ધરેાલ વંદર વાલેા લખ્યું છ.

સહી.